GROWING AND PROTECTING YOUR
MOST CHERISHED RELATIONSHIP

MARRIAGE

Two Best-Selling Books Complete in One Volume

TOWARD A GROWING MARRIAGE

BY GARY CHAPMAN

Author of The Five Love Languages

LOVING YOUR MARRIAGE ENOUGH TO PROTECT IT

BY JERRY B. JENKINS

Coauthor of the Left Behind series

INSPIRATIONAL PRESS

First Inspirational Press edition published in 2005.

Inspirational Press
A division of BBS Publishing Corporation
450 Raritan Center Parkway
Edison, New Jersey 08837

Inspirational Press is a registered trademark of
BBS Publishing Corporation.

Published by arrangement with Moody Press.

Distributed by World Publishing
Nashville, TN 37214
www.worldpublishing.com

Library of Congress Catalog Card number: 2003112270

ISBN: 0-88486-365-4

Printed in the United States of America.

MARRIAGE

CONTENTS

TOWARD A GROWING MARRIAGE

TOWARD
A GROWING
MARRIAGE

INTRODUCTION

She had been married six months. Like many other Christian young people, she had entered marriage with the vision of "heaven on earth." *Ours will be the greatest marriage ever,* she thought. "I'm a Christian, and he's a Christian, and we're in love" had been her rationale for marriage. What else could one ask? What else could one expect? Bells were ringing! Tingles ran up and down her spine when he touched her. It was thrilling!

"Counseling? Who needs counseling? That's for people who have problems. We don't have any problems; we're in love!" Then how about reading a book on marriage or doing a Bible study to discover biblical principles for family life? "We don't have time for that; we just want to get married. We'll read the books when we retire. This is the time for living."

This had been her attitude just half a year ago. But all of that was changed now as she sat in my office, crying. Her dreams were shattered. "I can't stand him," she said. "He's so selfish. He never thinks of me. He wants me to do everything his way. He never stays at home. I'm miserable." How could one's hopes plummet from the heights of Mt. Everest to the depths of Gehenna in only 180 days?

The material in this book is presented to those who are wise enough to know that marital happiness is not automatic, even when both partners are Christians and "in love." The separation and divorce rate among Christian couples continues to rise, while thousands of other Christian couples continue to live together in something far less than the "abundant life" that Jesus promised.

The blame for such unrest within Christian marriages

cannot be laid totally at the feet of the young couples involved. Far too often couples have been willing to receive guidance, but churches have failed to offer it. In our public preaching, almost all we ever say to our young people is that they should not marry non-Christians (2 Corinthians 6:14) and that they should not have sexual intercourse before marriage (1 Corinthians 6:18). Although both of these statements are biblical, they are both negative. Following both does not guarantee a fulfilling marriage. The Bible is far more positive than negative, but we have been slow to enunciate the positive principles of male/female relationships to our young people.

It is the author's hope that the material presented here will serve to stimulate interest among Christian couples, married and aspiring, in the tremendous help that the Bible gives in this area. It is not intended to be an end in itself. In areas where excellent materials are available, the author has indicated titles and sources. It is believed, however, that if a couple completes only this study, they will be well on the road to marital happiness. It should be noted that, as in all studies related to life, mere intellectual exposure to the truth bears little fruit. It is the practical application of truth that produces fruit. Therefore, the suggested assignments at the conclusion of each chapter are extremely important.

The book is divided into two sections: Premarital Growth and Marital Growth. The first section, as one would expect, is designed for people who are in the process of becoming the kind of persons who will be "fitting," or "suitable," marriage partners. The second section speaks to those couples who have already said "I do" and are now trying to fulfill that commitment. The engaged couple should work through the entire book before marriage and then review the Marital section within the first six months of marriage. Couples who have been married for longer periods of time will find the Marital section a stimulus to their own marital growth, and the Premarital section helpful as they counsel the unmarried.

Section One

℘REMARITAL GROWTH

1

The Purposes and Pitfalls of Dating

I have met many Christian college students who have given up on dating. They have found it to be a road strewn with heart-hurt, physical frustration, misunderstanding, and untold bother, all of which add up to a "bad trip."

"Why date? I'll just wait till God brings the right one into my life and avoid all the dating hassle," they reason. Are these young people right in their conclusions? Is it more biblical not to date?

To some, the very idea of not dating sounds unnatural, but for others it seems a viable alternative. What are the factors that must be considered?

First, let me remind you that dating is not a universal practice. In many cultures, literate and nonliterate alike, the very idea of a fellow and a girl arranging a series of times to get together, for whatever purpose, would be considered taboo. These cultures have many stable marriages. Therefore, dating is not a necessary part of the marriage process.

Having said this, however, we must be realistic and admit that dating is a very integral part of the American culture. In fact, some have referred to dating as America's favorite tribal custom. The fact that there are pitfalls in the system does not mean that the process itself is necessarily evil. On the contrary, it may be one of the most healthy social systems in our entire society.

PURPOSES OF DATING

What are the purposes of dating? The reason many young people have failed in the dating game is that they have never clearly understood the objectives. If you ask a group of students, "Why are you dating?" the answers would range from "to have a good time" to "to find a mate." In some general sense we know that the end of all this is to lead us to marriage, but we are not clear as to other specific objectives. Let me list a few and suggest that you add to the list as you give thought to your own personal objectives.

One of the purposes of dating is to get to know those of the opposite sex and to learn to relate to them as persons. Half the world is made up of individuals of the opposite sex. If I fail to learn the art of building wholesome relationships with "the other half," immediately I have limited my horizons considerably.

God made us male and female, and it is His desire that we relate to each other as fellow creatures who share His image. Our differences are numerous, but our basic needs are the same. If we are to minister to people, which is life's highest calling, then we must know them—male and female. Relationships cannot be built without some kind of social interaction. In America, dating provides the setting for such interaction.

Some years ago, a friend of mine told me his experience while serving in the military, stationed on the French Riviera. Daily he would look out his apartment window upon the female half of God's creation, clad almost as Eve before the Fall. His mind ran wild with lustful fantasies. Day after day this phenomenon occurred. The battle with lust waged hotter and hotter and eventually led him to ask advice from a Christian brother.

"What am I to do with this tremendous frustration within? I can't go on like this," he confided.

The friend made a very wise but unexpected suggestion.

"Go down to the beach and talk with some of those girls."

My friend resisted at first, thinking that was not the Christian thing to do, but at the insistence of his friend he finally consented. To his amazement, he found that his struggle with lust was not heightened but reduced. As he talked with those women, he found that they were persons, not things; persons, each with her own unique personality, history, and dreams; persons with whom he could communicate and discuss ideas and who in turn could relate to him as a person.

As long as he remained in his apartment and gazed upon them through the window, he saw them only as sex objects. When he came near, he found that they were persons. This is one of the purposes of dating.

A second purpose that dating serves is to aid in the development of one's own personality. All of us are in process. Someone has suggested that we ought to wear signs around our necks reading "Under Construction."

As we relate to others in the dating context, we begin to see various personality traits exhibited. This provokes healthy self-analysis that brings greater self-understanding. We recognize that some traits are more desirable than others. We come to see our own strengths and weaknesses. The knowledge of a weakness is the first step toward growth.

The fact is that all of us have strengths and weaknesses in our personalities. None of us is perfect. Maturity is not flawlessness. The Christian road, however, is a road winding upward. We are never to be satisfied with our present status of development. If we are overly withdrawn, we cannot minister freely to others. If, on the other hand, we are overly talkative, we may chase away those to whom we would minister. Relating to those of the opposite sex in a dating relationship has a way of helping us see ourselves and cooperate with the Holy Spirit in His plan of growth for our lives.

A number of years ago, a supertalkative young man said to me, "I never realized how obnoxious I must be, until I dated Mary. She talks all the time, and it drives me batty." The light had dawned; his eyes were opened. He saw in Mary his own weakness and was mature enough to take steps toward growth.

For him, this meant curbing his speech and developing his listening abilities, a prescription written long ago by the apostle James: "My dear brothers, take note of this: Everyone should be quick to listen, slow to speak and slow to become angry" (1:19). What we dislike in others is often a weakness in our own lives. Dating can help us see ourselves realistically.

Closely aligned to this is a third purpose for dating. It provides an opportunity for ministry to others. Christ is our example. He said He came not to be ministered unto but to minister (Mark 10:45). If we are to follow His example, then our theme must be "ministry." The word means "to serve." The ministry is not a position of lordship, but a practice of servanthood. "Whoever wants to become great among you must be your servant, and whoever wants to be first must be your slave" (Matthew 20:26–27).

I do not mean to convey the idea that dating should be done in a spirit of martyrdom—"Poor ole me, I have to do this service as my Christian duty." Ministry is different from martyrdom in that ministry is something we do for others, whereas martyrdom is something others bring upon us. Martyrdom is beyond our control. Ministry is not.

Dating for the Christian must always be a two-way street. The question is never simply, "What am I going to get out of this relationship?" but also, "What can I contribute to the life of the one whom I am dating?" We are called to minister to one another, and ministry is most effective at close range. Certainly we can teach the group, but where are the real needs met if not on the more personal plane?

Again, Christ is our best example. He ministered to the multitudes in His teaching and preaching, but He also ministered to individuals. Lest some argue that Jesus' personal ministry was always with the Twelve (those of the same sex), I would remind you of the woman at the well in John 4, and of His time with Mary and Martha in Bethany. Women were among the group who prayed after the crucifixion, and they were first at the open tomb. Jesus ministered to people, males and females, and this must also be our pattern.

How much could be accomplished throughout our lives if we could see ministry as one of the purposes of dating. Many a reserved fellow could be "drawn out" by the wise counsel of a Christian sister. Many a braggart could be calmed by the truth spoken in love.

You see, taking ministry seriously may change many of our attitudes toward dating. We are so trained to "put our best foot forward" that we often refuse to speak anything that we feel would put us in a bad light. But real ministry demands that we speak the truth in love.

We do not serve each other by avoiding one another's weaknesses. I know this is difficult, and I am not suggesting it as a norm for non-Christian dating. That is likely impossible. I am suggesting, however, that as Christians we are called upon to minister, and this ministry must be carried into our social life. When we touch the needs and weaknesses of others in the spiritual, intellectual, emotional, or social areas, and provoke growth, we are ministering indeed.

Julie had liked Tom from the moment she saw him in freshman English. In sophomore biology he finally asked her for a date.

By this time, however, Tom had a reputation for conserving natural resources, especially water. He took a bath only on Saturdays. Everyone knew it, but no one was willing to "speak the truth in love." Oh, there had been some backdoor approaches, like the time the men on the hall gave him nineteen bars of soap on his nineteenth birthday. But backdoor approaches seldom effect constructive change.

Julie wanted to help and decided to accept the date in spite of her roommate's needling comments about wearing a gas mask on a date. On the first date, in a very candid way, Julie told Tom the truth and suggested that a bath a day was normal and ecologically sound. She changed the behavior pattern of a young sophomore. We can help others if we care enough.

Another purpose of dating is to give us a realistic idea of the kind of person we need as a marriage partner. In the process of dating, it is to be hoped we have gone out with a variety of people with differing personalities. It is this process that gives us criteria for making wise judgments when we come to deciding upon a marriage partner.

One who has had limited dating experience is always plagued with the thought, *What are other women/men like? Would I have had a better marriage with another type of mate?* The question comes to almost all couples, especially when there is trouble in the marriage, but the individual who looks back on a well-rounded social life before marriage is better equipped to answer the question. He is not as likely to build a dream world, because experience has taught him that all of us are imperfect. We must grow with our mates rather than look for better ones.

Eventually, of course, the purpose of dating is to find the mate God has for you. Some Christians like to leave God out of this area, but the biblical account in the next chapter should establish clearly that God is vitally concerned with your finding the right mate.

Proverbs 3:5–6 says, "Trust in the Lord with all your heart; and lean not on your own understanding; in all your ways acknowledge him, and he will make your paths straight." Notice, it does not say that we are not to use our understanding, but rather that we are not to lean on it. That is, human reason alone is not to be the center of our decision-making process. Our trust is in God. The task is too big for us. What could be more difficult than finding someone with whom we can live in harmony and fulfillment for the next fifty years? The variables are too many. Human reason is not sufficient. God alone is capable of making such a monumental choice. He wants to help us and asks that we acknowledge His lordship. As we turn this area of our lives over to Him and constantly ask His direction, we can trust Him to direct our thinking and circumstances—in short, to direct our paths.

We are, indeed, to use our minds in determining God's will for us. But it is the mind committed to Him, not the mind apart from Him. The purpose of the next two chapters is to suggest biblical guidelines for understanding God's direction in this area. God has given us principles to follow in order that we may arrive at the proper destination.

CAUTION: DANGER AHEAD

The kind of purposeful dating of which we have been speaking is not without dangers. Chuckholes are marked by barriers and detour signs. Many persons have disregarded these, however, and have ended up with a badly damaged vehicle. If we are aware of the dangers, we can avoid them. To pinpoint some of these dangers is the purpose of this section.

Perhaps the most common danger in dating is to allow the physical aspect of the relationship to predominate. This seems to be the pattern for far too many Christian couples. Long hours are spent in close, physically charged activity, all of which was designed as a prelude for sexual intercourse. Since this conclusion is forbidden by Scripture, the Christian couple seeks to stop short of this point and ends the evening in tremendous frustration. When the physical aspect is the major part of the relationship, the personal growth of the individuals involved is stymied.

Often the question is raised by conscientious young people, "What physical expressions of love are appropriate, and when should these become a part of the dating relationship?" Any specific answer to that question would be arbitrary, but there are principles that will give guidance. First, since we know clearly that sexual intercourse outside marriage can never serve God's purposes, we must avoid any physical expressions that lead us close to intercourse. Second, since the physical area of a relationship so easily overpowers the spiritual, social, intellectual, and emotional elements, we must establish these more important areas before we move to any physical expression of love.

So how do we apply these principles? I believe that any physical expression of love beyond holding hands ought to be reserved for the time when both partners agree that there is interest in a long-term relationship, with marriage as a possibility. There is a wholesome place for kissing and embracing when the other areas of our relationship are in place and Christ is at the center of the relationship. How do we avoid sexual intercourse? Three simple rules: never take clothes off;

never put hands under clothes; never lie down together.

What I am suggesting is that we may have a ministry-centered relationship designed for mutual edification that would never include sexually motivated behavior. There may be wholesome nonsexually motivated behavior as a normal part of the ministering relationship, such as a warm embrace expressing joy or genuine sympathetic concern in a time of sorrow. The sexually motivated physical activity, however, ought to wait until some degree of maturity has been reached in the relationship. Some will find such a suggestion objectionable, but I believe that this principle will enhance greatly the ministry aspect of dating.

Assuming that you have followed these principles and are now dating someone you view as a potential mate, what part should the physical aspect play in the relationship? I believe that here we move on a continuum from little to much, depending on the degree of commitment and the date of the wedding, always committed to reserving sexual intercourse for marriage. The key word is "balance." We must not allow the physical to predominate over the spiritual, social, and intellectual.

The couple themselves must regularly evaluate their relationship. When they see the physical aspect getting out of balance, they must discuss the problem and decide upon ways and means of bringing balance. This may mean radically changing the type of date they are having, moving away from long periods alone, planning more social activities, and involving other couples more often.

A couple can avoid this danger if they choose to avoid it. We cannot blame our sexual drive nor our circumstances for failure in this area. We are masters of our own fate.

A second danger is to misread the interest of others. A quiet, withdrawn fellow may well jump to the wrong conclusion when a Christian girl expresses an interest in getting to know him. She may be thinking of ministry, but he reads matrimony.

"I want to help," she says, "but how can I keep from hurting him?" Most likely, she cannot! But then, being hurt is not the worst thing in the world. In fact, most growth is accompanied by pain. Better to have suffered and grown, than never to have suffered at all. God can use heartache as well as headache to help us grow.

We must not sit back and fail to minister to those of the opposite sex because we fear hurting them. We should, however, not seek to hurt. Perhaps the best answer to this problem is open communication early in the relationship. I do not mean that the girl should walk up to the fellow and say, "Now, I don't have any romantic interest in you, but I do want to help you. Would you have ice cream with me after the meeting tonight?"

But somehow we must communicate our real motives to each other. This is the surest way to avoid the misreading of interests. We cannot read each other's mind. Communication alone can reveal our thoughts and intentions. Some have found it helpful to talk of "brother-sister relationships" or of "friendships" rather than "dating." If we cannot rid "dating" of its romantic connotations, then perhaps we can call our get-togethers "friendship appointments."

A third danger, born most often of insecurity, is the danger of limiting our dating experience to one individual. Most of the purposes for dating that we have discussed will find minimal fulfillment if this becomes the pattern. By such action, we short cut the process and arrive at our destination too soon, void of many of life's most enriching experiences.

I know that there are notable exceptions, and I am happy for every exception. That is, there are couples who dated only each other from a very early age and yet have a happy marriage. I am not suggesting they go back and "make up for lost time." This is impossible and undesirable.

What I am saying is that if you are still unmarried and have followed this pattern, I feel that you would do yourself a great service to broaden your base of friendships by developing brother-sister relationships with other individuals. This can be done without undue jealousy in your present relationship if you both understand the purpose.

A fourth danger is that of romantic color blindness. I often confuse green and brown, pink and beige, and certain other color combinations. Many couples do the same in their dating relationships. Because they are caught up in the excitement of romance, they fail to see things as they really are. When we like someone, we are inclined to see only his or her strengths. We overlook weaknesses. The truth is that we all have strong points and weak points in our personality and behavior characteristics.

Usually in my premarital counseling program, I will ask the girl to list all the things she likes about her fiancé. I ask the fellow to do the same. With some thought, they can usually give a rather impressive list. Then I ask them to list the weaknesses of their potential partner—the things they do not particularly like or things they see as potential problems. Unless the couple can list at least some traits in this category, I tell them that they are not ready for marriage.

A mature relationship, one that is ready for marriage, will always be realistic enough to admit weakness in the other person. You will not marry a perfect person. We must understand this, not only theoretically, but personally. Spelling out these weaknesses helps us face reality.

A couple will find great profit in discussing openly the weaknesses that they perceive in each other. Can these weaknesses be changed? Most can if the individual chooses to change. If there is no change, what problem is this likely to cause in the marriage? Realistic discussion of these questions should be a part of the decision-making process regarding marriage.

Still another danger is the "in love illusion." Some time ago, I had a call from a young man who asked if I would perform his wedding ceremony. I inquired as to when he wanted to get married and found that the wedding date was less than a week away. I explained that I usually have from four to six counseling sessions with those who desire to be married.

His response was classic. "Well, to be honest with you, I don't think that we need any counseling. We really love each other, and I don't think we will have any problems." I smiled and then wept inwardly. Another victim of the "in love illusion."

Most couples do not get married unless they think they are in love. And most feel the basis for marriage is being in love. I often ask couples who come for premarital counseling, "Why do you want to get married?" After looking at each other, giggling, and smiling, they say in their own way, "We love each other!"

But when I press to find out what they mean by "love," I find that few are able to describe it. Most end up by saying something about a deep feeling that they have for each other. It has persisted for some time, and is in some nebulous way different from what they have felt for other dating partners.

I am reminded of the African animal hunt. A hole is dug in the midst of the animal's path to the water hole, then camouflaged with branches and leaves. The poor animal runs along, minding its own business, then all of a sudden it falls into the pit and is trapped.

This is the manner in which we speak of love. We are walking along doing our normal duties, when all of a sudden one day we look across the room or down the hall and there she/he is—*wham-o*, we "fall in love." There is nothing we can do about it. It is completely beyond our control. Only one course of action is considered. Get married! The sooner the better. So we tell our friends, and because they operate upon the same principle, they agree that if we are "in love," we may as well get married.

No one considers the fact that our social, spiritual, and intellectual interests are miles apart. Our value systems and goals are contradictory, but we are "in love." The great tragedy stemming from this illusion is that six months later we sit in the counselor's office and say, "We don't love each other anymore." Therefore, we are ready to separate. After all, if "love" is gone, then we cannot stay together.

I have a word for the above described emotional experience, but it is not "love." I call it the "tingles." Now, I think the tingles are important. They are real, and I am in favor of their survival, but they are not the basis for a satisfactory marriage. In chapter 2, I discuss what I feel is the true basis for marriage. Here, however, I am simply saying that we must not allow our culture to squeeze us into the mold of believing that the tingles are all we need for a happy marriage.

I am not suggesting that one should marry without the tingles. That warm, excited feeling, the chill bumps, that sense of acceptance, the excitement of the touch, and so on that make up the tingles serve as the cherry on top of the sundae, but you cannot have a sundae with only the cherry. The many other factors that we discuss in the next two chapters must be of vital consideration in making a decision about marriage.

We may have the tingles with many people of the opposite sex before we meet the one whom we should marry. Many Christians would testify that it is also possible to feel the tingles for someone other than your mate even after you are married. That does not mean that we follow the tingles and get involved with someone else.

On the contrary, we admit our feelings, but thank God that we do not have to follow our feelings. In His power, we commit ourselves to our partner and go on developing our relationship. The tingles are temporary and should never be dictators of our actions.

Genuine love, which is discussed more fully in chapter 5, is a vital factor in deciding upon marriage. This kind of love is observed by actions rather than by feelings. Love is kind, patient, considerate, courteous, never demanding its own way, says the apostle (1 Corinthians 13:4–8). You can tell if your partner loves you by the way he/she treats you. You do not always know your partner's feelings, but you can always observe his actions. Yes, love should be a prerequisite for marriage, but it should be love in action, not emotions only. This reminds me of the little verse:

> He held me close—
> a chill ran down my spine.
> I thought it was love,
> but it was just his Popsicle melting.

Lest I be misunderstood, let me clearly state that I believe there ought to be a strong, warm, emotional feeling toward the one you marry. We are emotional creatures, and our emotions ought to be involved in any decision as meaningful as marriage. Yes, we ought to have the "tingles," but we must not make a decision for marriage based only upon the tingles. Marriage ought to be a rational decision as well as an emotional decision. Emotion alone is a poor instructor. Emotion and reason give us the insight we need.

The last danger that I would like to mention is the danger of attempting the impossible. Dreaming is great, but unrealistic dreaming is folly. God has warned us that we are not to try to blend light and darkness. That is impossible, and God wants to spare us the wasted energy. As stated by Paul in 2 Corinthians 6:14–15, the principle reads, "Do not be yoked together with unbelievers. For what do righteousness and wickedness have in common? Or what fellowship can light have with darkness? What harmony is there between Christ and Belial? What does a believer have in common with an unbeliever "

Someone will object, "But I know a Christian girl who married a non-Christian fellow, and after they were married he became a Christian, and they are extremely happy." Thank God! We must know, however, that that girl has experienced the exceptional. That is not the rule, as many would testify. Do not count on being the exception.

Others would object, "But I know a Christian who is married to a non-Christian, and they have a happy marriage." Thank God! I am in favor of happy marriages wherever they are found. As we will discuss later, however, the essence of marriage is oneness—that deep sense of being one in every area of life, that sense of freely sharing all life's experiences. A Christian and a non-Christian cannot share in the deepest of life's experiences—personal fellowship with the living God. One entire area of life goes unshared, and because this area is so important, it affects other areas.

No, a Christian/non-Christian alliance cannot experience all that God intended in marriage. It is not that this oneness is difficult to obtain; it is impossible to obtain. God's prohibitions are designed for our benefit.

A common question raised by conscientious Christian young people is "Should I date a non-Christian?" Some would answer with a strong and definite no! Those who hold this position usually emphasize that dating leads to marriage. "Never date a non-Christian, and you will not marry a non-Christian," they sometimes say.

It would be difficult to argue with the truth of that statement. The surest way to avoid "attempting the impossible" would be to refuse to date a non-Christian.

However, if we take the ministry aspect of dating seriously, and if we believe that non-Christians need Christ, we may minister to non-Christians in the dating context. We may be God's instruments to bring them to Christ. Many Christians would testify that they came to Christ through the loving witness of a Christian dating partner.

The biblical principle is "Be not unequally yoked together with unbelievers." I do not see ministry-centered dating as a yoke. A yoke involves commitment. The initial stages of dating require no commitment. A date is only an agreement to spend a specified amount of time in conversation with another person, perhaps accompanied by some other social activity such as eating or bowling. If this is commitment, it is very minimal commitment.

The danger for the single Christian is to rationalize that the date is ministry-centered when in reality it is not. If Christ is not presented and spiritual issues are not discussed on the first or second date, you are fooling yourself. If you express your faith in Christ, and there is no interest in further discussion of the matter, you are foolish to go on developing other aspects of the relationship. To allow thoughts and feelings of a long-term relationship with this person to reside in your heart is to court disaster. For the Christian, the spiritual aspect of life is central and all-pervasive. This truth must be faced realistically in dating relationships.

Why not evaluate your own dating record? Do you agree with the purposes presented in this chapter? What purposes would you add? Do you understand the dangers discussed? Are you presently involved in any of these dangers? What could you do about it? The following suggestions are designed to help you experience personal growth.

GROWTH ASSIGNMENTS

For the Unmarried:

1. Take the self-analysis test on the following page to see if you are making the most of your dating experience. (If you are presently dating someone whom you consider a prospective mate, you should both write your answers to these questions and then use them as a stimulus for discussion.)

2. Discuss your answers to the self-analysis test with a trusted friend who will honestly help you evaluate the relationship.

3. In the light of your self-understanding, what changes should you make in your dating relationship? List these as specifically as possible and take immediate action to effect change. Such change may involve the following:
   a. terminating the relationship
   b. changing the manner in which you use your time when you are together
   c. discussing openly your purpose in the relationship
   d. taking steps to avoid pitfalls

4. If your dating record is nonexistent, you may want to read *258 Great Dates While You Wait,* by Susie Shellenberger and Greg Johnson, for practical help on getting started (see Appendix).

For the Married:

1. Be realistic. You cannot go back and start over. The sign of maturity is to begin with the present and work toward the future.

2. Confess past failures, accepting God's forgiveness. Do not allow forgiven failures to live in your closet. Such skeletons should be buried.

3. Commit yourself to a genuine study of the principles in this book, with a view to making the most of your marriage.

4. As an adult, accept your responsibility to give guidance to the next generation. With whom could you share the content of this chapter on dating?

SELF-ANALYSIS TEST ON DATING

1. To what degree am I relaxed with members of the opposite sex (i.e., do I relate to them as persons)?

   _____extremely well _____average _____below average

2. In what specific way or ways has my personality improved through my dating experience?

   _____

   _____

   _____

   _____

   _____

3. Make a list of the contributions that you believe you are making to the person whom you are dating. It might be helpful to arrange these in categories: spiritual, intellectual, emotional, social, other.

4. What are the qualities and characteristics that I am looking for in a prospective mate?

5. What role does physical involvement play in our relationship?
   _____too much _____wholesome _____none

6. Do I have a realistic picture of our relationship? How does my partner see the relationship? How do I view the relationship?

7. Has my dating experience been limited largely to one individual? (If "Yes," then why? What are my reasons for believing this is best for us?)

8. What are the weaknesses or potential weaknesses in my dating partner? Have we discussed these openly? What progress is being made?

9. Are my emotions leading me toward a relationship that is not realistic?

10. Are we attempting the impossible? Do we agree on spiritual matters?

2

*H*ow to *F*ind a *M*ate

*D*id anyone ever get married in biblical times? "Don't be foolish," someone will say. "Obviously, many people were married in biblical times."

What I mean is, does the Bible tell us how it happened? How did boy meet girl, and what transpired from that point? Many will remember the story of Ruth and Boaz, and it is a beautiful love story, but there is a lesser-known story that gives more details of God's bringing male and female together. It is the account of Isaac and Rebekah, recorded in Genesis, chapter 24. The whole chapter is devoted to the subject "How does a man get a wife?" or "How does a woman get a husband?" Sixty-seven verses give minute details of the process, yet many of us have never even read it.

I suggest that before you go further you read this fascinating account. Note that the culture was radically different from ours, but the principles are the same. For example, it was the servant of Abraham who actually went on the journey to secure a wife for Isaac, while Isaac remained at home.

Here is the account from Genesis 24:1–67:

Abraham was now old and well advanced in years, and the Lord had blessed him in every way. He said to the chief servant in his household, the one in charge of all that he had, "Put your hand under my thigh. I want you to swear by the Lord, the God of heaven and the God of earth, that you will not get a wife for my son from the daughters of the Canaanites, among whom I am living, but will go to my country and my own relatives and get a wife for my son Isaac."

The servant asked him, "What if the woman is unwilling to come back with me to this land? Shall I then take your son back to the country you came from?"

"Make sure that you do not take my son back there," Abraham said. "The Lord, the God of heaven, who brought me out of my father's household and my native land and who spoke to me and promised me on oath, saying, 'To your offspring I will give this land'—he will send his angel before you so that you can get a wife for my son from there. If the woman is unwilling to come back with you, then you will be released from this oath of mine. Only do not take my son back there." So the servant put his hand under the thigh of his master Abraham and swore an oath to him concerning this matter.

Then the servant took ten of his master's camels and left, taking with him all kinds of good things from his master. He set out for Aram Naharaim and made his way to the town of Nahor. He had the camels kneel down near the well outside the town; it was toward evening, the time the women go out to draw water.

Then he prayed, "O Lord, God of my master Abraham, give me success today, and show kindness to my master Abraham. See, I am standing beside this spring, and the daughters of the townspeople are coming out to draw water. May it be that when I say to a girl, 'Please let down your jar that I may have a drink,' and she says, 'Drink, and I'll water your camels too'—let her be the one you have chosen for your servant Isaac. By this I will know that you have shown kindness to my master."

Before he had finished praying, Rebekah came out with her jar on her shoulder. She was the daughter of Bethuel son of Milcah, who was the wife of Abraham's brother Nahor. The girl was very beautiful, a virgin; no man had ever lain with her. She went down to the spring, filled her jar and came up again.

The servant hurried to meet her and said, "Please give me a little water from your jar."

"Drink, my lord," she said, and quickly lowered the jar to her hands and gave him a drink.

After she had given him a drink, she said, "I'll draw water for your camels too, until they have finished drinking." So she quickly emptied her jar into the trough, ran back to the well to draw more water, and drew enough for all his camels. Without saying a word, the man watched her closely to learn whether or not the Lord had made his journey successful.

When the camels had finished drinking, the man took out a gold nose ring weighing a beka and two gold bracelets weighing ten shekels. Then he asked, "Whose daughter are you? Please tell me, is there room in your father's house for us to spend the night?"

She answered him, "I am the daughter of Bethuel, the son that Milcah bore to Nahor." And she added, "We have plenty of straw and fodder, as well as room for you to spend the night."

Then the man bowed down and worshiped the Lord, saying, "Praise be to the Lord, the God of my master Abraham, who has not abandoned his kindness and faithfulness to my master. As for me, the Lord has led me on the journey to the house of my master's relatives."

The girl ran and told her mother's household about these things. Now Rebekah had a brother named Laban, and he hurried out to the man at the spring. As soon as he had seen the nose ring, and the bracelets on his sister's arms, and had heard Rebekah tell what the man said to her, he went out to the man and found him standing by the camels near the spring. "Come, you who are blessed by the Lord," he said. "Why are you standing out here? I have prepared the house and a place for the camels."

So the man went to the house, and the camels were unloaded. Straw and fodder were brought for the camels, and water for him and his men to wash their feet. Then food was set before him, but he said, "I will not eat until I have told you what I have to say."

"Then tell us," Laban said.

So he said, "I am Abraham's servant. The Lord has blessed my master abundantly, and he has become wealthy. He has given him sheep and cattle, silver and gold, menservants and maidservants, and camels and donkeys. My master's wife Sarah has borne him a son in her old age, and he has given him everything he owns. And my master made me swear an oath, and said, 'You must not get a wife for my son from the daughters of the Canaanites, in whose land I live, but go to my father's family and to my own clan, and get a wife for my son.'

"Then I asked my master, 'What if the woman will not come back with me?'

"He replied, 'The Lord, before whom I have walked, will send his angel with you and make your journey a success, so that you can get a wife for my son from my own clan and from my father's family. Then, when you go to my clan, you will be released from my oath even if they refuse to give her to you—you will be released from my oath.

"When I came to the spring today, I said, 'O Lord, God of my master Abraham, if you will, please grant success to the journey on which I have come. See, I am standing beside this spring; if a maiden comes out to draw water and I say to her, "Please let me drink a little water from your jar," and if she says to me, "Drink, and I'll draw water for your camels too," let her be the one the Lord has chosen for my master's son.'

"Before I finished praying in my heart, Rebekah came out, with her jar on her shoulder. She went down to the spring and drew water, and I said to her, 'Please give me a drink.'

"She quickly lowered her jar from her shoulder and said, 'Drink, and I'll water your camels too.' So I drank, and she watered the camels also.

"I asked her, 'Whose daughter are you?'

"She said, 'The daughter of Bethuel son of Nahor, whom Milcah bore to him.'

"Then I put the ring in her nose and the bracelets on her arms, and I bowed down and worshiped the Lord. I praised the Lord, the God of my master Abraham, who had led me on the right road to get the granddaughter of my master's brother for his son. Now if you will show kindness and faithfulness to my master, tell me; and if not, tell me, so I may know which way to turn."

Laban and Bethuel answered, "This is from the Lord; we can say nothing to you one way or the other. Here is Rebekah; take her and go, and let her become the wife of your master's son, as the Lord has directed."

When Abraham's servant heard what they said, he bowed down to the ground before the Lord. Then the servant brought out gold and silver jewelry and articles of clothing and gave them to Rebekah; he also gave costly gifts to her brother and to her mother. Then he and the men who were with him ate and drank and spent the night there.

When they got up the next morning, he said, "Send me on my way to my master."

But her brother and her mother replied, "Let the girl remain with us ten days or so; then you may go."

But he said to them, "Do not detain me, now that the Lord has granted success to my journey. Send me on my way so I may go to my master."

Then they said, "Let's call the girl and ask her about it." So they called Rebekah and asked her, "Will you go with this man?"

"I will go," she said.

So they sent their sister Rebekah on her way, along with her nurse and Abraham's servant and his men. And they blessed Rebekah and said to her, "Our sister, may you increase to thousands upon thousands; may your offspring possess the gates of their enemies."

Then Rebekah and her maids got ready and mounted their camels and went back with the man. So the servant took Rebekah and left.

Now Isaac had come from Beer Lahai Roi, for he was living in the Negev. He went out to the field one evening to meditate, and as he looked up, he saw camels approaching. Rebekah also looked up and saw Isaac. She got down from her camel and asked the servant, "Who is that man in the field coming to meet us?"

"He is my master," the servant answered. So she took her veil and covered herself.

Then the servant told Isaac all he had done. Isaac brought her into the tent of his mother Sarah, and he married Rebekah. So she became his wife, and he loved her; and Isaac was comforted after his mother's death.

This story is packed with practical guidelines for any man or woman in pursuit of a marriage partner. First, I want to observe with you some of the general guidelines, then give suggestions to men and women about their specific roles in the thrilling adventure of "operation marriage."

GENERAL GUIDELINES

We shall look at these as they unfold in the biblical account, but not necessarily in the order of their importance. The first principle is the Principle of Mutuality.

Principle of Mutuality

The more you hold in common, the better the foundation. Abraham said to his servant, " That you will not get a wife for my son from the daughters of the Canaanites, among whom I am living, but will go to my country and my own relatives and get a wife for my son Isaac" (vv. 3–4).

What was Abraham's great concern? The welfare of his son. He wanted the best possible marriage for Isaac, and he recognized the need for a common foundation. The culture, religion, language, and moral values of the Canaanites were vastly different from those of Abraham's kindred. The gap was too broad to bridge. The degenerate nature of the Canaanites' values was so cancerous that God eventually ordered surgery on the entire culture. Abraham recognized that marital oneness cannot be obtained if the partners have no common foundation on which to build.

What are the implications of this principle for us? Basically, it means that we must examine our relationship to evaluate whether or not we have a sufficient foundation for marriage. As we look at the intellectual, social, spiritual, and physical aspects of our relationship, do we have a common base? I do not mean that we must be identical, but we must be walking close enough to hold hands.

He is a Ph.D. candidate and strongly "in love" with a sweet, beautiful blonde. Three weeks after marriage, he finds that she cannot read. Given such an intellectual barrier, what are the chances of a mutually satisfying marriage? Or, she is deeply and genuinely committed to Jesus Christ as Lord. He is a "Sunday morning Christian" whose religion is only skin deep. How can they walk together?

This is the point at which students usually ask me for my views on interracial marriages. And this is the principle that I feel must be considered by those who would contemplate such. This passage cannot be taken as a dogmatic statement against interracial marriage. The issue was not race, but culture. Racially (that is, physically), the Canaanites and the inhabitants of Ur (Abraham's homeland) likely were very similar. The issue was culture—religion, language, social customs, and values. That is still the issue. If you ask me point-blank, "Do you advise interracial marriages?" my answer is no. I think the cultural barriers are formidable. But I must add that I believe every Christian must make his or her own decision on the matter.

I would not say that God never leads committed Christians to marry across racial lines. To say this would be to judge some of the world's greatest missionary leaders. I would say, however, that such marriages would be the exception, not the rule. A couple who contemplates such ought to thoroughly acquaint themselves with each other's culture by lengthy, in-depth time spent in each other's home and social setting.

We must make sure that we are not seeking to build a bridge over an impossibly wide chasm. Ultimately, "God's will" is the answer that any Christian young person must seek. We must not, however, allow a superficial understanding of "God's will" to erase our consideration of the principle of mutuality.

I want to explore this principle further when we come to the discussion on the purpose of marriage, but at this point we must examine the intellectual, social, physical, and spiritual aspects of our relationship. A marriage cannot be built upon one area alone. A common foundation in these areas does not guarantee a happy marriage, but it certainly enhances the probability of such.

Principle of Divine Activity

You are not alone in your search for a mate. Neither is the process left to mere chance. Abraham said, "God will send his angel before you, and you shall take a wife unto my son." Do you think God was any more concerned about Isaac than about you? He is no respecter of persons. God's secret agents are on your side, too.

I know some of you are wishing those agents would "get on the stick," but let me remind you that God does not work His staff overtime. Everything is on schedule. Perhaps you are concentrating too much on *finding* the right person and not enough on *being* the right person.

Of course, it is not God's plan for every believer to be married. What a loss to the world if we removed from history all those single saints who through the ages have given their lives in select service to God. That is another whole subject, but I feel very strongly that marriage is not a higher calling than the single state. Happy indeed are those people, married or single, who have discovered that happiness is not found in marriage, but in a right relationship with God.

Marriage is the norm, however, in the sense that it is the lifestyle that God intends for most of his children. The Bible, from beginning to end, speaks of marriage and family. I think you can assume that marriage is God's plan for you unless it is revealed otherwise in His time.

Not only is it God's plan for most, but God is actively involved in the process. If an angel went before Abraham's servant (and the rest of the chapter leaves little doubt of that), then we can count on supernatural help in our pursuit, also. This ought to give a great deal of encouragement to those uncertain souls who believe they do not have as firm a grip on the social graces as do their peers. This is not merely a human pursuit. God is active, and God will guide.

This principle of Divine Activity implies a practical response on our part—pray, pray, pray! I say it three times because in the chapter before us, the servant of Abraham prayed three times. That is, three prayers are recorded. He may have prayed even more. It is significant, however, that in this brief account we have three recorded times of prayer. He prayed first of all before he met the girl (vv. 12–14). He prayed again after some initial signs of progress (vv. 26–27). He bowed in a prayer of praise later after her parents said yes.

The pattern? Pray before you date. Pray while you are dating. Pray after the engagement. The whole adventure of finding a mate is to be done in constant fellowship with God. It is not a private or secular pursuit. Many couples do themselves a disservice by locking God out of this area of their lives. Why go it on your own when you can have all the help of heaven?

Principle of Beauty

The person you marry ought to be "good looking," at least to you. The text says of Rebekah, "The girl was very beautiful" (v. 16). Now, I do not mean to foster the beauty cult of our day, in which beauty is worshiped above all else. I am not suggesting that you must marry a beauty queen or a prince in shining armor. What I am suggesting is that the person you marry should be attractive to you. You should feel good about the way he or she looks.

I am not calling for hypocrisy. You need not say that she is the most beautiful or he the most handsome person you have ever seen. Most of us are too sophisticated to be deceived by that anyway. No, I am not talking about flattery but about a good, solid feeling that this person is someone upon whom you can look with pleasure for the next forty years of your life.

Of course, beauty is far more than physical features. Sometimes those who do not at first appeal to us as beautiful become beautiful as we get to know them. Character, attitude, love, and other internal characteristics have a way of making the most homely person beautiful.

Therefore, when I say your mate should be beautiful, I am thinking of the total person. This does not mean, however, that this principle is unimportant. We are aesthetic creatures. We have the ability to appreciate beauty, and a good foundation for marriage includes the conviction that the person you are about to marry is a beautiful person.

Principle of Morality

In the story of Isaac and Rebekah some very personal details are recorded. Having said that Rebekah was "very beautiful," the author adds that she was "a virgin." And lest there be any question about what is meant, he explains, "No man had ever lain with her" (v. 16).

Let there be no mistake; God's plan is for men and women to come to marriage without having had sexual intercourse. God did not give us this principle to hurt us but to help us. He was not trying to make it hard on us but to make it good for us. From beginning to end, the Bible makes this principle clear. If you have any question on this point, examine the data for yourself. Get a concordance and examine all those passages that speak of "fornication." That is the biblical word most commonly used for sexual intercourse before marriage. It is always condemned in the Old and New Testaments. God's ideal is always chastity before marriage.

I would be naive if I failed to deal with the fact that for many young people of our day this ideal is no longer a possibility. That is, they have already failed with regard to this biblical ideal. What are they to do? My answer is the same as I would give if the problem were in any other area of failure. Repentance and faith in Jesus Christ are still the answer to man's falling short of the mark.

Do not allow past failure to cause you to give up the warfare. To lose a battle does not mean that the war is lost. We cannot retrace our steps. We cannot undo the past. We can, however, chart our course for the future. Do not excuse present behavior because of past failure. Confess your wrong and accept God's forgiveness (1 John 1:9).

Such action on your part does not mean that all the results of your wrong will be eradicated. God forgives, but the natural results of sin are not removed totally. A man who gets intoxicated and slams his car into a telephone pole, resulting in a broken arm and a demolished car, may have God's forgiveness before he gets to the hospital, but his arm is still broken and his car lost. Thus, in our moral failures, the scars of wrong are not totally removed by confession. What, then, are we to do with these scars?

I believe the biblical injunction is "honesty in all things" (see Ephesians 4:15, 25). If we have failed in the past, and now under God's control we want the best in marriage, we must be honest with our potential mate. Disclose fully what has happened in the past. Marriage has no closets for skeletons. God has forgiven if you have confessed. Now trust your partner to forgive and accept you as you are, not as he or she might wish you were. If such acceptance cannot be experienced, then marriage should not be consummated. You must enter marriage with all the cards on the table.

In addition to the acceptance of your potential mate, you must also accept yourself and overcome your own past. If, for example, you have a negative attitude toward sex because of past failures, you must not sweep this under the rug and go on as though this attitude does not exist. Face it, and deal with it.

The starting point for overcoming such a negative attitude is an in-depth study of what the Scriptures say about sex. One cannot come away from such a study without the impression that the biblical view of sexual intercourse within marriage is positive. It is wholesome, beautiful, and ordained of God. An understanding of the truth will liberate from negative attitudes. Thank God for the truth and ask Him to change feelings to coincide with the truth.

No, the results of sin are never erased. You are never better for having sinned, but there is substantial healing. That is the message of the grace of God. You are not destined to fail in marriage because of past sin. You will have roadblocks to overcome that would not be there if you had followed God's ideal, but the Holy Spirit has come to heal our infirmities and help us reach our potential.

The non-Christian does not have such help. Therefore, premarital sexual experience for the non-Christian has long-lasting detrimental results. Contrary to many popular ideas, secular research indicates that sexual promiscuity before marriage has a positive correlation with extramarital sexual relationships within marriage.[1] Living together before marriage does not increase the degree of fidelity in marriage but, rather, weakens that possibility. God, who made us, also gave us the rules. We do ourselves a great disservice when we disregard them.

Principle of Parental Relationships

Parents are important. Someone has said, "God gave us a lot of guidance when He gave us parents." That statement is true even when those parents are non-Christian. Without them we would not have made it this far. When we come to marriage, we must not circumvent their guidance. We need the blessing of our parents if at all possible.

It is interesting that of the sixty-seven verses recording the union of Isaac and Rebekah, over half of them deal with their relationship to their parents (vv. 1–9; 28–60). Abraham was active in giving basic guidelines, and Rebekah's parents were consulted fully with regard to their willingness to give Rebekah as a wife for Isaac.

I know that the cultural setting was radically different from our own. The role of the parents was far greater than in Western society, but even when we make allowances for cultural differences, the Bible still puts a strong emphasis upon maintaining healthy relationships with parents.

It is true that in marriage we leave our parents and commit ourselves to each other, and I want to talk about that later, but that leaving is never in an absolute sense. First Timothy, chapter 5, makes clear that our responsibility to our parents is lifelong.

What does this mean for the young couple contemplating marriage? It means that such plans should be shared fully with parents. Having met Abraham's servant at the well, the next thing Rebekah did was to tell her parents what had happened (v. 28). Later, the servant fully informed her parents why he believed Rebekah was the one for Isaac. He also assured them that Isaac was capable of meeting the financial needs of their daughter. He spoke of the deep spiritual commitment of Isaac, as the son of Abraham, friend of God. Having related all of that, he waited for further confirmation that this was God's plan—

the affirmative response of her parents (v. 49).

If at all possible, a couple should have the blessing of both sets of parents. I am not saying that a couple should never get married when their parents object. I am saying that if there are objections, I believe the couple should wait and give God time to change attitudes.

Parents need to know that we respect their judgment and that we want their blessing. We should never convey the idea that what they think is unimportant to us. Life is too short and fragile to build it upon broken relationships. We need the emotional stability that comes from a positive and wholesome attitude toward our parents and those of our spouse.

If your parents do object to your marriage, how long do you wait for their approval? That is a question born out of struggle, and it deserves a good answer. I am sorry that I do not have a good answer to give. I could say until you are twenty-three, but that would be arbitrary. Only you can answer that question, but most who have married against their parents' wishes could have waited several years and profited from the wait. Could it be that your parents' disapproval is God's way of slowing you down?

Principle of Timing

There are two principles relating to timing in this account, each equally important. The first is "Don't jump the gun!" How easy it is to go too fast, to assume too much. Abraham's servant had prayed a very specific prayer. He had asked that, as he stood by the community well and asked the young ladies for a drink, the one whom God intended would not only give him a drink, but also would offer to draw water for his camels. While he was still praying, Rebekah came out, and he set the plan into motion by asking for a drink. Rebekah gladly responded. Then the butterflies started to fly as Rebekah said, "I'll draw some water for your camels also" (v. 19).

That was exactly what he had prayed for. God had

answered his prayer. This has got to be the one! Let us announce our engagement! Tell everybody, "I've found the one for me." That is the way many of us would have responded.

But that is not the way the servant responded. Rather, "without saying a word, the man watched her closely to learn whether or not the Lord had made his journey successful" (v. 21). Had God answered his prayer? It certainly appeared so. But you see, an assurance of God's will is not gained by one little test.

"O Lord, if this is the one, then let him ask me to go home with him at Christmas." That is fine, but that is not enough. I am not opposed to such prayers, but we must not exalt them out of proportion. I have known couples who felt they should get married because some such prayer seemed to be answered, even when all other signs pointed in the opposite direction.

Abraham's servant did not "jump the gun." He waited to make sure that this was of God. One sign was not enough. He moved on to the more meaningful signs: Is she interested, and are her parents willing? The next twenty-seven verses deal with gifts; conversations with mother, father, brother, and others; consideration of finances, living arrangements, spiritual matters, and so on. Even after all this, we still find an openness on the part of the servant. "Now if you will show kindness and faithfulness to my master, tell me; and if not, tell me, so I may know which way to turn" (v. 49). Many signs now seemed to be positive, but he wanted one more: her parents' blessing, which we have already discussed.

This spirit of openness to God's leadership is sadly lacking in the relationship of many couples. By nature, we are prone to run too fast, to assume that because we feel what we feel, and that this is true or that is true, we should get married. Far too little consideration is given to the weightier matters of intellectual, social, spiritual, and cultural mutuality. God's leadership is not usually against reason. Take your time. Do not say everything you think.

Discuss issues. Explore the foundation. Do not make a decision in the dark. It is the truth that sets us free.

To parallel this emphasis, there is another principle related to time. "Once the green lights are flashing, don't wait for a vision in the night!" I say this especially for those timid souls who have difficulty deciding what kind of peanut butter to buy. I mean those who are so slow in decision making that by the time they decide, the decision is no longer necessary. Most of you do not need this principle, but for some it is important. Once the servant had the positive response of Rebekah's parents, coupled with all the other green lights discussed above, he was ready to move. Her mother and brother tried to talk him into delaying the trip for ten days or so, but he said, "Do not detain me" (v. 56). Let me go. Wedding bells are ringing in the chapel.

Marriage is a big step. Some prefer the word *leap*. If you have had difficulty in making decisions all your life, then I can assure you that you are going to have cold feet when you near the wedding altar. (It took him two years to decide that he wanted to go to college and six years to get his degree because he changed his major five times. Look out, because he will go into trauma if the possibility of marriage arises.)

What am I trying to say? When you have a Christ-centered relationship with a member of the opposite sex and a string of green lights from here to Chicago, then do not wait for the handwriting on the wall. At some point, you have to make a decision. Do not misunderstand me. If there are still some bright red lights flashing, some things that really bother you, some unresolved hurdles, I am not suggesting that you ignore them. Such lights are always for our warning. We need to work at the problems until the lights are green, or else we need to turn aside. If all the signs are green lights, then trust God and move forward.

Principle of God's Will

God's will supersedes "love" as a basis for marriage.

As noted earlier, I usually ask couples who come for premarital counseling why they want to get married. It seems
a logical question to me. Most seem stunned that I would
ask such a question, but when they decide that I am serious they usually respond, "Because we love each other."
That is supposed to be the reason for getting married. The
Christian and the non-Christian seem to agree that love is
the basis for marriage. When I press them for definitions, I
find that often the Christian and the non-Christian differ
little in their view of love.

If love were the basis for marriage, then Isaac and
Rebekah would not have gotten married. They never saw
each other until the wedding day. The Scriptures say, "So
she became his wife, and he loved her" (v. 67). It was in
that order. Love came after marriage for them. There was
no opportunity before marriage. Now, I like our system
better. At least we have the possibility for love to develop
before marriage. Since our pattern is not universal, there
must be something more fundamental as a basis for
Christian marriage. I believe that basis is the will of
God—the plan of the Creator.

The Christian should get married because he or she is
deeply convinced that this marriage is the work of God,
that God in His infinite wisdom has brought the couple
together and intends that they live their lives in union with
each other and with Him. Anything less than this conviction is something less than a biblical basis for marriage.
All other foundations for marriage are changeable. Even
love, by whatever definition, comes and goes, but the will
of God is constant.

God will not lead you into a marriage for the purpose
of failure. If you have His choice in your mate, you have
the highest potential for fulfillment in marriage. This does
not mean that God will not help you if you turn to Him
later in life. You may not have known Him at the time of
marriage and thus could not have had the benefit of His
guidance. God always wants to take us where we are and
help us reach our greatest potential from that point. There

is hope for every marriage in which the couple will turn to Him for guidance. If you are not yet married, however, why would you want less than God's best?

How, then, do you discern God's will? This is the purpose of the entire first section of this volume. God's leadership, as noted above, is according to reason. God gave us a means of guidance when He gave us our minds. When our minds are committed to Him, when we are using His principles in the search for a mate, He will guide us to a confident assurance of His will. It is this confidence that will keep us growing together when the storm hits. "Yes, we have a problem, but God has called us together, so there is an answer." This will be your reasoning, and you will find that answer and go on from conflict to growth.

SUGGESTIONS

In addition to the general principles listed above, there are also some practical suggestions to both men and women that can be observed in this account of Isaac and Rebekah. I want to speak first to the men.

For Men

Make much of gifts. The number of gifts that were given in this account is amazing. It is obvious that gifts were very important to Abraham's servant, for he made the journey laden with them. He knew that when he found the right girl, he was going to give gifts. His first gift came rather soon after the first indication that this was the girl of God's choice. After his first prayer was answered, he gave two bracelets and a ring, all gold (v. 22). Later on, after her parents had expressed their willingness, he gave more gifts to Rebekah and also gifts to her mother and brother (v. 53).

I know that the type of gift and place for gifts will vary from culture to culture, but in all my study of various cultures, I have never discovered a culture where gift-giving is not a part of the marriage process. There is something about the giving of gifts that expresses love and worth.

I do not suggest that in our society a man should give gifts lightly and freely. The spendthrift who gives expensive gifts to every girl he dates will probably be thought foolish rather than someone to be admired. It is the rare girl, however, who does not appreciate a gift from that special man in her life if it is accompanied with an attitude of love. In my opinion, gifts should be reserved for that person for whom I have a special attraction and some reason to believe that this may be God's selection for me.

Gifts become more important as the relationship develops. Some men make a serious mistake at this point. After engagement and marriage they come to take their mates for granted and suppose that gifts are unimportant. The exact opposite ought to be true. The more you know each other, the more you love each other, the more you ought to give gifts.

They do not need to be expensive gifts. The old adage "It's the thought that counts" is certainly true. You should not, however, use this as an excuse for hoarding money. Some of the best investments you will ever make will be those investments in gifts for your partner.

Go where the girls are. When you think of it, the servant of Abraham was given a colossal assignment: to go back to Abraham's homeland and secure a bride for Isaac. Where in the world would one begin? Your assignment is even more colossal. Because of the population explosion the possibilities are expanded. How in all the world do you find the woman for you?

Well, here is one simple, but profound, guideline: go where the women are! The Scriptures say of Abraham's servant, "He had the camels kneel down near the well outside the town; it was toward evening, the time the women go out to draw water" (v. 11). He began by going to the place in that community where the women came each evening—the community well. Now, we do not have wells in our society, but we do have libraries, ball games, church activities, Bible studies, and many other places where Christian women go regularly. It seems to me that these would be logical places for a man to go if he wants God's direction in finding a marriage partner.

I am not intending to dictate any pattern of operation. Nor do I wish to communicate that a man should be walking through the library every evening, straining as an animal about to spring on its prey. What I do want to say is that we need to relate normally and naturally to women in the social settings that our society provides. It is most likely that when God chooses to bring you into contact with His choice for you, it will be in this context. Why make it difficult for God by sitting in your room every night reading Shakespeare? Go where the girls are!

I know there is a school of thought that says dedicated Christian men ought to stay away from women and concentrate upon their spiritual growth. I do not question the motive of such, but I do question the results. Spirituality cannot be developed in a vacuum. One may feel that he is making great spiritual progress, but when confronted with the real world, falls flat on his face. I believe that normal Christian growth is best achieved in the context of social interaction with members of the opposite sex.

Make the spiritual central. This is a good place to talk about the role of the spiritual life in dating relationships. One cannot read the account of Isaac and Rebekah without sensing that God was central in their consideration. From beginning to end the servant spoke freely of his master's faith in God. He prayed in private and in the presence of Rebekah's family. He told her parents clearly of Isaac's faith in God and how God had led him to his decision about Rebekah.

You will do well to follow the servant's example. Your relationship with God is the most important aspect of your life. You dare not leave Him at church when you date. Conversation ought to be genuine and open regarding your relationship with God.

I believe that couples who are moving toward marriage ought to be regularly praying together, studying the Scriptures together, attending worship services together, and discussing their aspirations and visions together. It is through this kind of freedom to interact that one determines the cornerstone of marriage—spiritual mutuality. Together you dig to find your individual spiritual foundation and then help each other grow. If Christ is kept at the center of the relationship before marriage, He is likely to remain there after marriage.

Several excellent Bible studies for couples are available. In the assignment section of this chapter, I suggest one that has helped many couples examine their relationship from a biblical perspective and grow in the process.

For Women

Be faithful in the routine. I wonder how many times Rebekah had gone to that well? I doubt that she went there with the special agenda of finding a husband. She was doing the routine—drawing water for her family. In her culture, it was one of her regular chores, not an abnormal, unnatural thing, just one of those duties that she did daily.

Do you sometimes become bored with the routine? Do you take an apathetic attitude toward life simply because things seem to remain the same day after day? Could it be that you are making God's job more difficult because of your attitude and behavior? It is very likely that you will meet the man who is to be your husband in some unromantic place like the college dining hall, the library, a Sunday school class, or a coed Bible study.

The daily details are important. Paul admonishes us to do everything with a wholehearted attitude, as though we were doing it for Christ Himself (Colossians 3:23). If you will commit yourself to this philosophy and apply it to those routine assignments that are yours day by day, you will put yourself in the best possible position to cooperate with God in His purposes for your life.

The routine is never merely routine when it is done

with God. All of life is meant to be lived in fellowship with Him. How sad that so many of us simply *do* things, rather than do things *with Him*. His presence makes all the difference in the world. He wants our fellowship all along the way as He unfolds His plans for our lives. On one of those routine days, when you are ready, He will bring the right man to the well.

Be kind. We learned it as children. It is too bad that we forget it as adults. Pure old unadulterated kindness is one of the great qualities of the truly liberated woman. Rebekah was not so self-centered that she was unable to serve others.

True freedom does not mean that we live unto ourselves. Rather, it means that we are freed from the bondage of selfishness and have the liberty to invest our lives in the good of others. It was a little matter, to be sure—simply watering the camels—a deed very much akin to making brownies or complimenting a man for having a clean car. Not much, but an expression of kindness. What could one do that would speak more eloquently?

Kindness is still a virtue to be cultivated. It is one of the longest arms of love and is always appropriate. It is never in poor taste to be kind. It is in the expressing of kindness that many a girl has ignited a spark that has grown into a flame. Unending in its value, kindness will serve the purposes of oneness as long as you live. No husband is ever too old to appreciate kindness, and no wife unable to extend it.

Share your joys with your parents. When Rebekah had her first indication that God was about to do something, she told her parents (v. 28). I have mentioned this earlier, but I say it again here because I believe many women keep their mothers from great joy by failing to tell freely of God's work in their lives. If your parents are alive, they are concerned about your welfare. They rejoice when you rejoice and weep when you weep. Perhaps you do not want to see them weep, but surely you wish them to share your joy. You can add much to their lives by sharing the joy of premarital growth.

WARNING!

I must make one clarifying statement lest the content of this chapter be misunderstood. The Christian is never to drop all other pursuits and set out on a journey to "find a wife" or to "find a husband." Such a journey was necessary in Isaac's case because of the geographical and cultural factors discussed above. For most of us, however, God's choice will be revealed in the context of normal pursuits.

As noted, most of us need to concentrate upon *becoming* the right person, rather than upon *finding* the right person. When we are ready, it is a very easy matter for God to work out the logistics of bringing us together.

Too many Christians have contracted the disease commonly known by college students as "senior panic" and have made unwise and unguided decisions. Do not get too eager. God's timing is as important as God's person.

Marriage is not the answer to all of one's inadequacies. God is! As we get to know God, He seeks to give us help in every area of life. He does not, however, make decisions for us. That responsibility He has delegated to us. The principles in this chapter are designed to make us wise decision makers.

GROWTH ASSIGNMENTS

For the Unmarried:

1. If you are engaged or moving with your partner steadily in that direction, read and discuss each of the "General Guidelines" in this chapter. Use this as a facilitator for honesty and openness in these areas.

2. If, afterwards, you are still committed to continuing your relationship, begin a weekly or biweekly Bible study session together. I would suggest *Before You Marry*, by J. Allan Peterson (see Appendix). Complete your Bible study individually and discuss the concepts when you are together.

3. Begin praying together at least once a week.

4. Take notes on the biblical messages that you hear and discuss them with each other.

5. Those who are not dating anyone seriously should give special attention to those sections entitled "Go where the girls are" and "Be faithful in the routine." What steps can you take to make these principles practical in your own life?

For the Married:

1. This chapter may appear to have no application to your life inasmuch as you have already found a mate. As you have read the chapter, your reaction has likely been one of the following: a sense of gratitude and joy as you remember the manner in which God led you to your mate or a sense of despair as you realize how little you knew of God's ways before you were married. What is your honest response at this point?

2. The marvelous message of the Bible is that God wants to take us as we are, where we are, and lead us to where we ought to be. Are you honestly open to growth in your marital relationship?

3. What act of kindness will you do for your mate this week? What gift will you give?

4. Read Colossians 3:23–24. Does your attitude toward your daily responsibilities need to be changed? Are you willing to ask for God's help?

3

The Goal of Marriage

*B*efore we launch into a study of marriage, perhaps we ought to pause long enough to ask, "What is the purpose of marriage?" To those trained in decision making and goal setting, this will seem an obvious first question. For others, with ideas firmly set, this will seem a useless question. After all, everyone knows the purpose of marriage—or does he? If you asked a dozen friends that question and asked them to write their answers privately, how many different answers do you think you would receive? I would like to list some of the answers that I have received from both singles and marrieds:

- sex
- companionship
- love
- to provide a home for children
- social acceptance
- economic advantage
- security

"But can't these objectives be accomplished outside marriage?" asks modern man. Indeed, the social and economic advantages of marriage have been called into question in our day. Certainly our society has demonstrated that sexual relations need not be limited to marriage. What of love, security, companionship, and a home for children? Can these not be accomplished to some degree without marriage? Then why marriage?

These are the reasonings of modern secular man. What does the Bible say? Does God speak to this question? What is the purpose of marriage according to the Scriptures?

The biblical picture of marriage is the blending of two lives in the deepest possible way into a new unit that will both satisfy the individuals involved and serve the purposes of God in the highest possible manner. The heart of mankind cries out for unity. We are social creatures. God Himself said of Adam, "It is not good for the man to be alone" (Genesis 2:18). I would remind you that this analysis was before the Fall of man, and that this man already had the warm, personal fellowship of God. Yet God said, "That is not enough!"

God's answer to man's need was to create woman, one who could be a suitable helper (Genesis 2:18). The Hebrew word used here is one that literally means "face to face." That is, God created one with whom man could have a face-to-face relationship. It speaks of that kind of in-depth personal relationship whereby the two are united in an unbreakable union that satisfies the deepest longings of the human heart. Marriage was God's answer for man's deepest human need—union of life with another.

As the pages of Scripture unfold man's history, we see that this unity is to encompass all of life. It is not simply a physical relationship. Nor is it simply the giving and receiving of emotional support. It is rather the total union of two lives on the intellectual, social, spiritual, emotional, and physical levels.

This kind of union cannot come without the deep and enduring commitment that God intends to accompany marriage. Marriage is not a contract to make sexual relationships legal. It is not merely a social institution to provide for the care of children. It is not merely a psychological clinic where we gain the emotional support we need. It is not a means for gaining social status or economic security. The ultimate purpose of marriage is not even achieved when it is a vehicle for love and companionship, as valuable as these are.

The supreme purpose of marriage is the union of two individuals at the deepest possible level and in all areas, which in turn brings the greatest possible sense of fulfillment to the couple and at the same time serves best the purposes of God for their lives.

THE NATURE OF MARITAL UNITY

Obviously, getting married does not give a couple this kind of unity. There is a difference between "being united" and "unity." As the old country preacher used to say, "When you tie the tails of two cats together and hang them across the fence, you have united them, but then unity is a different matter."

Perhaps the best biblical example that we have of this kind of unity is God Himself. It is interesting that the word used for "one" in Genesis 2:24, where God says, "For this reason a man will leave his father and mother and be united to his wife, and they will become *one* flesh" (italics added), is the same Hebrew word used of God Himself in Deuteronomy 6:4 where we read, "Hear, O Israel: The Lord our God, the Lord is *one*" (italics added).

The word "one" speaks of composite unity as opposed to absolute unity. The Scriptures reveal God to be Father, Son, and Spirit, yet one. We do not have three Gods but one God, triune in nature. Illustrations of the Trinity are many, and all break down at some point, but let me use a very common one to illustrate some of the implications of this unity.

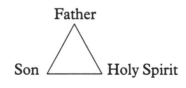

The triangle may be placed on any side, and the Father, Son, and Spirit labels moved to any position. It makes no difference, for God is one. What we cannot do is erase one side or remove one title. It must all stand together. God is triune, and God is one. We cannot fully understand this statement, yet we must speak of God in this manner, because this is the manner in which He has revealed Himself. We would not know that God is triune unless God had revealed Himself as triune. We would not know that the Trinity is a unity except that God has revealed it as such.

God is unity. On the other hand, God is diversity. We cannot rightly say that there are no distinctions among the Trinity. Strictly speaking, the Holy Spirit did not die for us upon the cross. That was the work of the Son. As believers, we are not indwelt by the Father, but by the Spirit. The Members of the Trinity do have varying roles, yet unity. It is unthinkable that members of the Trinity would ever operate as separate entities. From Genesis 1:26 where God said, "Let *us* make man in *our* image" (italics added) to Revelation 22:16–21, we find the Trinity working together as composite unity.

What implications does this divine unity have for marriage? Let me use a second triangle to illustrate.

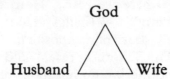

This time the triangle may not be tilted to rest on another side. God must remain at the apex of a Christian marriage. We can, however, exchange the labels "husband" and "wife," for they are to be one. Their objective is to cooperate with God in developing their unity. This does not mean that the wife will lose her identity as a person any more than the Holy Spirit loses His identity in the Trinity.

Marital unity is not the kind of unity that eradicates personality. Rather, it is the kind of unity that frees you to express your own diversity, yet experience complete oneness with your mate. You are free to be all that God intends you to be, while experiencing all that God intended when He made us male and female. No truth could be more liberating and satisfying.

IMPLICATIONS FOR THE UNMARRIED

If the goal of marriage is the deep union of two individuals in every area of life, then what implications does this goal have for an individual who is contemplating marriage? It seems to me that such an understanding should open many avenues of exploration.

If our goal is oneness, then the key question before marriage ought to be "What reasons do we have for believing that we could become one?" As we examine the intellectual, social, emotional, physical, and spiritual areas of life, what do we find? Do we hold enough in common in these areas to provide a foundation for oneness? No house should be built without a suitable foundation. Likewise, no marriage should be initiated until the couple has explored the foundation.

What does this mean in a practical sense? It means that couples thinking of marriage ought to spend quality time discussing each basic area of life in order to determine where they are. It is amazing how many couples marry with very little understanding of each other's intellectual interests. Many marry with only a superficial understanding of each other's personality or emotional makeup. Others marry thinking that religious and moral values are unimportant and, therefore, give little time to their consideration. If you want the most out of marriage, does it not make sense to consider the foundation?

Intellectual Oneness

Let me make some practical suggestions for unmarried couples. Set aside specific dating time to discuss each of the major areas of life. For example, discuss with each other the kinds of books you read. This reveals something of your intellectual interest. If one reads no books, this also is revealing. Do you read the newspaper regularly? What magazines do you read? What kind of television programs do you enjoy most? The answers to all these questions will indicate something of your intellectual interests.

Grades in school should also be considered. This does not mean that you must have the same areas of intellectual interest, but you ought to be able to communicate with each other on somewhat the same intellectual plane. Many couples have awakened a short time after they have married to discover that this entire area of life was off-limits because of inability to understand each other. Before marriage, they never considered it.

I am not talking about perfection, but foundations. Do you hold enough in common intellectually so that you have a basis for growth? This may best be answered by attempting some growth exercises. Agree to read the same book and spend some quality time discussing its concepts. Read one lead article in the newspaper each day and discuss its merits and implications. This will reveal a great deal regarding your present status and potential for future growth.

Social Oneness

Or take the social area. I remember the young wife who said, "He wants to have that dumb country and western music on all the time, and I can't stand it!" It had never seemed important before marriage. I wonder why. Could it have been the "in love illusion"?

We are social creatures, but we do have different social interests. You owe it to yourself to explore the foundation. Is he an athletics fan? How many hours each week does he spend in front of the tube? (Do not think he is going to change after marriage.) What are your musical interests? What about opera, ballet, and gospel songs? What kind of recreational activities do you enjoy? Have you ever heard of "golf widows"? Do you enjoy parties? And what kind of parties? These are questions that cannot afford to go unanswered.

"Must we have the same social interests?" you ask. No, but you must have a foundation. Do you hold enough in common that you can begin to grow together? Such social growth ought to begin before marriage. If it does not, it is not likely to begin afterward. Stretch yourself. Go to things that you have not learned to enjoy before. See if you can learn to enjoy some of the same things. If you find that you are marching in two different directions socially, remember that the goal of marriage is oneness. Ask yourself, "If he never changes his present social interests, will I be happy to live with him the rest of my life?"

What about your personality? Could you write a descriptive paragraph about the kind of person you are? Then why not do it and have your prospective mate do the same? Share these with each other and discuss your self-concept as compared with how you appear to others.

"Opposites attract each other," so they say. True, but opposites do not always get along with each other. Do you understand each other enough to believe that you can work as a team? Surely your personality can complement his, but does he want to be complemented?

What clashes have you encountered in your dating relationship? What do you see as potential problem areas when you think of living life together? Discuss these openly. Can you make progress in overcoming these difficulties before marriage? If it is an unresolved problem before marriage, it will be magnified after marriage.

This does not mean that your personalities should be identical. That could make for a boring marriage. There should, however, be a basic understanding of each other's personality and some idea of how you will relate to each other. I am amazed at couples at odds with each other before marriage because of personality clashes who think that marriage will erase the problem.

Spiritual Oneness

Spiritual foundations are often the least excavated, even by couples who attend church regularly. Many married couples find that their greatest disappointment in marriage is that there is so little oneness in this area. "We never pray together," said one wife. "Church is like something we do individually. Even though we sit together, we never discuss what has gone on," said another. Instead of oneness, there is growing isolation, the exact opposite of God's design for marriage.

Too many premarital discussions on religion deal only with church attendance and other external matters and fail to grapple with the far more basic and important issues of God and our personal relationship to Him. "Is your fiancé a Christian?" I often ask. The normal reply is, "Oh, yes, he's a member at St. Marks." I am not talking about church membership versus non-church membership. I am talking about a spiritual foundation for marriage. Do you agree that there is an infinite, personal God? Do you know this God? Tell me about it. These questions get at the heart of the matter.

We have discussed elsewhere the impossibility of a Christian being one with a non-Christian. But let us assume that both parties are genuine Christians, in that they both acknowledge Jesus Christ as Savior and have accepted the gift of forgiveness and eternal life. Is this enough?

Suppose the man is committed to Christ as Lord and senses God's direction into mission work, but the woman has visions of summer cottages, Cadillacs, and mink stoles. Do they have an adequate foundation for marriage?

Do your hearts beat together spiritually? Are you encouraging each other in spiritual growth, or is one pulling gently but consistently in the opposite direction? Spiritual foundations are important. In fact, they are most important. Without the guidance of the Creator, we are unable to attain our potential as married creatures.

Physical Oneness

What of the foundation for physical oneness? Usually this is not a problem. Building upon that foundation may be a problem, but we will discuss that in the Marital Growth section. If you are physically attracted to each other, you probably have the foundation for physical oneness. But there is an interesting fact about sexual oneness. It can never be separated from emotional, spiritual, and social oneness. In fact, the problems that develop in the sexual aspect of marriage almost always have their root in one of these other areas. Physical incompatibility is almost nonexistent. The problem lies in other areas; it is only expressed in the sexual area.

There are, however, a few things that ought to be done in order to determine the nature of the foundation in this area. A thorough physical examination for both partners is an essential. If there are physical problems, they will usually be discovered here and can usually be corrected. If there are physical handicaps or disfigurements of the body that are not readily observable, these should be discussed with your prospective mate. If this is the person God has for you, he will be willing to accept you as you are. You should never begin a marriage with deceit in any form.

In chapter 2 we dealt with the problem of what to do if there has been moral failure in the past. The suggestions given there are extremely important in building a proper foundation for physical oneness. Let me suggest practical help for what may well be the biggest problem that single adult Christians face—the problem of controlling their natural God-given sexual desires.

It should be clearly understood that sex was God's idea. Hugh Hefner did not originate it; he only exploited it. God made us male and female and then judged that all he·had made "was very good" (Genesis 1:26–31). Therefore, those physical-emotional desires that we have toward members of the opposite sex are wholesome. It is only when we misuse them or fail to follow the "Manufactur-

er's guidelines" that we get into trouble. Those desires are
to find their fulfillment in the context of marriage as an
expression of our love for each other. Therein lies the
problem for single adults. This strong sexual urge increas-
es in the middle and late teens, but the time for marriage
in our society is usually several years away. What is one to
do in the meantime?

When God created man, He did not ask my advice.
Had He asked me, I would have suggested a different
timetable for man's sexuality. I would have waited until
the man was twenty-four, B.A. and M.A. in hand. Then I
would have turned him on sexually, opened his eyes to the
"other half," and introduced his Eve, with the wedding
date set three months hence. You will have to admit that
would surely seem the easier way.

But God does not always choose the easy way. In fact,
not many things of value are effected easily. I have often
asked myself and others, "Why do you suppose God made
us with the sexual time clock set as it is?" The only answer
I have found is that He wanted to extend His trust and
teach us the joy of self-control.

Therein lies our greatest help. God's desire is that I
control those sexual desires, not that I deny them. He has
clearly delineated that the full satisfaction of those desires
is to be reserved for marriage, and I must not ignore that
guideline. My responsibility, with the aid of the Holy Spirit, is to respect those desires as wholesome but, at the
same time, to control them in a responsible manner.

How then do I establish a Christian control program
in this area? One help is Rick Stedman's book *Pure Joy:
The Positive Side of Single Sexuality* (see Appendix). Stedman takes a biblical approach to the subject of sexuality
and deals extensively with the physical differences
between males and females. He talks realistically about
masturbation and self-stimulation. His practical program
of self-control can be of immense help to single adults.

As a couple moves toward marriage, there should also
be time spent in a refresher course on the physical aspect

of marriage. Along the way, most of us pick up a great deal of misinformation. Before marriage, we need to reexamine the validity of our ideas about sex. We need to understand our own bodies and how they function, as well as the sexual nature of our mates.

For this purpose, I recommend Ed and Gaye Wheat's book *Intended for Pleasure,* intimate sex counsel from a Christian physician and his wife (see Appendix). This book should be read by every engaged couple prior to marriage and again sometime during the first three months of marriage. It is also extremely helpful for those who may have been married many years.

We are discussing foundations for marital oneness. If sex is your only goal, then the matters discussed above may be relatively unimportant. If you only want someone to cook your meals or pay the rent, then all you need is a willing partner. If, on the other hand, your goal is total unity of life, then you ought to examine the foundation closely. Jesus noted the folly of building a house upon sand (Matthew 7:24–27).

"God through his Holy Spirit seeks our best welfare and happiness. He seldom does this by supernatural act. Instead He seeks to permeate our thinking until our judgments are His."[1]

IMPLICATIONS FOR THE MARRIED

I can hear many married individuals who have read to this point saying, "You're too late! I'm already married. Why didn't you give me all these ideas twenty years ago? I made a poor choice, and I am destined to misery and unhappiness." Now, hold on! I am coming to you. The second half of this volume is dedicated to your well-being.

All hope is not gone; miracles do still happen. I have written these chapters to the unmarried because I believe that preventive medicine is greatly needed by single adults, but I want to remind you that disease and death

are not synonymous. Your marriage may be sick, but it is
far too early to call the morgue.

I hope that you have clearly in mind the goal of marriage—unity on the deepest possible level in all areas of
life. Maybe that is only a dream for you, but if you are
willing to work at it, it can become reality. Can you imagine what it would be like to have a degree of intellectual
oneness? social oneness? spiritual oneness? physical oneness? Do not give up. You may be on the brink of a new
discovery.

"But my partner is not interested in working with me,"
you say. "I can't do it all by myself." True, but you can do
something by yourself. And that something just may be
used of God to stimulate change in your mate. I believe
that the principle discussed in the following chapter is the
number one principle for marital happiness and good
health. Read carefully, think clearly, and do not forget the
assignment at the end of the chapter.

GROWTH ASSIGNMENTS

For the Unmarried:

1. If you are considering marriage to the person you are
   now dating, take time to examine your foundation for
   marriage. On a separate sheet, make four parallel
   columns with the following headings:

   Intellectual   Social   Physical   Spiritual

   Under each of these headings, list the factors that you
   feel you hold in common with your prospective mate.
   In which area is the foundation weakest? Is the foundation strong enough to bear the weight of marriage?

2. Suggest that your partner make a similar list and answer
   the same questions. Use this as a stimulus for discussion
   about your relationship.

3. The above steps should help you to realistically evaluate your relationship. After identifying your weak areas, go back and read the appropriate section in this chapter. Each section gives practical suggestions for growth. Decide upon some specific steps that you will take to stabilize your foundation. Agree upon these steps and evaluate your growth in one month.

4. If you cannot experience growth over a period of time, perhaps you should reevaluate your intention to marry. If you cannot grow in oneness before marriage, it is not likely that marriage will initiate growth.

For the Married:

1. Take a good look at your marriage. We must recognize weaknesses before we can initiate improvements. On a separate sheet, make four parallel columns with the following headings:

   Intellectual   Social   Physical   Spiritual

   Under each of these headings, list the characteristics you feel you hold in common with your mate. In which area is your oneness weakest? What could you do to stimulate growth in this area? What will you do?

2. Suggest that your mate read the chapter, make a similar list, and answer the above questions. When you are both feeling good and open to growth, share your results and agree upon action that will increase your oneness. Concentrate on one area at a time.

Section Two

MARITAL GROWTH

4

"If My Wife Would Just Shape Up"

"What seems to be the problem?" I asked.

"Well, it's my marriage. We just can't seem to get along with each other."

"What are the problem areas?"

"Well, for one thing my wife listens to her mother too much. She's easily influenced, and her mother is wrecking our marriage."

"Any other areas?" I inquired.

"Yes, my wife thinks money grows on trees. I make good money, but she thinks we never have enough. She has gotten us so far in debt I don't know if we will ever get out."

"So you have the problem with her mother and the problem with money. Any other problem areas?"

"Just a lot of little things. She just irritates me to death. Always on my back to do something. When I come home from work, she acts like I'm her slave. She is never satisfied with anything."

After listening to several more areas of complaint about his wife, I asked, "Do you have any idea as to how to solve these problems?"

He responded, "I really don't. I wish I did. If she would just understand that I am human too. I have needs, too, but she doesn't seem to consider me at all." Then, looking at me, he said, "If someone could just get through to her."

Sound familiar? Sometimes it is the wife giving similar criticisms against the husband, but the pattern is the same. We pour out our feelings against our mates. We describe our problems in terms of our mates' failures. What we are really saying is, "My problem is my wife/husband. You see, I am basically a nice person, but my partner has made me miserable."

Often in my counseling procedures, I give the couple paper and pencils and ask them to write for me the things they dislike about their partner. You should see the lists. Some have to request additional paper. They write furiously and freely. Then, a bit later, I ask that they list for me what they feel to be their own weaknesses. Their response is amusing. Usually they can think of one weakness right away, so they write that one down. Then they have to really think to come up with that second one. Some never find it. Is that not amazing? Only one little thing is wrong with me (or at most three or four), but my mate has dozens of failures.

"BEHOLD THE BEAM"

If my partner would just get straightened out, we could have a happy marriage, we reason. So we nag, we fuss, we demand, we cry, we withdraw, we despair—all to no avail.

My partner does not change, and therefore I am destined to misery. Do not believe it! Your marriage can improve, and improvement can begin today, regardless of your partner's attitude.

There is a strategy for improvement, spoken by Jesus and recorded in Matthew 7:1–5. In the following quotation, I am substituting "partner" for the word "brother" so that we may see the principle at work in marriage.

Do not judge, or you too will be judged. For in the same way you judge others, you will be judged. . . . Why do you look at the speck of sawdust in your [partner's] eye and pay no attention to the plank in your own eye? How can you say to your [partner], "Let me take the speck out of your eye," when all the time there is a plank in your own eye? You hypocrite, first take the plank out of your own eye, and then you will see clearly to remove the speck from your [partner's] eye.

Now, please, do not misunderstand. I am not calling anyone a hypocrite. I am simply quoting a principle of Jesus. Jesus is saying that if one tries to improve his marriage by getting his partner to change (working hard to get the speck out of his eye), energies are being expended in the wrong direction. The place to begin is with one's own failures (the plank or beam in one's own eye).

I am not suggesting that the partner does not have weaknesses or faults. What I am saying is that trying to deal with the faults of the partner is not the place to begin. The first question for any of us when we are in a marital storm is "What's wrong with me? What are my faults?"

This approach may seem strange to you, for after all, your partner is 95 percent of the problem. Right? You are not perfect, but your failure is only minimal. Certainly not more than 5 percent. Let us assume that this is true, though the percentages may change as you begin reflection. Even if you are only 5 percent of the problem, the key to improvement lies with you. Jesus said, "First take the plank out of your own eye."

What are the mechanics for doing this? How do you go about extracting a "plank" from your eye? I suggest that you get alone with God, preferably in a place where you can talk aloud. (If you really feel strong hostility toward your mate, you may want to make a written list of his/her faults beforehand. This may help free the mind psychologically, so that you can deal with your own failures.)

Now, alone with God, simply ask, "Lord, what's wrong with me? What are my faults? What are my sins? I know that my mate has many, and I have already written those down, but right now what I want to know is, what are *my* sins?" Get your pencil and paper ready, for that is a prayer God will answer. Make a list of your sins.

You may find the sin of bitterness, which is condemned in Ephesians 4:31: "Get rid of all bitterness, rage and anger, brawling and slander, along with every form of malice." Certainly your partner may have triggered your negative attitude, but you are the one who allowed bitterness to develop. It is always wrong to be bitter toward one of God's creatures.

You may find the sin of unkindness, which is in violation of the command of Ephesians 4:32: "Be kind and compassionate to one another, forgiving each other, just as in Christ God forgave you." "But my mate has not stimulated kindness from me," you reason. True, but you are the one who decides to be kind or unkind. Absence of kindness is always wrong for the Christian.

You may discover lack of love toward your mate. We will discuss this further in chapter 5, but let me say here that love as described in 1 Corinthians 13 is an act or attitude more than an emotion. "Love is patient . . . kind . . . never boastful, nor conceited, nor rude; never selfish, not quick to take offense. Love keeps no score of wrongs" (NEB). When you fail to express love to your partner, you have sinned.

The Holy Spirit may bring many sins to your mind. Write them down one by one until you can think of no other, then open your Bible and read 1 John 1:9: "If we confess our sins, he is faithful and just and will forgive us our sins and purify us from all unrighteousness." In making your list you have really confessed your sin, for you have agreed with God that these things are wrong in your life.

I suggest, however, that you go back over the list and agree again with God that these are wrong and, at the same time, thank Him for the Cross and therefore for forgiveness. In your own words you are saying, "Father, this is wrong—so wrong. How could I be so foolish? But I want to thank You for the Cross—that Christ has paid for this sin, and I can be forgiven. Thank You, Father, for forgiveness."

Work through your list and accept God's forgiveness for every past failure. You may want to destroy your list as a symbol of God's forgiveness. God does not intend us to live under the emotional load of past failures. We can be forgiven.

A CLEAR CONSCIENCE

After the acceptance of God's forgiveness, there is a second step toward a growing marriage. The apostle Paul states it in Acts 24:16 as a basic principle in his own life: "So I strive always to keep my conscience clear before God and man."

I believe that in this statement we have the most important principle of mental health and, consequently, of marital health. Paul is not saying that he never did anything wrong, but rather that, having done wrong, he has also voided, or emptied, his conscience first toward God and then toward men. We empty our conscience toward God when we confess our sin. We empty our conscience toward a partner when we go to him or her and confess our failures.

"But what if my partner isn't willing to forgive me?" That is his problem and not yours. Your responsibility is to admit the wrong you carry and ask forgiveness. Your partner's response is not your responsibility. You have done what you can do by dealing with your wrong. You have not done what you can do until you have dealt with your own offenses. You see, you cannot confess your partner's sin, but you can deal with your 5 percent.

You can say to your partner in your own words, after a good meal, "Babe [or whatever title you prefer], God has dealt with me today, and I now realize that I have been wrong in so many things. I have confessed them to God and want to ask your forgiveness. I have been very selfish in demanding that you . . . I have not been very kind in . . . I have failed in meeting your needs for . . . And I want to ask, will you forgive me?" Be as specific with your partner as you have been with God. Give him or her a chance to respond.

What will happen when you do this? It may be the dawning of a new day. On the other hand, your partner may say, "Oh, yeah, I've heard that before, and I don't believe it." What you do at this point will determine whether you must have another confession session with God, or whether you will go on to improve your marriage. If you explode with tears, words, or flying saucers, you will need to retreat to ask God's forgiveness for another failure.

Why not respond by saying, "I can understand your feelings. I know that I have confessed before, and I know that I have failed many times to be what I want to be. So I understand that you find it hard to believe that things will be any different this time."

Do not make any rash promises about the future. Right now, you are dealing with the past. Seal your confession with an embrace and a kiss. Smile even if you are pushed away.

Do not worry about your partner's response to your confession. Do not think he should fall on his knees and confess his own wrong. He may, and if so, great! You will have a tender evening. But negative feelings may not capitulate that easily. Personal pride stands as a hurdle for all of us. Allow time for God's work in your mate. When you have confessed your wrong and emptied your conscience toward God and your partner, you have done the greatest thing you could do for your mate. He may not respond in like manner, but you have made it much easier for him to admit wrong.

We cannot manipulate people. Every person has a free will. We can choose to be hateful, cutting, mean, even in the face of confession. But your marriage will be better even if your partner never confesses his wrong, because now you are free to move out to be a positive stimulus for good in the relationship. You are now free to be a part of the solution instead of a part of the problem.

Many couples are at a stalemate because they have

allowed a wall to develop between them. Walls are always erected a block at a time. One partner fails in a particular matter. It may be as small a matter as failing to carry out the garbage or as large as failing to meet sexual needs. Instead of dealing with that failure, we ignore it. We excuse ourselves, thinking, *After all, what does he expect? I'm doing my part! Why doesn't he think of my needs?*

For whatever reason, one failure after another is ignored until a long, high, thick wall develops between two people who started out "in love." Communication grinds to a halt, and only resentment remains.

How is such a wall to be destroyed? By tearing down those blocks of failure, one by one. As we admit our failures as specifically as possible, we destroy the barrier to growth. Granted, the walls must be torn down from both sides if the relationship is to be ideal, but if you will tear down your side, you make it easier for your partner to begin demolition. If both are willing to tear down the wall of separation, you can build on the rubble a beautiful relationship.

Once the wall is destroyed by confession and forgiveness, we must practice immediate confession of subsequent failures. We must never allow the wall to be erected again. Confession must become a way of life.

Some months ago, in one of those frenzied attempts to get the children to school on time, I said to my wife, "Karolyn, where is my briefcase?"

To which she replied, "I don't know."

I repeated with greater volume, "Come on, Karolyn, I'm in a hurry. Where is my briefcase? I put it right in there by the dresser last night, and it's gone. Where did you put it?"

"Gary, I don't know where your briefcase is," she emphatically replied.

We had about two more rounds of this—same message, higher volume. By this time, I was really upset. Obviously she had moved my briefcase, but she was not concerned enough to even think about where she had put it. In anger, I rushed the children out the door and sped them off to school. I talked to them kindly about their school work, but after I let them out, I returned to the business of being furious with Karolyn for misplacing my briefcase. I spent the entire nine miles from my children's school to my office thinking, *How could I have married such a scatterbrain? My briefcase is important. In fact, I can't operate without it. What am I going to do today?*

That question was answered the moment I walked into my office. There sat my briefcase, right where I had left it the day before.

At that point, I had an option. I could sweep the matter under the rug, promise myself that I would never let her know where I had found my briefcase, and hope that she would never ask. I could rationalize that my response to her was because of lack of sleep, exercise, and so on. Or I could practice what I preach—behold the plank, confess my sin, and ask forgiveness.

So I turned to God and said, "O God, how could I be so foolish? Forgive me for the horrible way in which I treated Karolyn—for the lack of love, the unkind, critical, accusing words, the bitter spirit. Thank You, Father, for the Cross. Thank You that the penalty has been paid. Thank You for forgiveness." My conscience was emptied toward God.

Next was the phone call. "Karolyn, I—uh—I—uh—found my briefcase."

"Yes," she said.

"It was here at the office," I haltingly continued. "I'm really sorry about the way I talked to you. It was horrible, and it was wrong, and I want to ask, Will you forgive me?"

Do you know what she said? "I thought you'd call!"

Why? Because we have committed ourselves to keeping the wall down. She knew that I would not go long with that failure unresolved. Life is too short to let walls develop. Why waste life? A wall will never be built if you deal with each failure as it occurs.

THE MINISTRY OF THE HOLY SPIRIT

A third step must accompany the first two. In fact, if we do not acknowledge the third, it is not likely that we will take the first two.

I speak of the ministry of the Holy Spirit in the life of the Christian. It is the Holy Spirit who rebukes us when we are wrong (Hebrews 12:5) and motivates confession. He is, indeed, "God with us" and indwells every believer (Romans 8:9). He is called the Comforter who abides with us forever (John 14:16). He is also called "the Spirit of truth," whose job it is to remind us of the truth so that we can order our lives accordingly (John 14:17; 16:13). He becomes our teacher and brings to our minds the teachings of Jesus (John 14:26). It is His task to produce in us the qualities and characteristics seen in the life of Jesus and called by Paul the "fruit of the Spirit," which is "love, joy, peace, patience, kindness, goodness, faithfulness, gentleness and self-control" (Galatians 5:22–23).

Notice that these characteristics are called the "fruit of the Spirit" rather than the fruit of self-effort. The Christian life is not a commitment to try to be like Jesus. Rather, it is yielding our lives to the Holy Spirit so that He can express the qualities of Jesus through us.

We cannot work hard enough to produce peace. Peace comes as a by-product of yielding our lives fully to the Holy Spirit. The same is true of joy, patience, gentleness, goodness, and all the other qualities listed above. The key to the Christian's victory is recognizing and accepting the control of the Holy Spirit.

We are admonished in Ephesians 5:18 to not be drunk with wine but be "led by the Spirit," or "filled with the Spirit" (KJV). That is, we are not to be controlled by wine but controlled by the Holy Spirit. This is a command and it is expected of every Christian. Just as a person may choose by an act of his will to put himself under the control of wine, so the Christian is to choose by an act of his will to put himself under the control of the Holy Spirit.

To be filled with the Spirit is not some bizarre emotional experience, though our emotions may be involved. It is, rather, an act of the will in which we yield control of our lives to the Holy Spirit. All Christians are already indwelt by the Spirit (Romans 8:9), but not all Christians are controlled by the Spirit. This is the challenge of Ephesians 5:18.

How then are we filled with the Holy Spirit, or controlled by the Holy Spirit? Having confessed our sins and accepted God's forgiveness, we then ask Him to fill us, or control us, totally by His Spirit. That is, we ask the Holy Spirit to ascend the throne of our lives. That is a prayer God will answer because He has promised, "If we ask anything according to his will," He will hear us and grant our petition (1 John 5:14–15). We know it is "according to His will" to fill us with His Spirit because of the command in Ephesians 5:18: "Be filled with the Spirit." Therefore, when we ask Him to fill us, or control us, we know that He will.

We accept the Spirit's control over our lives by faith. We do not wait and plead for some great emotional experience. Having confessed our sins and asked for His control, we simply believe that He is on the throne of our lives, and we move out to do the things we know should be done. We rely upon the Spirit to give us the ability needed to relate to our mates in a redemptive way.

Normally, the sequence of events in applying these principles to one's marriage is as follows:

1. I realize that my marriage is not what it should be.
2. I stop blaming my mate and ask God to show me where I am at fault.
3. I confess my sin and accept God's forgiveness, according to 1 John 1:9.
4. I ask Him to fill me with His Spirit and give me the power to make constructive changes in my life.
5. In His power, I go to my mate, confess my failures, and ask forgiveness.

6. In His power I go on to change my behavior, words, and attitudes, according to the principles that I discover in Scripture.

Such activity is bound to improve a marriage.

HELPING YOUR MATE WITH THE MOTE

I do not wish to communicate the idea that you are not to discuss the faults of your mate. Let me give a personal illustration that indicates the role of confession as it relates to discussion of faults.

One Saturday last summer, my wife and I were having lunch with our two children, enjoying the beauty of the view outside our window. Birds were singing, flowers blooming, and our hearts were glad—glad, until my wife made the announcement that she was going to take our son to the shopping center and get him some shoes. Rather soon after the announcement, she left. Dirty dishes were still on the table.

Being a mature person, of course I did not say anything, but as she drove off down the street I retreated to the back porch, made myself comfortable in my rocker, and proceeded to get angry with her. With the aid of my melancholic personality, I thought all kinds of morose thoughts.

After all, this is my only day off. I always try to be at home on Saturdays. She doesn't work outside the home. She had every day of the week to go shopping. Why wait until Saturday? Obviously, she doesn't love me or she would not leave me alone. Well, she didn't really leave me alone. There are all those dirty dishes on the table. The least she could have done was to have cleaned up the table. I guess she expects me to do that. Well, I'll show her. I am not her servant.

The thoughts went from bad to worse, and I succeeded in making myself miserable in the presence of singing birds and blooming flowers. Then there came to my mind very quietly—almost as though God hesitated to disturb my misery—the title of my lecture "Behold the Beam" and Jesus' words "First take the plank out of your own eye."

Turning to God, I said, "O Lord, how foolish! How stupid! What's wrong with me that I can get so upset over my wife going to the shopping center?" The answer came quickly. First, I was judging my wife's motives for her decision, saying that she left because she did not love me or think of me. Such judging is condemned by Jesus in Matthew 7:1. (Incidentally, such judging is also foolish, for no one can know the motives of another unless that person chooses to reveal them.) Second, my attitude was very selfish. Having confessed these and accepted God's forgiveness, I yielded the throne of my life to the Holy Spirit and was able to wash the dishes with an optimistic spirit and a positive attitude toward my wife.

That evening, after the children were in bed, I had a chance to relate to my wife my afternoon problem. "You know, Babe," I said, "I had a real struggle this afternoon. So much of a struggle, in fact, that I sinned and God had to deal with me about it. Now, I've confessed it, and God has forgiven me, but I thought you might like to know about it."

How could she resist? I proceeded to tell her about my attitudes and thoughts, and that I had seen how wrong they were. I did not need to confess to her because she had not even seen me at my point of failure. My confession had been to God, but I told her because our goal is oneness. Oneness is attained only as we are willing to confide failures as well as successes. When I disclosed my problem and my confession to God, my wife was very open to discuss her action, and we agreed upon some guidelines for the future that were mutually acceptable. You see, my confession had paved the way for a constructive conversation about her action.

It should be noted that in this illustration my wife had done nothing morally wrong. Shopping on Saturday is not a sin. I was the one who had sinned. When I acknowledged my problem, rather than pointing an accusing finger at her, she was free emotionally to discuss her action and ask, "What can I do to help with this problem?"

How different the results would have been had I decided to continue in my misery and allowed bitterness to grow! When she came home, I could have plowed into her with condemnation or given her the silent treatment and let her beg me to reveal the reason for my animosity. It could have been swept under the rug and become a part of a growing collection of negative feelings toward her. How foolish for us to respond in any such manner.

Whenever a relationship breaks down, both people are a part of the breakdown. One may bear more of the responsibility than the other, but either can move to restore it. They must each deal with the wrong they personally bear, and, indeed, that is *all* either party can do. Confession is a personal act. We must allow each other the freedom to decide whether or not to confess. In the meantime, we can confess our failure, and this may be the stimulus that triggers confession on the part of our mate.

SUMMARY

In this chapter, we have discussed a strategy for growth in marriage. The steps suggested above have turned many marriages around and started them on a road toward growth. These principles will have application as long as two people live together.

After the first major confession, you will not need to make a list of your faults, but you should deal with them one by one as they occur. On any given day when you become aware of friction, ill feelings, and lack of oneness in your relationship, the first questions should be "Lord, what's wrong with me? Why should I be so upset over that? What did I do or fail to do that may have stimulated that action from my mate? Even if she is totally wrong in her action, what about my attitude? Is my response to that action right or wrong?"

As you see where you are wrong, confess it, accept

God's forgiveness, and ask His Spirit to control you. People do not "make us miserable." We choose to be miserable. The immediate emotion that arises after the action of your partner may be automatic and beyond your control, but what you do with that emotion is your decision. If you are willing to search your own heart and confess any wrong discovered, then, as a liberated person, you can rejoice with internal peace, even though you are not particularly happy with the situation at hand. As one who is at peace with himself, you are more likely to be a constructive factor in the relationship rather than one who compounds the problem.

Your marriage can be improved even if your partner never changes. One partner can change a marriage for the better even when the other has no desire for improvement. I am not saying that you can have an ideal marriage, fully satisfying in every area. That, indeed, takes the work of two individuals under God. But you can see substantial growth in your marriage, if only you are willing to change.

If you will take the kind of action suggested in this chapter, you will be taking the first and most strategic steps toward a growing marriage. Who knows what God will do with your mate if you serve as a helper instead of a hinderer?

GROWTH ASSIGNMENTS

For the Married:

1. Make a list of the weaknesses of your partner. Where is he/she failing? (We will talk later about how to use this list. For the present, simply make the list so that you can free your mind to look at your own needs.)

2. Read in your Bible the following: Matthew 7:1–5; Acts 24:16; 1 John 1:9.

3. Make a list of your own sins and confess them to God in the manner described in this chapter.

4. Ask for, and accept by faith, the control of the Holy Spirit over your life.

5. As a person forgiven by God and controlled by the Spirit, disclose your failures to your mate and ask his/her forgiveness.

6. Whenever you have a wrong attitude or action, judge it immediately and experience forgiveness. Discipline yourself to live with a clear conscience toward God and your partner.

7. Life is too short to be at odds with anyone. You deserve the liberty of a clear conscience. Confession of wrong and asking for forgiveness is the road to liberation. Why wait?

For the Unmarried:

1. The principle of a clear conscience has application before marriage as well as afterward. Examine your own attitudes and actions. What do you need to confess to God? To your dating partner? Do it now.

2. Is your life yielded to the control of the Holy Spirit? He is your greatest ally. Why not accept His control right now?

3. Perhaps there are others in your life (parents, employers, roommates, etc.) toward whom you have bitter or resentful attitudes or to whom you have expressed harsh words or actions. Failures are not handled by ignoring them but by confessing them, first to God and then to the person involved. Take action to free your conscience from past failures.

4. Discuss this principle with your dating partner. Can you agree to accept this pattern of confession as a principle for life?

5. If we deal with our failures by confessing them, they can become stepping-stones to growth. If we sweep our failures under the rug, they become mounds of irritation that cause us to stumble. Does your living room need to be vacuumed?

5

"I Don't Love Her Anymore"

We have talked about the role of love in an earlier discussion of dating and premarital relationships. Now we want to look at the role of love in the context of marriage. For the past several years I have asked various seminar study groups to give me their definitions of love. Definitions have varied greatly. Some have placed a strong emphasis upon the emotional-physical aspect of love, whereas others have emphasized the altruistic, or self-giving, nature of love. One I like best is: "Love is a four-letter word composed of two consonants, *L* and *V*; two vowels, *O* and *E*; and two fools, you and me."

Without trying to define love further at this point, I want to point out two very strange statements in Scripture. In Ephesians 5:25, husbands are admonished, "Love your wives," and in Titus 2:3–4, the elderly women are advised, "Train the younger women to love their husbands." I would remind you that the grammatical construction in Ephesians 5:25 is the same as that in verse 18 where we read, "Be filled with the Spirit." It is a command.

Why would a man have to be commanded to love his wife, and a wife have to be taught to love her husband? Is that not what marriage is all about? Is this not why you got married in the first place? That is what most couples tell me when they come to discuss marriage. Why then after marriage do we have to be commanded to love?

Could it be that what we have called love is not love at all? Could it be that for most couples, love comes after the wedding, if indeed it is ever realized? Conduct your own survey among married couples. Provide anonymity and ask them to rate themselves on a continuum from one to ten regarding their own motivation for getting married. Tell them that you want them to be as honest as possible.

On the continuum, let one represent self-interest and ten represent the welfare of one's mate. What really was their motivation for marriage? Let me know what you find. I predict that you will find, as I have found, that few will rate themselves above five. If we are honest, most of us are thinking about what we are going to get out of the relationship—how wonderful it is going to be for us. Now I raise the question, Is that love?

Let us look at 1 Corinthians 13:4–8 for the best description (not definition) of love that I have ever found. Read it slowly in a modern translation, with thought as to what implications it would have in marriage. Most people like to feel the flow of its poetry but fail to see its practical implications.

"Love is patient; love is kind and envies no one. Love is never boastful, nor conceited, nor rude; never selfish, not quick to take offense. Love keeps no score of wrongs; does not gloat over other men's sins, but delights in the truth. There is nothing love cannot face; there is no limit to its faith, its hope, and its endurance. Love will never come to an end" (NEB).

The passage is too strong to digest at one sitting, so just take a few of the key ideas. Love is patient and kind, never demanding its own way; not a "know-it-all," but understanding, slow to take offense; courteous; and exhibiting a positive attitude toward problems. All these characteristics of love are directed toward the well-being of the one loved.

I would raise a further question. Do these qualities of

love require a warm "feeling" toward the one loved? Do not answer too hurriedly. How warm do you have to feel to be kind? Earlier, I referred to the "tingles," that bubbly, emotional/physical attraction that we sometimes have for members of the opposite sex. Must we have the "tingles" in order to be courteous? Can we be patient toward our mate without a warm feeling? You see, the kind of love described in 1 Corinthians 13 does not emphasize emotion but attitude and action. Attitude and behavior are not beyond our control.

Often couples come to me in the midst of marriage difficulty. They are at the point of separating, and when I ask why, they make known their points of contention and conclude with the clincher, "Well, we just don't love each other anymore." That is supposed to settle it. Divorce is the only alternative. After all, we cannot help it. We have simply "lost our love." Or, "It's beyond our control." "I wish I could love her," one husband said, "but it's too late. Too much has happened."

Do you want to know something? I do not believe that. If you want sympathy with that view, do not come to see me. I would do you a great disservice if I led you to believe that your marital happiness is "beyond your control."

Let me give you the second half of a sentence I pointed out earlier. In Ephesians 5:25 we read, "Husbands, love your wives, just as Christ loved the church and gave himself up for her." Are you ready for a question? What was the attitude of the church when Christ gave Himself for it? Were those whom He loved kind, considerate, and patient toward Him? On the contrary, the best among them cursed and said, "I don't even know him" (Matthew 26:74 TLB). Romans 5:8 states that God showed His love toward us in that while we were filthy, selfish, and hateful, Christ died for us.

God loved us when we were very unlovely. So, a husband is commanded to love his wife when she exhibits the same negative attitudes. Does anyone have a wife who qualifies? You see, any man can love a woman who loves

him. You do not need to be commanded to do that. That is
the kind of love we knew before we got married. I was
lovely to her because she was lovely to me, but how am I
to respond now that my partner is not lovely? This is
where the biblical admonition gives us help.

I am commanded to love my wife, and she is instruct-
ed to love me, regardless of how either of us responds. It is
this kind of love that is most likely to beget a positive
response from my partner. That is, if I respond with kindness, understanding, patience, and courtesy, I am making
it as easy as possible for her to respond in like manner.

Now this does not mean that she must respond with
love. She has the freedom not to love. That is why the ultimate success of a marriage cannot be achieved by the acts
of one partner only. It takes two loving individuals to
attain ultimate satisfaction in a relationship. But if I, as
one individual, choose to love, things will improve. I can
always improve my marriage, and love is my greatest
weapon.

I would be unfair if I did not express clearly my deep
doubts that you will ever be able to express such self-giving
love without the aid of the Holy Spirit. The Scriptures say,
"God has poured out his love into our hearts by the Holy Spirit" (Romans 5:5). The ability to respond in love comes
from God. I have the opportunity to be God's agent of love
to my wife. No one in all the universe is in a better position
to love my wife than I. I must not forfeit that opportunity. If
I am willing to turn to God, admitting my lack of love, yes,
even my bitterness and hatred, and accept His forgiveness
and ask Him to love my wife through me, I can become a
lover par excellence.

What happens usually is this. My wife does something
that I think is wrong or, worse yet, fails to do something
that I think she should have done. Immediately, my emotions toward her are negative. These negative emotions
may well be spontaneous and beyond my control. But
what I do with those emotions is not beyond my control.

If I follow my basic nature, I will express those emotions with cutting words or the painful silent treatment, either of which will accomplish the job of making both of us miserable. My negative actions will tend to elicit negative reactions from her.

If, however, I choose not to follow my negative emotions, I can be an agent of love. That is, I can thank God that in His power I do not have to be negative just because I feel negative and thus can ask for His ability to express love and turn the whole situation around.

Contrary to some popular psychological notions, all of our negative emotions do not need to be expressed. Some need to be starved. Only when I feed my negative emotions with meditation and action do I become guilty of error. The world is filled with couples who have come to the breaking point because they expressed all their negative emotions toward each other. I do not mean that we are to deny that we have such emotions, but rather that we are to express them to God and thank Him that we do not have to follow them.

Some will say, "All right. You are telling me to love my mate regardless of how I feel toward him. Isn't that hypocritical?"

No, there is nothing hypocritical about that unless you are claiming to feel something that you do not feel. When you express kindness by a thoughtful act or a gift, you do not have to claim any warm emotional feeling. You are simply being kind. You may not feel anything, or indeed your feelings may be negative. But it is in the act of expressing love that you are most likely to receive love from your mate, which in turn affects your emotions in a positive manner. Negative feelings are most often alleviated when they are ignored rather than pampered.

Thousands of marriages could have been redeemed if one partner had discovered the principle of love as we have discussed it. Should you forget everything else taught in this book, remember to love "1 Corinthians 13 style." Love is the greatest of all and is available to all.

Let us assume that you choose to love. Though your

feelings may be apathetic or even negative, you choose to be God's channel of love to your mate. How would you express such love? There are two basic ways: by words and by deeds.

LOVING WITH WORDS

In 1 Corinthians 8:1 we read, "Love edifies" (NASB). The word *edify* means "to build up." The noun form is our word "edifice," or "building." Therefore, to love my mate means to "build up" my mate. One of the most powerful means of edification is the compliment. Find something, small or great, that you like about your mate and express appreciation.

The story is told of a woman who went to a marriage counselor for advice. "I want to divorce my husband," she confided, "and I want to hurt him all I can." "In that case," the counselor advised, "start showering him with compliments. When you have become indispensable to him—when he thinks you love him devotedly—then start the divorce action. That's the way to hurt him most." Some months later the wife returned to report that she had followed the suggested course. "Good," was the reply. "Now's the time to file for divorce." "Divorce!" said the woman indignantly. "Never! I've fallen in love with him." She had the "tingles" again!

"How can I compliment him when he is treating me so horribly?" the wife asks. By the help of the Holy Spirit, the Bible replies. Is this not the admonition of Jesus when He says in Matthew 5:44, "Love your enemies and pray for those who persecute you"? If we love in the face of ill treatment, we may likely redeem our marriage.

If we could learn the tremendous power of the compliment, we would seldom again revert to complaint. Let me give an illustration.

The wife looks out the window and observes that her husband has almost completed mowing the front yard. She decides, *This is the time to strike.* She goes outside, cups her hands to her mouth, and screams above the noise of the lawn mower, "Do you think you will get around to the gutters this afternoon?" Imagine—her husband has just spent an exhausting two hours mowing the grass, and all she offers is another job assignment. I cannot tell you what he will say, but I can tell you what he will think: *Woman, get off my back!* How much better he would feel if she would come out with a glass of lemonade and tell him how nice the yard looks.

I will not guarantee that your husband will volunteer to clean the gutters, but I will guarantee that the compliment will be received with joy. A husband is far more motivated to attend to household tasks when rewarded by a compliment.

Of course, it works for the husband as well. Some time ago a lady in her sixties said to me, "My husband often tells me how nice I look in a new dress as we get into the car." Then she added, "You know, it does an old lady good to get a compliment once in a while." I would add that the same is true for a young lady or a middle-aged lady.

A second way to express love by words is to speak with kindness. Love is kind (1 Corinthians 13:4). This has to do with the manner in which you speak. "A gentle answer turns away wrath, but a harsh word stirs up anger" (Proverbs 15:1). Why do you scream when you talk to your mate? Why do you speak harshly? Because you are following your negative emotions. You can speak kindly even with negative feelings if you choose God's help.

There is nothing wrong with admitting your feelings to your mate if you speak with kindness. The husband says to his wife, "Darling, right now I have strong negative feelings toward you, but I want to say this with kindness— would you please wash this shirt that has been lying here for three weeks? You are a great wife!" It never hurts to throw in a compliment with your kind request.

A third way to speak with love is to use entreaty rather than command. Love does not demand its own way (1 Corinthians 13:5). "What do you think of this?" "How

about this?" "Is this possible?" "Could we do this?" These
are words of entreaty, as opposed to "See that this gets
done today!"

Another way to express love is with words of acceptance. Assure your mate that he/she can express ideas
without being put down. A wife says, "I feel that you don't
really love me like you used to." By nature, the husband
responds, "How could you say that? Don't you remember
the coat I bought you three years ago and the time I took
you out to dinner last summer?" What is he doing? He is
condemning her for her feelings. How much better to say,
"How's that, Babe? What is it that makes you feel that
way?" Give her a chance to express her feelings, and then
accept her words. Look for ways to minister to those feelings, rather than condemning them.

Speaking with love also means that we use present
tense words. Love does not keep a score of wrongs, does
not review the past with each new crisis. If past failures
have been confessed, then why bring them up again? Love
speaks only of present facts and does not seek to build a
case by referring to every past imperfection. Some couples
club each other to death with past failures. This never
leads to marital growth.

LOVING WITH DEEDS

John admonishes us to love not "with words [only] but
with actions" (1 John 3:18). The old adage "Actions speak
louder than words" may well be true. Certainly we ought
to couple our loving words with loving actions.

Love is patient. Therefore, if we want to express love in
our behavior we must have patient behavior. The implications here are tremendous. This would eliminate your pac-
ing the floor while your wife gets ready to go. Why not sit
down and relax? Your impatient behavior does not
increase her speed. It simply agitates your own spirit. You
do not have to be impatient. You have the choice. Why not
love?

Love is kind. Acts of kindness are one of love's strongest voices. One is limited only by his imagination and will. Flowers either bought or clipped from the yard say "I love you" to all but the wife who is allergic to flowers. That phone call in the middle of the day to say "You are the greatest husband in the world" may well make it so. A dinner together at the special restaurant communicates "You are special" to a wife who regularly prepares meals for the family.

How long has it been since you wrote your mate a love letter? "Don't be silly," someone will say. "I see him every day. Why write a letter?" Because you will say some things in a love letter that you do not say in verbal conversation. A love letter a month will keep a marriage alive and growing. A letter is an act of kindness.

Why not set some new goals for yourself in the area of kindness? Think of something you can do every day to express your love to your mate. Having completed the deed, say verbally, "I love you!" Do not be like the man who told me: "I told my wife I loved her when I asked her to marry me. If I ever change my mind, I'll let her know." Love is not a once-for-all act. It is a way of life.

Love is courteous. The word courteous means "of court-like manners, polite." Have you forgotten the little things? Do you treat others with more courtesy than you do your mate? Perhaps your wife does not want you to open the car door for her, but you ought to ask her before coming to that conclusion. It is a small act, but to some women it adds that touch of dignity that they need.

My wife trained me well in this art. When we were first married, she simply refused to get out of the car until I opened the door. One Sunday morning, I found myself in the lobby of the church looking back to see that she was still in the car!

Telephoning to say "I'll be late" is not more than you would do for anyone else with whom you have an appointment. Why not treat your mate with as much courtesy and respect as you do others? Love is courteous.

Love is unselfish. Love looks out for the best interest of the person loved. If a husband lived with a view to helping his wife reach her potential, and the wife lived with a view to helping her husband reach his potential, we would be following the biblical ideal.

Perhaps the pattern of love that we have discussed seems supernatural to you. It is! The human norm is to love those who love you. Jesus said, "If you love those who love you, what reward have you? Do not even the tax collectors do the same?" (Matthew 5:46 RSV). You do not need God's help to love a husband or wife who loves you. That is natural. But Jesus calls us to "love [our] enemies" (Matthew 5:44).

Surely your mate could not be worse than an enemy. Then your responsibility is clear. God wants to express His love through you. Will you give Him a chance to demonstrate the power of love? Let your emotions alone; do not condemn yourself for your negative feelings. In the power of the Holy Spirit express love in word and in deed, and your emotions will catch up with you. If in time your mate reciprocates your love, the "tingles" may even return. Love is not beyond your grasp if you are a Christian.

ONE FINAL CHALLENGE

Finally, 1 Peter 4:8 reads, "Love covers a multitude of sins" (NASB). If I could paraphrase the verse, I would say, "Love accepts many imperfections." Love does not demand perfection from one's mate. There are some things that your mate either cannot or will not change. These I am calling imperfections. They may not be moral in nature but are simply things that you do not like. May I illustrate from my own marriage?

We had been married several years before I realized that my wife was a "drawer opener," but not a "drawer closer." I do not know if I had been blinded to that fact the first three or four years or if it was a new behavior pattern for her, but at any rate it irritated me greatly.

I did what I thought was the "adult" thing to do. I confronted her with my displeasure in the matter and asked for change. The next week, I observed carefully each time I entered our apartment, but to my dismay there was no change.

Each time I saw an open drawer, I fumed. Sometimes I exploded. My basic pattern was to vacillate between days of verbal explosion and days of quiet smoldering, but all the while I was furious.

After a couple of months, I decided to use my educational expertise. I would give her a visual demonstration along with my lecture. I went home and took everything out of the top bathroom drawer, removed the drawer, and showed her the little wheel on the bottom and how it fit into the track, and explained what a marvelous invention that was. This time, I knew that she understood how the drawer worked and how serious I was about the matter.

The next week, I eagerly anticipated change. But no change came! For several weeks, I had internal combustion every time I saw an open drawer.

Then one day, I came home to discover that our eighteen-month-old daughter had fallen and cut the corner of her eye on the edge of an open drawer. Karolyn had taken her to the hospital. There she had gone through the ordeal of watching the surgeon stitch up that open wound and wondering if it would leave a scar or impair vision.

She told me the whole story, and I contained my emotions while I listened. I was proud of myself. I did not even mention the open drawer, but on the inside I was saying, *I bet she'll close those drawers now!* I knew this would be the clincher. She had to change now! But she did not.

After another week or two, the thought crossed my mind, *I don't believe she will ever change!* I sat down to analyze my alternatives. I wrote them down: (1) I could leave her! (2) I could be miserable every time I looked at an open drawer from now until the time I die or she dies, or (3) I could accept her as a "drawer opener" and take for myself the task of closing drawers.

As I analyzed these alternatives, I ruled out number one right away. As I looked at number two, I realized that if I were going to be miserable every time I saw an open drawer from now until I die, I would spend a great deal of my life in misery. I reasoned that the best of my alternatives was number three: accept this as one of her imperfections.

I made my decision and went home to announce it. "Karolyn," I said, "you know the thing about the drawers?"

"Gary, please don't bring that up again," she replied.

"No," I said, "I have the answer. From now on, you don't have to worry about it. You don't ever have to close another drawer. I'm going to accept that as one of my jobs. Our drawer problem is over!"

From that day to this, open drawers have never bothered me. I feel no emotion, no hostility. I simply close them. That is my job. When I get home tonight, I can guarantee the open drawers will be waiting for me. I shall close them, and all will be well.

What am I suggesting by this illustration? That in marriage you will discover things that you do not like about your mate. It may be the way he hangs towels, squeezes toothpaste, or installs the toilet paper.

The first course of action is to request change. (If you can change, why not? It is a small matter to make your partner happy.) However, I can assure you that there are some things that your mate either cannot or will not change. This is the point at which "love accepts many imperfections." You decide where the point of acceptance will come.

Some of you have had running battles for twenty years over things as simple as open drawers. Could this be the time to call a cease-fire and make a list of things that you will accept as imperfections? I do not want to discourage you, but your mate will never be perfect. He or she will never do everything that you desire. Your best alternative is the acceptance of love!

GROWTH ASSIGNMENTS

For the Married:

1. Having confessed your failures and accepted God's forgiveness and having asked your partner to forgive you, ask God to let you be His agent for loving your partner. Ask Him to fill you with His Spirit and His love. (God will answer this prayer because He has already told us that this is His will, Ephesians 5:18, 25; Titus 2:3–4.)

2. Forget about your feelings. You do not have to feel anything to love your partner. Feelings may change because of your actions, but feelings should not dictate your actions. Choose to love your mate, no matter how you feel.

3. Express love to your mate by word or action once each day for the next month. Read again the sections "Loving with Words" and "Loving with Deeds." Perhaps you could begin with a compliment each day for the next week.

4. Do not allow your mate's reaction to stifle your love. Nothing your mate does can stop your love as long as you choose to love. Why stop when love is your greatest weapon for good and growth?

5. Consider the possibility of accepting in your mate some imperfection that has irritated you for years. If you decide to accept it, be sure to tell your mate. Such acceptance can be a positive step in your own emotional growth.

6. Few individuals can resist genuine, unconditional love for more than a year. Why not start today? Make this the greatest year of your marriage. Many have found that in less than a month, love has begotten love, and their whole marriage has been turned around.

For the Unmarried:

1. Analyze the role that love plays in your dating relationship. On a separate sheet, list the following words at the
   head of parallel columns:

   • Patience • Kindness • Courtesy • Forgiving Spirit
   • Positive Attitude

   Under each column list the evidence of these qualities
   in your own actions toward your partner. Be specific.
   In what way have you shown these qualities?

2. On a separate sheet, do the same for the person whom
   you are dating. What evidence do you see in his/her
   actions that he/she loves you? If he/she were being tried
   by a jury, would there be enough evidence to convince
   the jury that he/she loves you?

3. Suggest that your partner read this chapter and make
   the same analysis of your love. Use your analysis as a
   basis for further discussion of this matter. Is your love
   growing? What makes you think it will grow after you are
   married?

6

Communication in Marriage

To communicate or not to communicate, that is the question. And herein lies the key to success or failure in growing oneness in marriage. Norman Wright indicates that in the experience of family counselors, 50 percent of those couples who come for help have as their major problem an uncommunicative husband.[1] One wonders if lack of communication is also the missing link for those unhappy couples who do not go for counseling. I do not wish to point a condemning finger at husbands, for wives too may be guilty of living unto themselves.

When we fail to communicate, we dam up the stream of life and tend to create a stagnant pool of self-pity. We feel alone because we are alone. We have put our mate outside and refuse to share life. We may still live in the same house, but we live as two lonely people rather than as a unit. This is precisely the opposite of what God intended. In the beginning He said, "It is not good for the man to be alone [cut off]" (Genesis 2:18). Many individuals have found themselves "cut off" in the midst of marriage. It is never good to be alone.

Contrary to those lofty ideals that we had before marriage, communication does not come naturally. On the other hand, neither is it, as some couples have concluded, impossible to attain. If we are to become one and enjoy

that warm flow of life that is the deepest of all human sat-
isfactions, we *must* communicate. We cannot know each
other unless we confide in each other. The apostle Paul
put his finger on this truth when he addressed the church
at Corinth: "For who among men knows the thoughts of a
man except the man's spirit within him? In the same way no
one knows the thoughts of God except the Spirit of God"
(1 Corinthians 2:11).

Just as we would never know what God is like if He
had not chosen to communicate Himself through His
Spirit, so we cannot know each other unless we choose to
communicate. "I can read him like a book" may be true
after fifty years of free communication, but it is not true in
the early years of marriage.

No, your wife cannot read your mind, as you very well
know. If she is going to know what is going on in your life,
you must choose to tell her. You must let her in. If your
husband is to know the anxieties or joys of your life, you
must take the initiative and communicate.

Communication is an act of the will. This is illustrated
in 2 Corinthians 6:11–13, where Paul says to the Corinthians "Our heart is opened wide. . . . Open wide [your hearts] to
us also (NASB)." We communicate or do not communicate
by deliberate act. We cannot truthfully say, "I do not communicate with my partner because of my personality. I am
an uncommunicative person by nature; therefore, I cannot
communicate with my mate."

It is true that some of us have what might be called a
"Dead Sea personality." We can have many thoughts, feelings, and experiences and be perfectly content not to
express them to anyone. We have no compulsion to talk.
Others have the "babbling brook personality"; everything
that enters the mind comes out the mouth, and usually
there is not a sixty-second lapse between the two. The
"Dead Sea personality" will have greater difficulty
expressing himself than will the "babbling brook." On the
other hand, the "babbling brook" has the equally difficult
problem of learning to listen.

Both talking and listening are required for effective communication. Each of us tends to lean toward one of these two extremes in basic personality orientation. Therefore, we each have our own difficulty in communication, but we *can* communicate. Communication is basically an act of the will, not a matter of the personality.

Our personalities may be an asset or a liability to communication, but they never render us bankrupt. Either I choose to share my heart, or I choose to keep the door closed. I cannot blame my personality, my mate's response, or anything else. If I live unto myself, I do so by choice and in deliberate disobedience to the command of God for oneness between marriage partners. Marriage cannot reach its ideal unless both partners choose to communicate.

LEVELS OF COMMUNICATION

There are various levels of communication, all of which are important, but some are more difficult than others. I suggest that you begin with the easiest—communicating the day-to-day events.

Some time ago a woman told me of a problem. Her husband had a job schedule that required three days at home and then three days out of town. When he would return after being away three days, she would ask, "How did things go?"

He would respond, "Fine."

"Three days away," she said, "and all I get is 'Fine.' Now that doesn't tell me much."

Do you understand what she is saying? She is separated from the events in her husband's life by three days, and "fine" does not bridge the distance. His response every husband will appreciate: "I want to leave my work at work. I don't want to bring it home and hash it over again."

Though every husband can identify with that feeling, there is one important factor that is overlooked—oneness with his wife. That goal is worth the energy it takes to rerun the events of the day to a wife who wants to share his life.

My suggestion to young marrieds and to others who have problems with this level of communication is to "lean over backwards" for a few weeks to communicate the details: "Well, dear, I got in the car and drove to the stop sign, turned left, and so on. When I got to the office, I hung my coat on the rack by the back door. . . ." Of course, I am speaking in hyperbole, but you get the point. Relate in great detail what is going on in your life. After a couple of days of this, you will be able to mention only the more important events of the day. Begin to express your feelings as well as the events. The process of such sharing will bring a fresh sense of oneness to your mate. He/she will begin to feel a part of what you are doing. Your vocation is not simply a job to "bring home the bacon," but is a part of your life. If it goes unshared, then a great deal of your life is unshared.

The wife should feel no less responsible to share her life with her husband. Whether at home or at work, you have spent several hours away from your husband. He cannot share this time unless you choose to communicate.

It is also helpful for each partner to visit the location of the other's employment, if both are working. "One picture is worth a thousand words." With a visual image of your work setting, your mate will be better able to identify with you as you describe events of the day.

Introduce each other to your close associates at work so that, when you come home and say "George was really in a foul mood today," your mate has a mental image of George and what he must look like when he is in a foul mood. This, again, enhances identification with your vocation.

Questions become an important stimulus to such communication. If the husband comes home and the wife does not ask, "How did things go?" perhaps she is communicating, "I don't care how things went." If a husband never inquires about the wife's experiences, she may feel rejected and unloved. We must evaluate our commitment to oneness. If we want the most from marriage, we must choose to communicate. Asking questions about the day-to-day affairs is the easiest and best place to start.

A second level of communication is that of problem solving or decision making. Since an entire chapter is devoted to the decision-making process, I will not discuss this level of communication except to say that this is often the first point of conflict in marriage.

I have often counseled couples having trouble in communication. When I ask, "Did you have trouble communicating before marriage?" they respond, "Oh, no. We could talk freely about everything."

Why is it that these free talkers have "clammed up"? Before marriage, no decision had to be made. They could discuss freely any issue and then each could go home and do his own thing. Now they are together and working at unity. They can no longer simply discuss. Following that discussion, a decision must be made, a decision that affects both. Because they do not agree on that decision, communication comes to a halt, and all kinds of problems arise.

The third level of communication is communicating when "the pressure is on." When the temperature rises, reason declines, emotion ascends the throne, and chaos results. How do we prevent chaos and bring unity out of those pressure moments?

One warm August day several years ago, my wife-to-be and I made a visit to the minister who was to perform our wedding ceremony. We ate dinner under an aged oak tree, and he presented this bit of advice, which I have never forgotten: "When you are angry, take turns talking." He went on to explain that I should take three to five minutes to state my ideas on the issue while my wife remained silent (no butting in allowed). Then she should be given three to five minutes to state her understanding of the issue. This process should continue as long as necessary.

On that warm August day, I could not imagine that I would ever need to use such a strategy with the perfect wife God had given me. Why should I ever get that angry at her? That question was soon to be answered, and I was to become proficient at "taking turns." I have suggested

the same to hundreds of couples since. Taking turns does
not solve the problem, but it does allay the heat so that
you can get at the problem. Norman Wright relates the
following on solving problems:

> There is an old story about a sheep herder in Wyoming who would
> observe the behavior of wild animals during the winter. Packs of
> wolves, for example, would sweep into the valley and attack the
> bands of wild horses. The horses would form a circle with their
> heads at the center of the circle and kick out at the wolves, driving
> them away. Then the sheep herder saw the wolves attack a band of
> wild jackasses. The animals also formed a circle, but they formed it
> with their heads out toward the wolves. When they began to kick
> they ended up kicking one another. People have a choice between
> being as smart as a wild horse or as stupid as a wild jackass. They
> can kick the problem or they can kick one another.[2]

Let me suggest other guidelines for taking turns. When
your partner is talking, you should be listening. One of the
great discoveries of communication is the awesome power
of the listening ear.[3] Most of us have never reached our
potential as listeners. James said, "Everyone should be
quick to listen" (James 1:19). Talking is of little value
unless someone is listening. When your partner is talking,
it is your turn to listen. Do not sit there and reload your
guns. You cannot concentrate on what she is saying if you
are marshaling your own forces. Your ideas will come back
to you when it is your turn. Do not worry about your
ideas. Concentrate on those of your mate.

Listen to the facts and the feelings being expressed. In
light of what she is saying, try to understand how she
came to feel that way. If you can understand, then a statement to that effect could be a powerful medication. "I can
understand how you would feel that way; I really can. Let
me explain my action as I saw it." Then take your turn at
presenting the way things looked from your vantage point.
When you are truly wrong, be ready to admit your wrong-
ness, as discussed in chapter 4. There is no value in rationalization.

Ask yourself, What needs does my partner have that I am not meeting? Her complaint may be that you have been late for dinner for the past three nights, but her feeling may be that you do not love her as you should. After all, love is considerate. We all have the need to be loved. If she feels unloved, then for all practical purposes she is unloved. What can you do about it? You have the potential for meeting the needs of your mate. If you accept this as your goal, you will be following the biblical admonition of Philippians 2:3–4: "Do nothing out of selfish ambition or vain conceit, but in humility consider others better than yourselves. Each of you should look not only to your own interests, but also to the interests of others."

Discussions over hurt feelings and disappointing behavior should always aim at change in the lives of both partners. However, each must think in terms of his/her own change, not that of the partner. If something has become a source of irritation, it ought to be a stepping-stone toward oneness, not a stumbling block. A willingness for personal change is absolutely essential for growing oneness. Why should both of you continue to be miserable when you can choose to be understanding and open to change?

OVERCOMING BARRIERS
TO COMMUNICATION

The picture of marital oneness is beautiful, but the creation of such a portrait is another matter. It requires your greatest creativity and energies, but few things in life are more rewarding. Because there are common barriers to communication, I want to give practical suggestions that may speak to your own problem.

"My Mate Won't Talk"

Without doubt, the most common complaint I hear from troubled couples is that one partner refuses to talk.

More often than not it is the husband who is the silent one. It would be unfair, however, to convey the idea that this is characteristic only of males. Many women also find it more comfortable to draw the curtains of the soul. Let me say first of all that this tendency to keep things inside should not be viewed as a mental disorder. I have known husbands who have recognized their own reticence to open their hearts to anyone, their wives included, and who have allowed the problem to lead to depression and self-deprivation. Their conclusion has been that they are hopelessly mentally ill. Such is not the case.

We all have strengths and weaknesses in our personalities. Though we cannot correct the past, we are masters of the future. Throughout childhood, for whatever reason, we may have developed a withdrawn, inwardly directed personality, but that does not mean that we cannot learn to open our lives and experience the joy of unity with our mates. Any pattern that has developed can also be altered. We must decide that marital oneness is worth the pain of alteration. (And I assure you that it is.)

A beginning step to communication is to discuss the problem with your partner. Sit down with your partner in a comfortable setting, and in your own words say, "Darling, I know that the unity of our marriage is not what it could be. I know also that one of our big problems is my reluctance to talk with you. I keep things inside; I have difficulty saying what I really think or feel. I know that this makes it hard on you because you cannot read my mind. I really want to grow in this area, and I am asking for your help. I am not sure what you can do to help, but maybe you have some ideas." Give your mate a chance to respond. Perhaps she does have some ideas.

Continue by telling her some of the things that you believe make it difficult for you to be open. Tell her that when she keeps asking you to talk, she simply makes it harder for you to get started. (Many partners do not realize this.) Perhaps she could ask questions about specific matters. As one husband said, "Please don't stop asking questions just because I give a short answer. I really want to say more, but I just can't get it all out with the first question. Keep the questions coming and, it is hoped, I'll keep talking."

Perhaps your partner could help by asking your advice from time to time. Most of us talk more readily if someone asks for specific advice, especially if we believe that the person really wants it. Perhaps also, if she would develop some interest in your vocation or your hobbies, you would have something else in common about which you could talk. This may mean the reading of magazines, watching certain television programs, or taking an evening school course. If it enhances oneness, it is time and money well invested.

Some years ago a wife related this story: "My husband works as an electrical engineer. When he comes home he goes to the basement where he has an electrical shop and works until I call him for dinner. During our meal, he almost always reads the newspaper. Very seldom does he say anything to me. After dinner he returns to the basement where he stays until bedtime."

"Saturday finds him in the shop all day, and Sunday is spent reading the newspaper and watching television. We have virtually no communication."

"How long has this been going on?" I asked.

"Five years," she replied.

Five years of silence! "Tell me," I said, "what do you know about electronics?"

"Absolutely nothing!"

"I have a suggestion," I said. "The local technical institute offers a course called Introduction to Electronics. I want to suggest that next quarter you enroll in that course. Obviously, your husband is interested in electronics. I bet if you could ask a question about electronics, he would talk. Besides that, the course is offered in the evening while he is in the basement. He wouldn't even miss you!"

If something is really a barrier to communication, then why not disclose it? Perhaps it is something he has done or failed to do that you have never forgotten or forgiven. If it is still on your mind, you need to be open so that your partner can have a chance to correct it. No failure is worth a lifetime of misery. You must be willing to confess and forgive.

If you have difficulty verbalizing the problem, then write it in a letter and ask him to read it in your presence. Then discuss the matter. Sometimes you can say in writing what you have difficulty expressing aloud.

Unless you communicate, however, your partner may have no idea that you are still bothered with the past. You must destroy the barriers of the past so that you can build a new life together on the rubble.

Perhaps, also, your partner could help by examining his own flow of conversation. Maybe he is talking so much that you have no opportunity. Many partners ask a question and then proceed to answer it. The other partner feels unneeded. Some could profit greatly by applying the advice of James: "Everyone should be quick to listen, slow to speak" (James 1:19). You have heard the story of the little boy who was writing a paper entitled "Garden Clubs." He asked his father for help, and his father said, "Ask your mother." The boy replied, "I didn't want to know that much."

If you believe discussion of other areas would help communication, confide in each other. After all, your discussion is on communication. You are admitting your difficulty and looking for help, so any suggestion should be considered. Perhaps your sexual needs are not being met, and you have developed a very negative attitude toward your mate. You have never discussed it, but this may be a real barrier to your communication in other areas. This is the time to speak of it. It cannot hurt. It may help.

May I suggest, as a conclusion to this conversation about your problems in communication, that you join in prayer. You may or may not be able to pray aloud, but certainly you can pray silently. If it is to be silent prayer, then agree to hold hands while praying and say "Amen" when you have finished.

Such a conversation could be the beginning of a whole new life for any couple. The partner who has the reluctance to communicate should be the one to initiate the session. The ideas I have presented, however, may be helpful to your mate until such a session materializes. We can do many things to make it easier for our mates to communicate.

"I Have Such a Temper"

Anger is certainly a barrier to communication. It is difficult, if not impossible, to communicate when one is angry. The capacity for anger, however, must not be seen as an evil. As Dr. J. H. Jowett says, "A life incapable of anger is destitute of the needful energy for all reform."[4] It is the emotion of anger against injustice and inequity that gives rise to social reform. Jesus Himself was angry upon occasion (Mark 3:5).

Most of our anger, however, does not arise from a concern for righteousness but from a self-centered heart. Someone has rubbed us the wrong way, or we did not get our way. Such anger is condemned in Scripture (Ephesians 4:31). Even a righteous anger can very easily lead to wrong actions. Therefore, Paul warns us in Ephesians 4:26, "In your anger do not sin." We must not allow anger to control us and lead us to wrong actions.

The emotion of anger may be beyond our control, but our actions in response to anger are not. We have the ability to control anger instead of being controlled by it. We cannot rightfully excuse rash behavior by simply saying "I have a temper." We all have tempers, and we all have the responsibility to deal with our tempers.

In marital conflict, how then am I to control my anger? I suggest the simple technique of withdrawing for evaluation. When you feel anger arising (all of us are aware of what is happening to us), at that moment move to control it. A simple statement such as "Dear, I can feel myself getting angry. I don't want to get angry, and I know you do not want me to get angry. So, let's agree to stop discussion until I can get my feelings under control." (I am not talking about days, but perhaps minutes or at most a few hours.) The biblical admonition is "Do not let the sun go down while you are still angry" (Ephesians 4:26). This is not an avoidance of the conflict but a temporary withdrawal for the purpose of controlling emotions.

Having withdrawn from the source of heat, evaluate your thoughts, actions, and feelings with God. Never try to do this alone, or you will come to the wrong conclusions. "Lord, why would I get so upset over this matter?" might be an appropriate prayer. Admit and confess selfish motives, wrong attitudes, or any other failure—first to God, then to your mate.

With the emotion calmed, come back to discussing the problem, perhaps using the each-take-a-turn approach mentioned earlier. There are answers to all problems. Following your anger with harsh, cutting words or physical abuse only compounds the problem. It never solves it.

Anger may well reveal an area of your relationship that needs attention. If you respond constructively, it can stimulate growth in oneness. If, however, you allow anger to control you, it will lead to separation, not oneness. Anger always drives apart. Control of anger may well bring you closer together.

"My Partner Is So Selfish"

"But my partner is so selfish," someone says. "Even when he does communicate, it is to demand his own way. I am always wrong. 'Sit down and let me tell you how things are going to be' is his idea of communication."

Selfishness is the greatest barrier to oneness, and we are all afflicted with the disease. We are our own greatest enemy in attaining marital unity. By nature we lean in the opposite direction: "My side always appears right to me. Otherwise, it would not be my side. You don't think I would choose the wrong side, do you?"

It is an awareness of human nature that will help us at this point. Recognizing this flaw in our armor will help us evaluate every situation in a more realistic manner. I can expect myself to be selfish because this is my nature. But as a Christian, I have a new nature—the very real presence of the Holy Spirit in my life. Therefore, I have a choice. I do not have to bow to my old selfish nature. I have the live option of choosing to cooperate with the Holy Spirit in doing the unselfish thing. The opposite of selfishness is love, biblical love, which is self-giving and unconditional. This is the greatest gift I have to offer my mate. But I am not free to offer such love until I have decided against selfishness. The choice is mine.

It is true that you cannot deal with the selfishness of your mate. You can deal only with your own. If you deal with your own, however, you are giving your mate a model to emulate. (Most of us would respond positively to a loving model.) When you no longer fight the selfishness of your mate, you are free to concentrate upon the defeat of your own selfishness.

"I Don't Want to Hurt Him"

Many marriage partners have refrained from expressing themselves because they did not want to hurt their mates. They have believed that if they were honest, it would be more than the partners could stand. Thus, they are content to live with limited unity rather than splinter the relationship. The intent is worthy, and most of us have felt this tension at one time or another. We treat each other with "kid gloves," because, as best we can determine, we are "kids." This may be true, but how will we ever mature if we are not given adult responsibilities?

I do not mean that you should hit your mate with your whole tale of woe thirty minutes before dinner on Friday evening. A time and place should be selected carefully. There is also the principle of constructive communicating as opposed to destructive explosion. Romans 14:19 sug-

gests, "Let us therefore make every effort to do what leads
to peace and to mutual edification." The word *edify* means
to "build up." Your objective must be clearly in mind—to
build up your mate. "Love edifies" (1 Corinthians 8:1
NASB).

I am not encouraging the emptying of your negative
garbage upon your mate's head in the name of honesty.
The Christian plan is to speak the truth in love (Ephesians
4:15), and love edifies. We speak the truth, but we seek to
say it in such a way as to build up, rather than to destroy.

A good question to ask is "What is my motive in saying
this?" Are you doing it out of a bitter heart that wants to be
vindictive? Then it is wrong and will drive you apart rather
than draw you together. All of us have negative thoughts
and feelings toward our mates at certain times. Honesty
does not compel us to express all these feelings. We must
allow these feelings to go through the sieve of "edification."
If they come out as building blocks—great! Express them!
If they come out as bombs, then defuse them before you
have destroyed the very thing that you most desire.

Having said this, I want to remind you that certain
aspects of building up another are painful. Personal
growth does not come without pain. Look at your own
life. How much have you grown through the honest, loving, but painful, criticism of your friends? As Proverbs
27:6 notes, "Faithful are the wounds of a friend."

Genuine love moves out to stimulate growth even if it
must be accompanied with pain. No one enjoys pain, and
your mate will not likely be joyful over your expression of
truth; but if such pain can bring growth, it is worthwhile.
Surgery is never a pleasing thought, but the results may be
life itself. All of us need emotional, social, and spiritual
surgery along the way, and our mates may well be the chosen surgeons.

Certainly you will want to express your own disap-
pointments and frustrations. One is not always happy or
satisfied. A mature marriage will provide acceptance even
when the mate is "out of sorts." That is never the time for

criticism but rather for acceptance and understanding.

Never use honesty as a license to pour out all your unhappiness and blame it on your mate. Remember, happiness or unhappiness is a state of mind that you choose for yourself. It may be helped or hindered by your mate's attitudes and actions, but the choice is yours.

In conclusion, let me say that you must not be over-protective of your mate. What your mate needs is not another mother or father but a partner who loves him enough to speak the truth in love. Weigh your medication carefully. Do not give an overdose. None of us can face all our weaknesses on the same day. Medicine must be taken at regular intervals, not all at once. Find the best time—never when one is hungry, or late at night. Ask your mate if he thinks he could take a little constructive criticism. Do not give it unless he is ready. Make sure that your criticism is something to which your mate can respond positively.

Couple your criticism with compliments. The biblical pattern for criticism is found in Revelation 2:1–4. Christ said to the church at Ephesus, "I know your deeds . . . your hard work . . . your perseverance. . . . Yet I hold this against you." He then proceeded to give them one criticism.

Three compliments, one criticism is the pattern. It helps if the compliments are given in the same area as the criticism. For example, the husband may say, "Darling, you are a tremendous cook, and the way you keep the kitchen floor, I bet I'm the only guy in the community who can see himself in the floor, and the way you handled the spilt milk this morning—you have really grown in self-control. I am really proud of you! Are you ready, Babe?" (He waits for her response.) "That cobweb has been in the corner for three weeks!"

The compliments give me the assurance that I am not a failure. Basically, I am doing a pretty good job, so I am motivated to continue growth. If, however, you give me the criticism without the compliments, I am likely to give up. *I do everything I can to please him/her, and what do I get? Another criticism! I give up!* These are likely to be my thoughts.

"I Know That I Lack Self-Confidence"

Lack of self-esteem is one of the greatest barriers to communication. Many of us, for whatever reason, have grown up with the feeling of inadequacy. We look back at a string of failures and find our successes hard to remember. We view ourselves as threatened by every social encounter. Thus, when we come to marriage, we find it difficult to express our ideas for fear of further rejection and failure. Dr. James Dobson has said, "Low self-esteem is the most common source of depression among women. "[5] He further observes, "Lack of self-esteem produces more symptoms of psychiatric disorders than any other factor yet identified. "[6]

Is there no hope, then, for the one who perceives himself as weak and failing? If this were true, then a great segment of our society stands without help. How have we developed our self-concept? By judging ourselves by the value system of those around us. As Dr. Dobson observes, that value system has exalted beauty, brains, and athletic ability.[7] If we have failed in these three areas (most of which are beyond our control), then we see ourselves as failures.

But your self-concept could be wrong. So you may not be a beauty queen or have an IQ of 140 or be able to catch a ball before it smashes your nose—where does that leave you? It leaves you with the rest of us normal mortals made in the image of God. Hundreds around you have fought those same feelings of inadequacy and have won. So can you.

Surely, you have weaknesses. Surely, you have failed. But you also have strengths, and you can succeed in many things. You may not be able to pass the entrance exam to medical school, but you can do a commendable job painting your house. Your skills are not the same as others, nor should they be. God does not run a cookie factory where we all come out looking alike. His is a snowflake factory, noted for variety.

Be your best self under God's direction. Utilize your abilities; do not worry about those things that are beyond your control. You are a worthy person because you are made in the image of God. Your worth is not determined by what you have done or have not done. You can accomplish worthy goals. Do not let your emotions push you around. Admit your feelings of inadequacy to God, but thank Him that you can do all things through Christ, who strengthens you (Philippians 4:13).

How can a marriage partner help a mate with low self-esteem? By encouraging him/her to accept the past and to concentrate on the future and by the assurance of love and concern. That is what marriage is all about. One does not have to bear his burden alone (Galatians 6:2). Dr. Dobson verbalizes these ideas in the following statement:

> Life has been tough and you've had your share of suffering. To this point, you've faced your problems without much human support and there have been times when your despair has been overwhelming. Let me, now, share that burden. From this moment forward, I am interested in you as a person: you deserve and shall have my respect. As best as possible, I want you to quit worrying about your troubles. Instead, confide them to me. Our concentration will be on the present and the future, and together we will seek appropriate solutions.[8]

When a mate makes such a statement to a partner, he/she is conveying acceptance, love, understanding, encouragement, and direction. It calls for a positive attitude rather than despair. This is always the attitude for growth.

SUMMARY

Communication is not a luxury; it is a necessity. There can be no unity without communication. The barriers to communication are formidable but not unconquerable. The key is your own will to communicate. Motivated with the vision of oneness in marriage, you must choose to

communicate regardless of your emotions and past failures. The process will not be without pain, but then pain is
the handmaiden of growth. The following suggestions are
designed to help you, if you *"will"*!

GROWTH ASSIGNMENTS

For the Married:

1. Look at your own marriage and ask honestly: "Am I
    happy with the degree of communication that we have
    attained?" (If you are not, keep reading.)

2. Write down the areas where you feel communication is
    most needed in your marriage.

3. Who is the most talkative in your marriage?

4. If you find it very difficult to communicate your
    thoughts and feelings to your mate, consider an open
    discussion as suggested in the section entitled "My Mate
    Won't Talk." (Certainly, it will be hard to get started,
    but, as an ancient Chinese sage said, "The journey of a
    thousand miles begins with a first step.")

5. Reread each section of this chapter, and write down after
    each section ways in which you believe you could make a
    contribution toward growing communication with your
    mate. Seek to implement these on a regular basis.

6. Read each section aloud with your mate and discuss
    what you see about yourself in that particular section.
    (Do not mention what you see about your mate unless
    he/she asks you to do so.)

7. Ask your mate if he/she would like you to help in any
    area of communication. (Do not press the issue.)

For the Unmarried:

1. Evaluate the communication patterns that you have established with your dating partner. The following questions should prove helpful:
   a. Which of us is the more talkative?
   b. How do we communicate?
   c. Is our communication merely surface talk, or do we genuinely share in self-revelation?
   d. What have been barriers to our communication?

2. Scan each section of this chapter again and write down the ways in which you could stimulate growing communication with your prospective mate.

3. Read each section of this chapter aloud with your dating partner and discuss what you see about yourself in each section. Let your partner do the same.

4. Discuss with each other what you could do to enhance communication. Write down specific suggestions that you would like to try. Evaluate your progress one month from now.

7

Who Is Going to Clean the Commode?

*T*he honeymoon is over. Bill and Mary both have good jobs and have just taken the usual jesting from friends on their first day back at work. All day long they have been excited about their first evening together in their own little apartment.

Mary arrives home thirty minutes before Bill and, after a preliminary walk through the apartment, decides to begin dinner—her first! Before she has the carrots peeled, Bill walks in the door, goes straight to the kitchen, and sweeps her off her feet with a warm embrace and a passionate kiss. Before she has recovered, Bill is in the gold chair by the lamp, gazing at the sports page.

When dinner is ready, Mary calls him, and he bounces in with a big smile and says, "Boy, does this smell good!" A normal amount of chatter follows, mostly the relating of various comments of friends at the office, and dinner is ended. Bill excuses himself and rushes off to watch the Dallas Cowboys, while Mary proceeds to clear the table and wash dishes. By and by they get together and have a tender evening.

The next evening the procedure is much the same as that described above. The third evening brings Act III (the same as Acts I and II). The fourth evening Mary begins to wonder, *What is supposed to be so exciting about marriage?*

On the fifth evening she explodes. "Why don't you ever offer to help me? Who do you think I am? There's one thing I want you to know. I didn't marry you to be your slave . . . et cetera."

Bill does not know what hit him. "What brought all of this on? What in the world are you talking about? Do you mean that you want me to help you cook and wash dishes? That's the craziest thing I have ever heard . . . et cetera."

What is the problem with Bill and Mary? Confusion of responsibilities. Misunderstanding about who will do what. You see, in Mary's home her father always helped her mother in the preparation of dinner and always washed the dishes when he did not have an evening appointment. On the other hand, in Bill's home his father would never think of doing such things. Bill had heard "That's a woman's job" from his earliest childhood. Therefore, Bill and Mary came to their marriage with different role expectations. They had different mental images of what a husband was supposed to do. They had failed to discuss what the sociologists call "marriage roles."

Bill and Mary are not exceptions to the rule. They are demonstrating what happens in most homes sometime during the first three months of marriage, as the couple realizes that they have never agreed upon the answer to that all-important question: "Who will clean the commode?" Because he has assumed that it is her job and she has assumed that it is his job, the commode becomes a source of irritation in more ways than one. The same kind of conflict can appear on many fronts: the garbage, the mopping, the vacuuming, the laundry, cleaning the shower stall, washing the car, mowing the grass, and so on. The specific issue may be different, but the underlying problem is always the same—confusion of role expectations.

Usually we think of the word *role* as being related to the larger aspects of life, such as who will support the family financially. *Role*, however, means simply "the assumption of a responsibility." The particular responsibility may be major or minor. It may involve the task of financial provision, but it may also involve the more detailed matters mentioned above. Who will take the responsibility for what? That is the important question of roles.

Our society has undergone a great deal of change in the basic role expectations of the husband-wife unit. Traditionally, the husband has been the provider and the wife the homemaker. Currently, however, there are more wives working outside the home than there are those following the traditional role of domestic engineer. This has spawned fresh areas of conflict in marriage.

If the wife is going to work outside the home and play an equal role with the husband in financial provision, then will he take an equal degree of responsibility for household tasks that the wife formerly assumed? Most engaged couples discuss and agree upon the larger question, Will the wife work outside the home? Few, however, discuss who will clean the commode. Consequently, the greatest source of conflict in young marriages is not "provider versus homemaker" but the more nitty-gritty issues of daily life. Thus, the thrust of this chapter is to encourage the discussion of minor tasks as well as the major roles that each will play. Far too many unwarranted assumptions in this area are made by most couples.

Thus, discussion of roles before marriage and agreement upon roles within marriage are extremely important. Many conflicts could be eliminated if the couple would take time before marriage to discuss and agree upon responsibilities. Normally the problem is not the inability to agree upon responsibilities but rather the failure to even discuss the matter. Couples tend to feel that they both know what they will do when they get married. But how can one know what another thinks or envisions without open and thorough discussion?

Does the Bible give us any help in deciding what the husband should do and what the wife should do in the home? I once heard James Hatch of Columbia Bible College say facetiously, "The Bible makes it clear that the husband ought to wash the dishes. In 2 Kings 21:13, God

said, 'I will wipe Jerusalem as a man wipeth a dish (KJV).'"
That should settle the issue for you ladies.

In a more serious vein, we see the concept of varying
roles among equals when we look at God Himself. In
Ephesians 1, for example, we see God the Father planning
our salvation (vv. 3–4), God the Son shedding His blood
for our salvation (v. 7), and God the Holy Spirit sealing
our salvation (vv. 13–14). Each plays a different role in the
redemptive process, though they are one. Unity does not
mean that there is no diversity. Various roles work together
to perform the whole.

In a similar manner, the husband and wife perform
various responsibilities but work together as a unit. Acceptance of differing roles does not destroy unity but
enhances it. Responsibilities have nothing to do with
authority or worth but have everything to do with efficien-
cy and performance. There is no need to duplicate our
efforts; therefore, we agree to accept various responsibilities and work together toward the accepted goal.

In the very beginning, God assigned to Adam and Eve
an objective: "God blessed them and said to them, 'Be fruitful and increase in number; fill the earth and subdue it. Rule
over the fish of the sea and the birds of the air and over every
living creature that moves on the ground'" (Genesis 1:28).

The objective was twofold: to reproduce themselves
physically and to subdue, or have dominion over, the
earth with all its creatures. Notice that the objective was
given to the man and his wife. Both were to be a part of
accomplishing the goal, but obviously they could not both
play the same role. Physically, the woman was to be the
childbearer, but in this process man was to play a vital
role. Why? Because God's pattern is unity. It is always
God's plan that husband and wife work as a team. Physical birth demands such teamwork and is a model for all of
life.

Just as physical reproduction requires the cooperative
work of husband and wife, each playing a different role
but each necessary and both working together as a unit, so

in all other areas the pattern is to be varying responsibilities but unity of purpose. The players on an athletic team do not all do the same tasks, but they do have the same objective. Thus, the husband and wife do not perform identical roles, but they work toward a common objective as a team commissioned by God.

An allusion to the diversity of roles for Adam and Eve is seen in Genesis 3, where God pronounces judgment upon them for their sin:

> To the woman he said, "I will greatly increase your pains in childbearing; with pain you will give birth to children. Your desire will be for your husband, and he will rule over you." To Adam he said, "Because you listened to your wife and ate from the tree about which I commanded you, 'You must not eat of it,' "Cursed is the ground because of you; through painful toil you will eat of it all the days of your life. It will produce thorns and thistles for you, and you will eat the plants of the field. By the sweat of your brow you will eat your food until you return to the ground, since from it you were taken; for dust you are and to dust you will return" (Genesis 3:16–19).

God's judgment upon Eve was related to pain in childbirth. Childbirth was certainly a role unique to Eve. This judgment did not affect man's role in the reproductive process. When God placed a specific judgment upon Adam, He chose the earth, for Adam was a farmer. Thorns and thistles were to make the process of cultivation more difficult.

Both of these judgments would stand as a constant reminder of the results of sin, and each judgment was tailored to fit. That is, Eve's judgment met her in a role that was uniquely hers, and Adam's judgment faced him every day in the fields as he performed his major responsibility of providing food for his family.

If Eve was to accomplish her role in reaching God's objective ("Be fruitful, and increase in number"), then obviously she would not be able to till the fields. Since Adam's role in reproduction was different, he was free to focus his energies on the second aspect of God's objective, that of subduing the earth and having dominion over other living creatures. Thus, the emphasis was upon the wife as the childbearer and the husband as the provider.

These roles are not to be thought of as airtight compartments. Anyone who knows anything about an agrarian economy knows that the farmer's wife plays a vital role in the success of the farm. Also, Adam certainly had responsibilities related to child rearing. The biblical emphasis in child rearing is always on "parents," not "mothers." What we do have in this chapter is an introduction to the idea of varying responsibilities within marriage, with an emphasis on teamwork in reaching God's objectives.

Perhaps this passage would indicate that if the couple is to have children, then the traditional pattern of husband as provider and wife as homemaker would be the most logical. Some Christian couples today are deciding not to have children; they assume that the first half of God's command in Genesis 1:28—"Be fruitful and increase in number; [and] fill the earth"—has been fulfilled. If this is the case, there seems to be no logical reason why the wife should not be equally involved with her husband in helping fulfill the second half of God's command—"Subdue [the earth and] rule over [its creatures]."

Other couples who have children reason that in a nonagrarian society, the wife may well work outside the home and still maintain her role as a godly mother. The description of the godly woman in Proverbs 31 seems to lend credence to this position.

A wife of noble character who can find? She is worth far more than rubies. Her husband has full confidence in her and lacks nothing of value. She brings him good, not harm, all the days of her life. She selects wool and flax and works with eager hands. She is like the merchant ships, bringing her food from afar. She gets up while it is still dark; she provides food for her family and portions for her servant girls. She considers a field and buys it; out of her earnings she plants a vineyard. She sets about her work vigorously; her arms are strong for her tasks. She sees that her trading is profitable, and her lamp does not go out at night. In her hand she holds the distaff and grasps the spindle with her fingers. She opens her arms to the poor and extends her hands to the needy. When it snows, she has no fear for her household; for all of them are clothed in scarlet. She makes coverings for her bed; she is clothed in fine linen and purple. Her husband is respected at the city gate, where he takes his seat among the elders of the land. She makes linen garments and sells them, and supplies the merchants with sashes. She is clothed with strength and dignity; she can laugh at the days to come. She speaks with wisdom, and faithful instruction is on her tongue. She watches over the affairs of her household and does not eat the bread of idleness. Her children arise and call her blessed; her husband also, and he praises her. (vv. 10–28)

No one could read this chapter and conclude that the wife's role is to be limited to childbearing. Yet one profound impression is made—for this wife, the "center of gravity" was her home. She engaged in numerous and diverse activities: sewing, cooking , buying fields, planting vineyards, making and selling fine linen and girdles, caring for the poor and needy, and speaking with wisdom and kindness. This wife certainly contributed economically to the home. Yet all of these were directed toward the wellbeing of her family: her husband (vv. 11–12); her children (vv. 15, 21, 27); and herself (v. 22).

The results of such a life? "Her children arise and call her blessed; her husband also, and he praises her" (v. 28). I know scores of wives who have not made their homes central but have sought and obtained personal exaltation in various fields—and who would trade it all for this eulogy: "Her children call her blessed, and her husband praises her."

This Old Testament picture of a godly woman with a wholesome self-image and a dedication to ministry to her family became the New Testament ideal. I believe it is this picture Paul had in mind when he wrote that the older women were to instruct the younger women to be "keepers at home" (Titus 2:5 KJV). This does not mean that the

Christian wife must confine herself to any particular set of household duties, but it does mean that her family must be central in all her activities. When faced with a decision regarding a new responsibility, the questions ought always to be, How will it affect my family? My husband? My children? Myself? Our relationship with each other?

No personal achievement is worth sacrificing the unity of the family. I join with Socrates in the statement he made at about 450 B.C.: "If I could get to the highest place in Athens I would lift up my voice and say 'What mean ye, fellow citizens, that ye turn every stone to scrape wealth together, and take so little care of your children to whom ye must one day relinquish all?'"

The Christian wife has tremendous freedom. Many pursuits stand within the realm of opportunity for her, but her own satisfaction is best obtained in commitment to her family. What is a wife profited if she "gain the whole world" and lose her own family?

What of the husband's role as provider? Is seeing him as such simply an allusion to Genesis 3, or is the concept found elsewhere in Scripture? First Timothy 5:8 says, "If anyone does not provide for his relatives, and especially for his immediate family, he has denied the faith and is worse than an unbeliever." In the context, this passage is dealing with a man's responsibility to care for widows in his family, but certainly, if he is to care for widows, he has the same responsibility for his more immediate family.

Throughout the Scriptures, God is referred to as "Father," and various parallels are drawn between our heavenly Father and our earthly fathers. For example,

> Which of you, if his son asks for bread, will give him a stone? Or if he asks for a fish, will give him a snake? If you, then, though you are evil, know how to give good gifts to your children, how much more will your Father in heaven give good gifts to those who ask him? (Matthew 7:9–11)

If you wanted to describe God's role as Father in one word, which word would you choose? I would choose the word *Provider*. He has provided everything necessary for life and godliness (2 Peter 1:3). Not only has He given life, but He sustains life and meets all our needs. Likewise, the Bible depicts an earthly father as one who provides for his own.

That does not mean that the wife does not help in making provision for the family. Proverbs 31 dispels that idea. Husband and wife are a team, and they work together, but the scriptural pattern is for the husband to take the basic responsibility for meeting the physical needs of his family.

Some time ago I was pleasantly surprised to read the following in a secular magazine. Dr. Frances Welsing, the author, is a black female psychiatrist, an assistant professor of pediatrics at Howard University College of Medicine, and a member of the staff of Freedman's Hospital in Washington, D.C. Her insight into basic husband/wife roles is akin to the biblical pattern:

> It is within the family setting that black people can begin to alter the inferiorization dynamic and change it to a process for the maximal development of the young.
>
> The father's major specific task in relationship to the children is to teach adult male role functioning through daily example, with love and kindness expressed toward the children—the love and kindness being essential to efficient learning. Major adult role responsibility is breadwinning and protection of the family unit and the total people.
>
> The mother's major task in relationship to the children is to teach adult female role functioning through daily example, love and kindness. Major adult responsibility is child socialization and care of the home. These divisions of labor I see as fundamental and necessary for efficient and effective family functioning.
>
> I realize that there is much yelling and screaming about such role functioning priorities by mostly white women today, but we black people cannot allow whites to continue to set our priorities. If we ignore these necessities, we will do so at our peril.
>
> Black people can themselves begin to halt the process of the inferiorization of black people and black children if the now dysfunctional female-dominated "survival units" can be turned into true family units with a true balance and harmony established

between the adult male role of breadwinner and the female role of child socialization, with true equal respect returned to both adult roles.

Black females must begin to struggle for the same opportunity that the white female now has—to stay home while being adequately supported by her husband, and to provide adequate socialization and give the care and attention to black children that the white female can now give to her children, often with the assistance of a black female who had to leave her own children to take such a job.

Focusing on these external common objectives, black men and women will be freed from the now destructive practice of competing with one another and will instead learn to successfully compete as a team.[1]

Some years ago, I encountered a classic example of failure to reckon with this basic pattern. A wife who had been married for more than thirty years came for counseling. She described her present situation as "unbearable." For many years her husband had limited himself to three activities: his job, his hobby, and sleeping. Three meals were used to punctuate these activities. He took no responsibility in the home, did nothing with the children, and talked very little with his wife.

I inquired if this had always been his lifestyle. She answered, "Oh, no. For many years he did not work at all."

In the early years of their marriage he had been very irresponsible, working only a few days at any one job. They had bought a house with the help of parents but were in danger of losing it because of nonpayment on the mortgage loan. One day, she decided that if he would not work, she would. So she secured a job and began paying all the bills. From that day, she had assumed the leadership role in the home. He was free to continue his irresponsible behavior, which is exactly what he had done. Years later, he did secure and maintain regular employment, but he never regained a responsible position in the marriage. He felt unneeded and unwanted and had developed an introverted lifestyle.

As I presented the biblical pattern of the husband as provider, I saw the light dawn in the wife's mind. She saw her mistake and stated it in a way that I have never forgotten: "I saved my house, but I lost my marriage!"

What a revealing analysis! Her decision to become the provider had indeed saved her house but had also accepted her husband's failure as permanent. She had encouraged his pattern of irresponsible behavior. She further lamented, "I wish that I had let the house go. I have carried the load all these years. Now that he is providing the money, I don't know how to get him to be the leader. I want someone to lean on!"

In her effort to save material possessions, she had lost the more important possession—oneness with her husband according to God's pattern. What might she have done differently? For whatever reason, her husband was irresponsible at the time of their marriage. She did not help that pattern by removing the responsibility. One can only learn responsibility by accepting responsibility. Had she expressed not only her willingness to help but also her expectation that he be the provider, and had she been willing to live on what he provided, I believe that he would most likely have come to accept his new role of husband-provider. He needed pressure and encouragement to assume responsibility.

Certainly there are families in which, because of physical or mental disabilities, the wife must assume the role of provider. These are exceptions to the rule, and God will give strength and grace to these wives. Such a wife should, however, help her husband to see his role in the relationship. Remember, husband and wife constitute a team, and everyone on a team must have responsibility.

With these basic guidelines—(1) the husband is provider, and (2) the wife is homemaker—the Christian couple is free to work out their own particular pattern of responsibilities within the home. Again, let me emphasize that these guidelines are not to be thought of as airtight compartments.

The biblical pattern does not preclude the wife working outside the home, thus making a financial contribution to the family. It does mean, however, that this must not be done to the detriment of the family.

The wife and mother bears great responsibility in the home, but this must not be taken as excluding the father from household responsibilities. The physical role of the mother in childbearing and nurturing is basic, but the child needs also the warm emotional involvement of the father. The child needs both parents, and the father must be as concerned for the welfare of the child as is the mother. Fellowship and training of children cannot be delegated to the mother exclusively. Many Christian fathers have made this fatal mistake. Husband and wife are members of a team and must function as teammates.

As a team, the husband and wife are to work together under God to determine the roles each will play so that together they may accomplish God's purposes for their union. The specific roles will vary from family to family and may change within the same family from time to time, but the roles should be agreeable to each partner.

In my opinion, the gifts and abilities of the partners should be considered when determining responsibilities. One may be more qualified than the other. Since you are on the same team, why not use the player best qualified in that area? In my own life, I would hate to imagine the chaos that would result if I bought the groceries. That is my wife's department, and she is highly qualified. For other couples, however, the husband may be particularly equipped for that task.

None of the above should be taken to mean that once a responsibility is accepted the partner should never help with that task. Let us say that the wife accepts the responsibility for vacuuming the floor every Thursday. This does not mean that the husband should never help her. Love wants to help and often will. What the acceptance of that responsibility does mean is that, if the husband does not help her, she will not be hurt. She is not expecting him to vacuum because that is her duty. If he does help, she takes it as an act of love, and indeed it is.

The Scriptures do not tell us "who should clean the commode," but they do encourage us to agree upon an answer. Amos once asked, "Do two walk together unless they have agreed to do so?" (3:3). The answer is, "No, not very far and not very well." Agreement upon responsibilities is a relatively simple matter, but if it is overlooked, problems may burst forth like lava from a volcano.

GROWTH ASSIGNMENTS

For the Married:

1. In your marriage, who has the basic responsibility for providing financially?

   _____Wife _____Husband _____Shared

   Are you satisfied with the present arrangement? If no, write a brief description of the changes you would like to see.

2. Without discussing it with your partner, make a list of some of the items you consider to be your responsibility around the house. Make a separate list of those items you consider to be his/her responsibility. Include everything and be as specific as possible.

3. Have your partner read this chapter and complete assignments 1 and 2.

4. At an agreed-upon time, show your lists to each other. You may find:
   a. that you completely agree upon your roles.
   b. that you have specific items upon which you disagree (there is some area of confusion as to who has responsibility for what).

    c. that you agree on very little—thus, this is an area of real marital conflict.

5. Whatever you find, use this time to discuss and evaluate your roles. What are you doing that you believe your mate is better qualified to do? Would he/she be willing to accept this responsibility? Let him/her try it for one month.

6. Do not ever believe that responsibilities cannot be changed. If conflict arises over roles, it is time for discussion and evaluation.

For the Unmarried:

1. Likely you have already discussed and agreed upon who will accept the basic responsibility for financially providing for the family, but have you decided "who will clean the commode"? Agreeing upon major and minor responsibilities is extremely important.

2. After each of you has read the chapter, make a list of the items that you consider will be your responsibility around the house after marriage. Make a separate list of those items that you consider will be his/her responsibility. Include everything, and be as specific as possible.

3. When you have considerable time, compare these lists.
    a. What duplications do you have—items for which both of you feel responsible? (Make a list of these and tentatively agree upon a division of labor.)
    b. What omissions do you have—items for which neither of you feels responsible? (Make a list of these and tentatively agree upon a division of labor.)

4. Review these agreements shortly before you are married.

5. Remain open to evaluation and shifting of responsibilities after marriage.

8

"He Thinks He's Always Right"

As noted earlier, many couples who seem to have no difficulty communicating before marriage find communication coming to a standstill after marriage. The basic reason for this change is that, before marriage, no decisions had to be made. They talked freely about any issue and then departed, each to do his or her own thing. After marriage, however, they are attempting to experience oneness, and decisions must be made that will affect both partners. Because they cannot agree on the decision, communication grinds to a halt, and a wall of separation begins to grow between them.

Sociologists and family counselors admit that one of the greatest problems in marriage is the decision-making process. Visions of democracy dance in the minds of many young couples, but when there are only two voting members, democracy often results in deadlock. Few still hold to the old autocratic system where the husband rules "with a rod of iron" and the wife is more of a child than a partner.

An alternative is a matriarchal system. Here the mother calls all the plays from the sideline, and the husband is at most the quarterback, running the plays. One of the practical problems associated with this system is homosexuality. Researchers who have studied the home life of homosexuals and lesbians have discovered that almost always the pattern is a dominant mother and a passive father. The mother calls all the plays, and the father's influence in the home is negligible.

What then are we to do? How shall we make decisions? If these questions can be answered before marriage, the couple will save themselves great frustration. Most newly married couples assume that decisions will take care of themselves. They anticipate no great problems in this area. Such illusions will soon be shattered.

Does the Bible offer any help? If we wanted to follow the best possible pattern of decision making, what would it be? I want to suggest that the best example we have for decision making among equals is God Himself.

As noted earlier, God has revealed Himself as a Trinity. This Trinitarian God has made many decisions, some of which are recorded in the Bible. From the original "Let us make man in our image" (Genesis 1:26, italics added) to the final invitation of the Trinity in Revelation 22, God has made decisions. How were these decisions made?

Our information is limited, but in Matthew 26:36–46 we get to look in on a communication session between the Son and the Father. Jesus was facing the Cross and, naturally, was feeling physical and emotional pressure. In these verses, we find Him expressing fully His feelings and thoughts to the Father. "My Father, if it is possible, may this cup be taken from me" (v. 39). This is not meant to be a complete record of the prayer but rather its theme. There was no holding back, no facade, but utter openness with the Father. Three times the prayer was repeated, and each time Jesus concluded, "Yet not as I will, but as you will (v. 39; cf. vv. 42, 44).

Was this fatalism? Not at all. Jesus simply recognized the Father as the leader. Granted, the decision of the Cross had been made in eternity past, for Jesus is "the Lamb that was slain from the creation of the world" (Revelation 13:8). But now, as He faced the Cross in time and space, He voiced his human feelings to the Father.

Another verse explains this relationship even more clearly. In 1 Corinthians 11:3, Paul says, "Now I want you to realize that the head of every man is Christ, and the head of the woman is man, and the head of Christ is God." That last phrase—"the head of Christ is God"—is overlooked by many. Paul is obviously referring to God the Father.

"I thought the Father and the Son were equal." They are! Yet within the perfect unity of the Godhead there is order, and the Father is revealed as the leader. If we can understand something of the nature of this divine model, that is, how the Father relates to the Son and how the Son relates to the Father, then we will have a better understanding of what it means for the man to be the "head" of the woman.

Is the Father more valuable than the Son? Is a man more valuable than a woman? Is the Father more intelligent than the Son? Are men more intelligent than women? The obvious answer to these questions is no. The Father and the Son are equal in every respect. But equality does not mean that there are no distinctions. It was the Son who died on the cross, not the Father. Are men and women equal in value? Yes! Say it loudly and clearly. Let no one question where the Bible stands on this issue. Both male and female were made in the image of God and are of equal value. Does equality mean they are identical? No. There are differences, but differences do not mean deficiencies. When God indicates that the man is to be the head of the woman, He is simply establishing order for a relationship among equals, a relationship that is pictured by God Himself.

Is it conceivable that the Father would ever force the Son to do anything against His will? Is it conceivable that a husband who followed this pattern would ever force his wife to do anything against her will? Headship does not mean dictatorship. Would the Son ever walk off to "do His own thing" without consulting the Father? "Unthinkable," you say. Would a wife ever walk off to "do her own thing" without consulting her husband? I know that God is perfect, and that we are imperfect; therefore, we do not always do what we know to be right. We must, however, understand the pattern to which we are called.

The biblical concept of man as the "head of the house" has perhaps been the most exploited concept of the Bible. Christian husbands, full of self-will, have made all kinds of foolish demands of their wives under the authority of "The Bible says . . ." Headship does not mean that the husband has the right to make all the decisions and inform the wife of what is going to be done. That is unthinkable, if one looks seriously at the model of God the Father and God the Son.

What, then, is the biblical pattern for decision making? Let us allow the conversation between Jesus and the Father that occurred in Gethsemane just prior to the Crucifixion to be our example. "My Father, if it is possible, may this cup be taken from me. Yet not as I will, but as you will" (Matthew 26:39).

The pattern seems to be a discussion of ideas and feelings—expressed in honesty and love—with the husband as the recognized leader. The objective is always oneness in our decisions. The Trinity knows perfect unity in every decision. As imperfect beings, we may not always be able to attain the ideal, but that must always be our goal.

What about those times when we have each stated fully our ideas, and yet we cannot agree on a course of action? I suggest that if the decision can wait (and most of them can), then wait. While you are waiting, both should be praying and seeking new information that may shed light on the situation. A week later, discuss it again and see where you are.

"How long do we wait?" As long as you can! In my opinion, the only time that a husband should make a decision without mutual agreement is on those rare occasions when the decision must be made "today." There are few such decisions in life. Most things can wait. Unity is more important than haste. "But if I don't buy it today, the sale will be over!" A "bargain" at the expense of unity with your mate is costly indeed.

On those occasions when the decision must be made "today" and there is still no agreement between partners, I believe the husband has the responsibility to make the decision that he feels is best. He must also bear full responsibility for that decision.

At this point, the wife may feel the pain of submission, but she should also feel the security of a responsible husband, one who will make decisions when he must. In such decisions, the wife should not feel responsible for the husband's choice. On the other hand, neither should she work for its failure.

If, indeed, time reveals that it was a poor decision, the wife should never yield to the temptation to say, "I told you so. If you had listened to me, this would not have happened." When a man is down, he does not need someone to step on him. He needs a gentle arm and soft assurance that you are with him and that things will work out. "We goofed, but we're together, and we'll make it." These are the words of the wise wife.

I am well aware that some will reject the idea that the husband should be the decision maker, or leader, in the home. However, when one understands the biblical pattern of such leadership, it becomes more feasible. Male leadership in the home has nothing to do with superiority. It has to do with order among equals. Sooner or later, if one partner is not recognized as the leader, the couple will come to a stalemate and will be rendered ineffective when a crisis comes. We must strive for unity in all decisions, and with proper attitudes such will be attained 95 percent of the time—but someone must have the responsibility for making decisions when unity cannot be achieved.

Does this squeeze the wife into something less than a person? If it does, then somewhere you have missed the pattern. The headship of God the Father in no way diminishes the deity of the Son. Thus, we must never interpret the headship of the husband in such a way as to diminish the personhood of the wife. The wife has fully as much as the husband to contribute to the relationship. In many areas, her insight may be better than his. A man is a fool to make decisions without consulting his wife. Not only does such action destroy oneness, but it also ignores a tremendous source of wisdom.

Many couples need to be reminded that they are on the same team. Too often, partners are competing with each other, each defending his/her own ideas. Nothing could be more foolish. Share your ideas, by all means, but use those ideas to come to the *best* decision. Not my ideas versus your ideas, but *our* ideas and *our* decision. "We feel; we think; we decided." This is the language of unity.

WHAT THE HUSBAND'S
HEADSHIP DOES NOT MEAN

At the risk of sounding redundant, let me note carefully what the Scripture does *not* mean when it says, "The husband is the head of the wife" (Ephesians 5:23).

The statement does not mean that the husband is more intelligent than the wife. Certainly, a given husband might have a higher IQ than his wife or a given wife a higher IQ than her husband, but headship has nothing to do with intelligence. God the Father and God the Son are equally infinite in wisdom, yet the Father is the "head" of the Son. Generally speaking, men and women are both highly intelligent creatures (though one may wonder about that at times).

"The husband is the head of the wife" does not mean that the man is more valuable than the woman. Both men and women are made in the image of God and are of infinite worth. It is true that the Old Testament records the Jewish system, which exalted the male child as more valuable than the female, but we must not accept the Jewish cultural system as God's system. The angels in heaven do not rejoice more when a man is converted than when a woman is converted. In Christ "there is neither male nor female"; they "are all one" (Galatians 3:28 KJV).

"The husband is the head of the wife" does not mean

that the husband is to be a dictator, making independent decisions and telling his wife what to do. We certainly do not see that pattern between God the Father and God the Son. It is unthinkable that God the Father would make a decision and then call in the Son and inform Him. "The Lord our God, the Lord is one" (Deuteronomy 6:4). There is full and complete communication and absolute unity in every decision.

Many a Christian dictator has brought ulcers upon himself by carrying an inordinate load of responsibility. God did not intend the husband to make all the decisions alone. Remember, the wife was given to be a helper. How can she help when her husband does not even consult her? The great need of our day is for Christian leaders, not dictators.

WHAT THE WIFE'S
SUBMISSION DOES NOT MEAN

Many wives shudder when they hear the pastor say, "Turn in your Bible to Ephesians 5:22." They can feel it coming, and they do not like the sound of it. "Wives, submit to your husbands as to the Lord."

But you don't know my husband, they think. "But you don't understand submission," God must say. In this section, I want to allay some fears by discussing what submission does *not* mean.

Submission does not mean that the wife must do all the "giving." The verse that immediately precedes Ephesians 5:22 reads, "Submit to one another out of reverence for Christ." Submission is a mutual exercise. Neither husbands nor wives can have their own way and a successful marriage at the same time. That is why God instructs husbands to love their wives "as Christ loved the church" (Ephesians 5:25). The word translated "love" here indicates a self-giving love that seeks the benefit of the one loved.

For example, a husband may well submit to attending

a party that he has no personal desire to attend in order to enhance the marriage. Likewise, a wife may submit to attending a football game about which she understands little in order to share one of her husband's joys. Submission is the opposite of demanding one's own way and is required on the part of both husband and wife.

Submission does not mean that the wife cannot express her ideas. Why would God give a wife the capacity for ideas if she were not to express them? You are called to be a helper. How can you help when you refuse to share your wisdom?

"But my husband is not open to my ideas." That is his problem, not yours. Silence is never the road to unity. You may need to develop tact and exercise wisdom as to the time and manner in which you express yourself, but you must utilize the mind that God has given you. You have a responsibility. You cannot stand idly by and watch your husband fail. You must seek to be a constructive helper.

Finally, submission does not mean that the wife makes no decisions. We have talked mainly about major decisions in the home, and we have said that the basic pattern is mutual expression of ideas with a view to unity under the leadership of the husband. In the average home, however, there will be entire areas in which the couple agrees that the wife will make the decisions.

It would be poor stewardship of time if both partners gave attention to every detail of life. The sign of wisdom is to agree upon areas of responsibility in which the wife will make decisions at her own discretion. (Of course, she should feel free to ask her husband's advice as she desires.) The areas of her responsibility will vary from family to family but may involve food, clothing, home decorating, automobiles, education, and so on.

Proverbs 31:10–31, the description of a godly woman, contains a tremendous range of decision making that was committed to the wife. She certainly could not have felt that her abilities were not being utilized. I suggest that the wise and mature couple will give the wife all the responsibility she is capable of handling and willing to handle. A husband who is secure in his own self-esteem will not view his wife's efforts as competition. A wife who recognizes her own God-given self-worth will not have to prove her worth to anyone. A husband and a wife who work as a team, each encouraging the other to reach his/her maximum potential for God, will both find the rewards satisfying.

The couple may also agree that, if and when disagreement arises in a particular area, the wife will make the final decision. This would seem wise when the wife has expertise in a given sphere. This, however, is a far cry from the current emphasis on a wife's declaring her own individuality by defying her husband. How can we have a team when a self-exalting attitude exists? Marriage has to do with unity, and decision making ought to reflect that unity.

SUMMARY

In summary, I am suggesting that if a couple will agree on a pattern for decision making, they can avoid many battles. The biblical pattern I am suggesting is that of mutual and complete expression of ideas and feelings relating to the questions at hand, seeking to come to a unanimous decision—one that both agree is the best decision.

When such a consensus cannot be reached, wait and look for further guidance. Discuss the subject again later and seek unity. If indeed you have not reached such unity, and the decision *must* be made right away, then the husband should make the decision that he feels is best and bear the responsibility for that decision. The wife should admit her disagreement but express willingness to work with her husband and accept his leadership. Such an attitude will eventually bring a unity of heart that is far more important than any particular issue.

GROWTH ASSIGNMENTS

For the Married:

1. In one paragraph answer the following question: How are decisions made in our home? (Describe the process as clearly as possible.)

2. If you decided to follow the decision-making pattern discussed in this chapter, what changes would have to be made? Make a list of these changes.

3. Ask your partner to read the chapter and answer the two questions above.

4. When both of you have completed these assignments, agree upon a time to discuss decision making with a view to growth. The following questions may serve as a guide to your discussion:
   a. Do we agree that unity between husband and wife is our goal in decision making?
   b. What has been our most common problem in reaching unity of decisions?
   c. What do we need to change in order to overcome this problem?
   d. Have we agreed on who is to make the decision on those rare occasions when the decision must be made "today" and we still do not have unity?
   e. Are we asking God for help as we seek to grow in unity?

5. Read Philippians 2:2–4. What guidelines does this passage suggest for decision making in the home?

For the Unmarried:

1. Do you and your prospective mate agree upon the decision-making pattern discussed in this chapter?

2. What degree of unity do you experience in making decisions?

3. What have you done when you could not agree on a given decision?

4. After discussing the chapter with your dating partner, agree to try for one month the decision-making pattern discussed in the chapter. Perhaps you will encounter one of those "must decide today" situations, which will give the man some practice in shouldering responsibility and the woman the experience of helping in the success of a decision with which she does not fully agree.

9

"All He Thinks About Is Sex"

The dreams and hopes of a bride and groom are many, but perhaps none are brighter than the dream of sexual oneness in marriage. Many enter marriage with the vision of one great sex orgy—morning, noon, and night. Obviously, for thousands in our country those dreams are shattered and hopes never realized. Why is it that cultured, educated partners cannot find satisfaction in this very important area of marriage? Part of the answer lies in unrealistic expectations.

Our society has been unfair to us. Films, magazines, and novels have conveyed the idea that sexual thrill and mutual satisfaction are automatic when two bodies come together. We are told that all that is required for sexual fulfillment is two consenting parties. That is simply not true. Sex is far more intricate and wonderful than that. When we enter marriage with the misconception that fulfillment in this area will "come naturally," we are headed for disappointment.

Sexual oneness, by which I mean the mutual satisfaction of partners, both enjoying their sexuality and a wholesome sense of sexual fulfillment, does not come automatically. It requires the same degree of commitment and effort as does intellectual oneness or social oneness, which we discussed earlier.

Someone will say, "You mean we have to work at sex? I thought that came naturally!" I would reply, "It is that very misconception that will be your greatest barrier to sexual oneness." I am not saying that the sexual aspect of marriage is drudgery, something that requires hard, unrewarding labor. What I am saying is that the time and work invested in this area will pay you back many times over.

Those couples who grow toward maturity in this area will be the recipients of a smile from the Creator, who said, "And they will become one flesh" (Genesis 2:24). Those who do not obtain sexual oneness will never know the joy of total marriage. Anything less than a deep sense of fulfillment on the part of both partners is something less than what is available. What, then, are the guidelines that will lead us to such oneness?

A WHOLESOME ATTITUDE

One of the barriers to sexual oneness is a negative attitude toward sex in general and intercourse in particular. Such attitudes may have their origin in a poor parental example, a distorted sex education, an unfortunate sexual experience as a child, or sexual involvements as a teenager that brought disappointment and guilt. The origin is relatively unimportant. The important thing is to understand that we are masters of our attitudes. We do not need to be slaves to our negative feelings forever.

The first step in overcoming such negative attitudes is an exposure to the truth. Jesus said, "If you hold to my teaching . . . you will know the truth, and the truth will set you free" (John 8:31–32). What is the truth about sex?

The truth is that sex is God's idea. As we discussed earlier, it was God who made us male and female. Humanity has exploited sex, but humanity did not originate sex. A holy God, totally separate from sin, made us sexual beings. Therefore, sex is wholesome and good.

Our maleness and femaleness is a righteous idea. There is nothing dirty about our sexual organs. They are exactly as God intended them to be. He is a perfect Creator, and all that He has made is good. We must not relinquish the sanctity of sex because people have exploited and cheapened it by misuse. Sex is not the trademark of the world; it bears the personal label "Made by God."

Sometimes even the church has been guilty of distorting this truth. In our eagerness to condemn the misuse of sex, we have conveyed the idea that sex itself is evil. Such is not the case. Paul wrote, "The body is . . . for the Lord . . . [the] body is a temple of the Holy Spirit" (1 Corinthians 6:13, 19). All of our body is wholesome. All of our body is good and clean.

The second step in overcoming a negative attitude toward sex is to respond to the truth. If, indeed, sex is a gift of God, and sexual intercourse between husband and wife is God's desire for us, then I must not allow my distorted emotions to keep me from God's will. I must admit my feelings to God and to my mate and then thank God that I do not have to follow those feelings. Such a prayer might even be prayed audibly during the sex act itself. As I do God's will in fellowship with Him, my emotions and attitudes will change. If I foster these negative emotions by refusing to become involved in an expression of love through intercourse with my mate, I am failing to exercise my freedom to live above my emotions. Positive actions must precede positive emotions.

AN OPENNESS TO COMMUNICATE

If there is one word that is more important in gaining sexual oneness than any other, it is the word *communication*. Why are we so ready to discuss everything else and so reticent to communicate openly about this area of our lives? Your wife can never know your feelings, needs, and desires if you do not express them. Your husband will never know what pleases you if you do not communicate. I have never heard of a couple who gained sexual oneness without open communication about sexual matters.

A wife once stated in my office that she had been married for three years and had never had a sexual orgasm. She had never communicated this to her husband, however. She did not want to hurt him. Perhaps there was something wrong with her, she reasoned. She had inquired of her doctor and was assured that there was no physical problem. When she finally told all this to her husband, the problem was soon solved. A husband cannot work on a problem about which he is unaware. A husband, however, ought to be asking questions to determine the satisfaction of his wife.

In an attempt to foster communication in my family life seminars, I have periodically asked wives and husbands to write out the advice they would like to give their mates regarding the sex act. That is, "What suggestions would you make to your mate that you feel would make the sexual act more meaningful?" A collection of these suggestions is to be found at the end of this chapter. It is hoped that they will encourage you and your partner to renew communication in this area.

UNDERSTANDING THE PURPOSE OF SEX

Some couples have difficulty in growth because they do not understand the purpose of sex as revealed in Scripture. The most obvious purpose, but certainly not the only purpose, is that of procreation. Having created man, male and female, "God blessed them and said to them, "Be fruitful and increase in number; fill the earth" (Genesis 1:28). Sexual intercourse for the purpose of procreation is God's way of letting us share in the thrill of creation. There are few human thrills to equal that of looking into the face of a baby, the offspring of your love for your mate.

Children are always viewed in Scripture as the gift of God. "Lo, children are an heritage of the Lord: and the fruit of the womb is his reward" (Psalm 127:3 KJV). What, then, of contraception? Some would argue that the original command of God to "fill the earth" has now been accomplished. Therefore, we must stop "filling" the earth, lest we overflow the earth. When one looks realistically at the world's hunger problem, his sympathy for such a view rises.

There is, however, a higher principle involved. We are created responsible creatures. Throughout Scripture, parents are viewed as responsible for caring for the needs of children whom they "create." As a responsible parent, I must use reason in deciding how many children I can care for realistically. As God has given us medical help through the effort of dedicated men, so He has given us means of limiting births. It is interesting that such knowledge has come in the generations of greatest need as far as overpopulation is concerned. As Christians, we are to use all God's gifts in a responsible manner. Therefore, I believe that a couple should discuss and decide together when they will use birth control and what method of birth control they will use as responsible persons. This matter should be discussed with the doctor when the couple goes for premarital examinations.

The second purpose of sexual intercourse within marriage revealed in the Bible is to meet physical-emotional needs. Paul speaks to this point when he says:

> The husband should fulfill his marital duty to his wife, and likewise the wife to her husband. The wife's body does not belong to her alone but also to her husband. In the same way, the husband's body does not belong to him alone but also to his wife. Do not deprive each other except by mutual consent and for a time, so that you may devote yourselves to prayer. Then come together again so that Satan will not tempt you because of your lack of self-control. (1 Corinthians 7:3–5)

Paul is dealing with the reality of the strong physical-emotional need that the husband and wife have for each other. We are sexual beings, and we do have this strong desire for each other sexually. Indeed, as we discussed earlier, our greatest problem before marriage is controlling this strong sexual desire. But within marriage, that desire is to find full satisfaction in sexual intercourse.

Our sexual desires are normal and God-given. With the desire, God also gave us the pattern for fulfillment. That pattern is regular sexual expression within marriage. There are other wholesome ways to meet this need before marriage, as discussed in Rick Stedman's book *Pure Joy: The Positive Side of Single Sexuality* (see Appendix). Those who do not get married, for whatever reason, would follow those same patterns.

But the norm for the human race, as expressed in Scripture, is that these needs would be met by sexual intercourse in the context of marriage. When we refuse each other this privilege, we frustrate the expressed pattern that God has revealed. If, indeed, husbands and wives would take this responsibility seriously, the rate of extramarital affairs would be drastically lowered.

An honest wife will say, "But I don't feel like having intercourse as often as my husband desires." This is the point at which, as Charlie Shedd says, a wife has a chance to be a "missionary" to her husband. Openly and honestly express your feelings to your mate, but also let him know that you stand ready to meet his needs. You need not go through all the foreplay and energy-consuming activity if you are fatigued. Simply let him know that you love him and want to meet his needs. This can normally be done very shortly with a minimum of energy. The wife should not be forced to have an orgasm if she does not desire such. If needs are met, then one of the purposes of sex is accomplished.

A third purpose of sex revealed in Scripture is to provide pleasure. Those who feel that God wished to make life as miserable as possible for His subjects may have difficulty with this one. But Scripture makes clear that God's plans for us are always good: "'I know the plans I have for you,' declares the Lord, 'plans to prosper you and not to harm you, plans to give you hope and a future'" (Jeremiah 29:11). God did not have to make the sexual act pleasurable, but He did. It is one of those above-and-beyond acts for which God is noted.

The eighteenth chapter of Genesis records a very interesting event in the life of Abraham and Sarah. The messenger of God had come to proclaim that they were to have a son. A wonderful idea, but Abraham was one hundred years old, and Sarah was ninety! Abraham posed a reasonable question to this heavenly messenger, and the Scriptures say that in response "Sarah laughed to herself as she thought, 'After I am worn out and my master is old, will I now have this pleasure' ?" (Genesis 18:12). The word translated "pleasure" is not the normal Hebrew word for pleasure and is used only here in the Old Testament. Sarah is reflecting upon the pleasurable experience of the sex act. She is old. The body chemistry is not what it used to be, but she is not too old to remember that it was a pleasurable experience.

The Song of Solomon is replete with illustrations of the pleasurableness of the sexual aspect of marriage (6:1–9; 7:1–10). The descriptive phrases may be foreign to our culture, but the intent is clear. Maleness and femaleness are meant to be enjoyed by marriage partners.

Another interesting passage is found in Deuteronomy 24:5, where we are told, "If a man has recently married, he must not be sent to war or have any other duty laid on him. For one year he is to be free to stay at home and bring happiness to the wife he has married." The word translated "happiness" is elsewhere translated "pleasure" and is the same word that is used for sexual gratification. He is to stay home and "pleasure" his wife for one year. Talk about a honeymoon!

This is a good place to digress for a moment and say a word about the honeymoon. We try to crowd it into three days or a week at most. It is supposed to be heaven on earth, but for many it is a very disappointing time. If God suggested a year for pleasure, what makes us think we can have sexual paradise in three days? Let me reiterate that sexual oneness takes time.

The typical American honeymoon is a very pressured time. For weeks you have expended your energy in preparation for the wedding. The bachelor parties and showers are now over. The last handful of rice has beaten upon your heads, and now you are alone. Physical and emotional exhaustion are not the companions of a meaningful sexual experience. Sexual adjustment is begun with two strikes against you.

Do not expect too much from your honeymoon. At best, it is the mere beginning of what is to come. Your sexual enjoyment on the honeymoon will be minimal compared to that of a year later if you commit yourselves to growth in oneness.

Very closely related to the idea of pleasure is the concept of love. One of the desires of love is to give pleasure to the one loved. Therefore, sexual intercourse within marriage becomes a very meaningful method of expressing love. It is one of love's loudest voices. This means that each mate must think of the other's pleasure (Philippians 2:3–4). The husband is to "pleasure" his wife, and the wife is to "pleasure" her husband. It is in mutual self-giving that love finds its highest expression.

ATTAINING ONENESS

Attaining these biblical purposes will take time, but a mutual commitment to these purposes will channel your efforts toward oneness. An understanding of the physical-emotional differences between the sexes also aids in growth.

It should be noted, for example, that for the male the sex drive is more physically based than for the female. That is, the male gonads are continually producing sperm cells. These cells along with seminal fluid are stored in the seminal vesicles. When the seminal vesicles are full, there is a physical demand for release. There is nothing comparable to this in the female.

For the female, the sexual need is more emotional than physical. The implications of this difference are readily observed. For example, the husband would experience little difficulty in having sexual intercourse one hour after a "knock-down-drag-out" argument with his wife. The wife, on the other hand, would find this almost impossible. Her emotions are too involved. She cannot have meaningful sexual fulfillment when things are not right in other areas of the relationship.

The suggestions on the following pages will show that for the wife good sex relations begin in the morning and are enhanced with all those little positive expressions of thoughtfulness on the part of the husband throughout the day. Kindness and thoughtfulness on the part of the husband pave the way for meaningful sexual experiences.

We need to understand the differences in the physical-emotional responses of males and females in the act of sexual intercourse itself. The husband tends to come to an emotional-physical climax rather rapidly, and after the climax his emotions drop rapidly, whereas the wife is much more gradual in her emotional changes, both before and after climax. This difference has many implications for the husband and wife who wish to experience physical oneness. The suggestions given on the following pages indicate some of these implications.

It is beyond the purpose of this volume to deal with all the details of sexual adjustment. Excellent materials are available (see Appendix), and I highly recommend the following for additional resource information: *Sexual Happiness in Marriage,* by Dr. Herbert Miles, and *The Act of Marriage,* by Tim and Beverly LaHaye. Both books are written from a thoroughly biblical perspective and yet are realistic in dealing with practical problems of sexual adjustment.

I also recommend *Intended for Pleasure,* by Ed and Gaye Wheat. Dr. Wheat, an outstanding Christian physician, and his wife wrote this book for couples who want to experience God's best in physical oneness. All these resources are excellent and give practical help in sexual adjustment. They should be in the lending library of every Christian couple.

GROWTH ASSIGNMENTS

For the Married:

1. How would you rate the sexual aspect of your marriage?

   _____excellent _____good _____fair ____poor

2. In a short paragraph, write your attitude toward the sexual aspect of marriage.

3. If you are a wife, read "Suggestions Wives Have Made to Husbands: How to Make Sexual Relations More Meaningful." Check those items you would like to mention to your husband.

4. If you are a husband, read "Suggestions Husbands Have Made to Wives: How to Make Sexual Relations More Meaningful." Check those items you would like to mention to your wife.

5. When both of you are feeling good and are open to growth, discuss with each other the items you have checked. Concentrate on what your partner is saying, rather than on trying to defend yourself. The purpose of conversation is growth, not defense.

6. At another time, write down for yourself what you can and will do to grow in physical oneness with your mate. A month from now check your list to see what improvements you have made. Set new goals each month.

For the Unmarried:

1. What is your attitude toward your own maleness? femaleness?
   _____good ____bad _____indifferent

2. If you are engaged or moving in that direction, discuss

with your partner the biblical purposes of sex as noted in this chapter. Do you agree with these purposes?

3. What are your attitudes toward having children? Toward birth control? Does your partner agree?

4. Read Rick Stedman's book *Pure Joy: The Positive Side of Single Sexuality* and discuss the contents with your prospective marriage partner.

SUGGESTIONS HUSBANDS
HAVE MADE TO WIVES
How to Make Sexual Relations More Meaningful

1. Be attractive at bedtime—no hair rollers. Wear something besides granny gowns and pajamas.
2. Be aggressive occasionally.
3. Be innovative and imaginative.
4. Do not be ashamed to show that you are enjoying it.
5. Do not always be on a time schedule that results in our having sex when we are both physically tired.
6. Dress more appealingly when I am at home (no housecoats, slippers, and so on).
7. Do things to catch my attention; men are easily excited by sight.
8. Communicate more openly about sex; communicate readiness for the actual act once foreplay has excited sufficiently.
9. Go to bed earlier.
10. Do not make me feel guilty at night for my inconsistencies during the day (not being affectionate enough, and so on).
11. Prolong the sexual relationship at times.
12. Be more aware of my needs and desires as a man.
13. Participate more fully and freely in the sexual act; be more submissive and open.
14. Allow variety in the time for the sexual act (not always at night).

15. Show more desire, and understand that caressing and foreplay are as important to me as they are to you.
16. More varied positions; keep an open mind to variety.
17. Do not allow yourself to remain upset over everyday events that go wrong.
18. Relax together at least once a week.
19. Stop trying to look romantic rather than being romantic.
20. Do not always play "hard to get."
21. Clear your mind of daily things (today's and tomorrow's) and think about the matter at hand—love.
22. Do not say no too often.
23. Do not try to fake enjoyment.
24. Do not try to punish me by denying me sex or by giving it grudgingly.
25. Treat me like your lover.
26. Listen to my suggestions on what you can do to improve our sexual relationship.

SUGGESTIONS WIVES HAVE MADE TO HUSBANDS

How to Make Sexual Relations More Meaningful

1. Show more affection and attention throughout the day; come in after work and kiss my neck.
2. Spend more time in foreplay; love, play, and romantic remarks are important.
3. Encourage the sex act at various times, rather than always at night when we're tired.
4. Be more sympathetic when I am really sick.
5. Be the aggressive one instead of waiting for me to make the first move.
6. Accept me as I am; accept me even when you see the worst side of me.
7. Tell me that you love me at times other than when we are in bed; phone sometimes just to say "I love you!" Do not be ashamed to say "I love you" in front of others.

8. While I am showering, find soft music on the radio.
9. Treat me as your wife, not as one of the children.
10. Honor Christ as the Head of the home.
11. Write love notes occasionally; send homemade love cards.
12. Talk to me after intercourse; make caresses after intercourse.
13. Be sweet and loving at least one hour before initiating sex.
14. Show an interest in what I have to say in the morning.
15. Do not seem as though you are bored with me in the evening.
16. Help me wash the dinner dishes.
17. Go to bed at a decent hour, rather than watching television.
18. Say sweet little nothings and be silly.
19. Bring me a flower or candy occasionally, when you can afford to.
20. Occasionally buy me lingerie, perfume, and so forth.
21. Pay romantic attention to me (hold hands, kiss) even during relatively unromantic activities (television watching, car riding, and so on).
22. Help me feel that I am sexually and romantically attractive by complimenting me more often.
23. Tell me what you enjoy and when you are excited; express your desires more openly; share yourself more fully with me.
24. Try not to ejaculate so soon.
25. Express appreciation for the little things I have done that day. (For example, say the meal was good, appreciate the tidy house.)
26. Pray with me about the problems and victories you are having; let me express my own needs to you.
27. Appreciate the beauty of nature and share this appreciation with me.
28. Take more of the responsibility for getting the children settled so that I can relax and share more of the evening with you.

29. Be patient with me; do not ridicule my slowness to reach climax.
30. Do not approach lovemaking as a ritualistic activity; make each time a new experience. Do not let lovemaking get boring by doing the same things over and over; try new things or new places.
31. Never try to make love with me when you are harboring bad feelings toward me or you know things are not right; let there be harmony between us so that sexual intercourse can indeed be an act of love.
32. Make me feel that I have worth as a person (not just as a wife and mother), warts and all!
33. Think of something nice to say about me in front of others occasionally.
34. Demonstrate *agape* love as well as *eros*.
35. Spend some quiet times with me, sharing life.

10

"If You Only Knew, My Mother-in-Law"

*I*n our society, mother-in-law jokes have become so rampant that many people feel ashamed to admit they have a good relationship with their mother-in-law. The truth is that a godly mother-in-law is a treasure second only to a godly husband or wife. On the other hand, a self-centered mother-in-law can be a constant "thorn in the flesh."

What guidelines does the Bible give for in-law relationships? How should the married couple respond to parents' ideas, suggestions, and needs? What can we do when we see parents destroying our marital unity? Two principles must be kept in balance if we are to follow the biblical patterns in our relationships with in-laws: new allegiance and continued honor.

"LEAVING" PARENTS

In Genesis 2:24 we read, "For this reason a man will leave his father and mother and be united to his wife, and they will become one flesh." This principle is repeated in Ephesians 5:31. God's pattern for marriage involves the "leaving" of parents and the "cleaving" to one's mate. Marriage involves a change of allegiance. Before marriage, one's allegiance is to one's parents, but after marriage allegiance shifts to one's mate.

It is what the psychologists call "cutting the psychological apron strings." No longer does the individual lean on his parents, but rather on his mate. If there is a conflict of interest between a man's wife and his mother, the husband is to stand with his wife. This does not mean that the mother is to be treated unkindly. That is the second principle, which we will deal with shortly. The principle of separating from parents is, however, extremely important. No couple will reach their full potential in marriage without this psychological break from parents.

What does this principle mean in the practical realm? I believe that it suggests separate living arrangements for the newly married couple. While living with parents, the couple cannot develop independence as readily as when living alone. The dependency on parents is enhanced as long as they live with parents. Living in a meager apartment with the freedom to develop their own lifestyle under God is better than luxurious living in the shadow of parents. Parents should encourage such independence, and the ability to provide such living accommodations should be a factor in setting the wedding date.

The principle of "leaving" parents is also important in decision making. Your parents may have suggestions about many aspects of your married life. Each suggestion should be taken seriously, but, in the final analysis, you must make your own decision. You should no longer make decisions on the basis of what would make parents happy but on the basis of what would make your partner happy. Under God, you are a new unit, brought together by His Spirit to live for each other (Philippians 2:3–4).

This means that the time may come when a husband must sit down with his mother and say, "Mom, you know that I love you very much, but you also know that I am now married. I cannot break up my marriage in order to do what you desire. I love you, and I want to help you, but I must do what I believe is right for my wife and me. I hope you understand because I want to continue the warm relationship that we have had through the years. But if you do not understand, then that is a problem you must work through. I must give myself to the building of my marriage."

If such a statement sounds harsh to you, be thankful. It is because you have not encountered a stubborn, selfish, carnal mother-in-law. Such do exist, and firmness with love is the biblical answer to correcting the situation. A husband must not allow his mother to continue to control his life after marriage. Such is not the biblical pattern.

On the other hand, parents' suggestions should be given due consideration. They are older and perhaps wiser. A good example of the wisdom of a father-in-law is found in Exodus 18. Moses was working from morning till evening judging the people of Israel. The waiting room was always filled, and there was no time for coffee breaks. "Moses' father-in-law replied, 'What you are doing is not good. You and these people who come to you will only wear yourselves out. The work is too heavy for you; you cannot handle it alone. Listen now to me and I will give you some advice'" (vv. 17–19).

He went on to suggest that the crowds be divided into thousands, hundreds, fifties, and tens, and that authority be delegated to other qualified men who would judge those under their jurisdiction. Moses then would be free to spend more time with God and in teaching the people the law of God (vv. 19–20). Thus, his would be more of a "preventive" ministry rather than a "crisis" ministry. Only the difficult cases would be brought to him for judgment (v. 22).

Moses saw the wisdom of such a suggestion and adopted it. In so doing, he revealed his own maturity. He did not have to rebel against a good idea just because it came from his father-in-law. He was secure enough in his own self-worth that he could accept a good idea, regardless of its source.

The principle of separation from parents also has

implications when conflict arises in marriage. A young wife who has always leaned heavily on her mother will have a tendency to "run to mother" when problems arise in the marriage. The next day her husband recognizes that he was his wrong, asks forgiveness, and harmony is restored. The daughter fails to tell her mother this. The next time a conflict arises she again confides in Mom. This becomes a pattern, and before long, her mother has a bitter attitude toward the son-in-law and is encouraging the daughter to separate from him. The daughter has been very unfair to her husband and has failed to follow the principle of "leaving" parents.

If you have conflicts in your marriage (and most of us do), seek to solve them by direct confrontation with your mate. Conflict should be a stepping-stone to growth. If you find that you need outside help, then go to your pastor or a Christian marriage counselor. They are trained and equipped by God to give practical help. They can be objective and give biblical guidelines. Parents find it almost impossible to be objective.

HONORING PARENTS

The second principle relating to our relationship with parents is found in Exodus 20:12 and is one of the Ten Commandments: "Honor your father and your mother, so that you may live long in the land the Lord your God is giving you." It is repeated in Deuteronomy 5:16 and Ephesians 6:2.

The command to honor our parents has never been rescinded. As long as they live, it is right to honor them. In Ephesians 6:1, Paul says, "Children, obey your parents in the Lord, for this is right." Obedience to parents is the guideline from birth to marriage. Paul's second statement is, "Honor your father and mother—which is the first commandment with a promise—that it may go well with you and that you may enjoy long life on the earth" (vv. 2–3). Honor to parents is the guideline from birth to death. Honor was the original command and stands forever.

The word *honor* means "to show respect." It involves treating one with kindness and dignity. It is true that not all parents live respectable lives. Their actions may not be worthy of honor, but because they are made in the image of God, they are worthy of honor. You can respect them for their humanity and for their position as your parents, even when you cannot respect their actions. It is always right to honor your parents and those of your marriage partner. "Leaving" parents for the purpose of marriage does not erase the responsibility to honor them.

How is this honor expressed in daily life? You honor them in such practical actions as visiting, telephoning, and writing, whereby you communicate to them that you still love them and want to share life with them. "Leaving" must never be interpreted as "deserting." Regular contact is essential to honoring parents. Failure to communicate with parents is saying, in effect, "I no longer care."

A further word is necessary regarding communication with parents. Equal treatment of both sets of parents must be maintained. Remember, "For God does not show favoritism" (Romans 2:11). We must follow His example. In practice, this means that our letters, telephone calls, and visits must indicate our commitment to the principle of equality. If one set of parents is phoned once a month, then the other set should be phoned once a month. If one receives a letter once a week, then the other should receive the same. The couple should also seek to be equitable in visits, dinners, and vacations.

Perhaps the most sticky situations arise around holidays—Thanksgiving and Christmas. The wife's mother wants them home for Christmas Eve. The husband's mother wants them home for Christmas dinner. That may be possible if they live in the same town, but when they are five hundred miles apart, it becomes impossible. The solution must be based on the principle of equality. This may mean Christmas with one set of parents one year and with the other the following year.

To "honor" implies also that we speak kindly with parents and in-laws. Paul admonishes: "Do not rebuke an older man harshly, but exhort him as if he were your father" (1 Timothy 5:1). We are to be understanding and sympathetic. Certainly we are to speak the truth, but it must always be in love (Ephesians 4:15). The command of Ephesians 4:31–32 must be taken seriously in our relationship with parents: "Get rid of all bitterness, rage and anger, brawling and slander, along with every form of malice. Be kind and compassionate to one another, forgiving each other, just as in Christ God forgave you." A further implication of honor to parents is described in 1 Timothy 5:4: "But if a widow has children or grandchildren, these should learn first of all to put their religion into practice by caring for their own family and so repaying their parents and grandparents, for this is pleasing to God." When we were young, our parents met our physical needs. As they grow older, we may have to do the same for them. If and when the need arises, we must bear the responsibility of caring for the physical needs of our parents. To fail in this responsibility is to deny our faith in Christ (1 Timothy 5:8). By our actions, we must show our faith in Christ and honor for our parents.

If I could make some other practical suggestions, I would advise you to accept your in-laws as they are. Do not feel that it is your task to change them. If they are not Christians, certainly you will want to pray for them and look for opportunities to present Christ, but do not try to fit them into your mold. You are expecting them to give you independence to develop your own marriage. Give them the same.

Do not criticize your in-laws to your mate. The responsibility of your mate is to honor his parents. When you criticize them, you make it more difficult for him to follow this pattern. When your mate criticizes the weaknesses of his parents, point out their strengths. Accentuate their positive qualities and encourage honor.

The Bible gives some beautiful examples of wholesome relationships between individuals and their in-laws. Moses had such a wholesome relationship with Jethro, his father-in-law, that, when he informed him of God's call to leave Midian and lead the Israelites out of Egypt, Jethro said, "Go, and I wish you well" (Exodus 4:18). Later on, after the success of Moses' venture, his father-in-law came to see him.

"So Moses went out to meet his father-in-law and bowed down and kissed him. They greeted each other and then went into the tent" (Exodus 18:7). It was on this visit that Jethro gave Moses the advice that we discussed earlier. His openness to his father-in-law's suggestion shows something of the nature of their relationship.

Ruth and Naomi serve as an example of the devotion of a daughter-in-law to her mother-in-law after the death of both husbands. Jesus directed one of His miracles to the mother-in-law of Peter, and she in turn ministered to Jesus (Matthew 8:14–15).

Freedom and harmony are the biblical ideals for in-law relationships. The train of God's will for marriage must run on the parallel tracks of separation from parents and devotion to parents.

WHAT IF YOU ARE AN IN-LAW?

From the parents' vantage point, it will help to remember our objective. From the moment of their birth until their marriage, we have been training our children for independence, or at least we should have done so. We want them to be able to stand on their own feet and operate as mature persons under God. We have taught them how to cook meals, wash dishes, make beds, buy clothes, save money, and make responsible decisions. We have taught them respect for authority and the value of the individual. In short, we have sought to bring them to maturity.

At the time of their marriage, our training ends, and their independence reaches fruition. It is hoped that we have helped them move from a state of complete dependence on us, when infants, to complete independence as newlyweds. From this point, we must view them as adults who will chart their own course for better or for worse. We must never again impose our will upon them. We must respect them as equals.

This does not mean that we will no longer help them, but it means that all help must be given in a responsible manner that will enhance independence rather than dependence. That is, if we give financial help it should be with a view toward helping them attain their freedom from our support rather than making them dependent on it. We should not help them establish a lifestyle that they cannot afford to maintain.

The cardinal sin of parents is to use financial assistance to coerce the young couple into conforming to the parents' wishes: "We will buy you a bedroom suite if you move into the house next door." Gifts are fine if they are given out of love without strings attached, but gifts that are conditional become tools rather than gifts. Parents must diligently guard against such temptation.

Certainly, parents should feel freedom to give advice to the young couple (though it is always best to wait until advice is requested). Even so, parents should not seek to force their advice on a couple. Give suggestions if they are requested or if you feel you must, but then withdraw and allow the couple freedom to make their own decision. Most important, do not express resentment if they do not happen to follow your suggestion. Give them the advantage of your wisdom but the freedom to make their own mistakes.

A newly married couple needs the emotional warmth that comes from a wholesome relationship with both sets of parents, and parents need the emotional warmth that comes from the couple. Life is too short to live with broken relationships. The principle of confession and forgiveness discussed in chapter 4 applies to in-laws as well as to marriage partners. We do not have to agree with each other in order to have a wholesome relationship, but bitterness and resentment are always wrong (Ephesians 4:31). Mutual freedom and mutual respect should be the guiding principle for parents and their married children.

GROWTH ASSIGNMENTS

For the Married:

1. Do you have any problems with your parents or those of your spouse? If so, write these problems down in specific terms.

2. What principles discussed in this chapter have your parents or in-laws violated? Write these down. Be specific. (Read that section again if necessary.)

3. Which principles discussed in this chapter have you or your spouse violated with respect to your parents or in-laws? Write these down in specific terms.

4. What do you think should be done to correct the situation? Be specific.

5. Before discussing your analysis with your spouse, ask him/her to read the section on in-laws in this chapter and complete assignments 1–4 above.

6. At an appointed time, have a conference to discuss the problem. Read your statements of the problem to each other and see:
   a. if you agree on the problem
   b. if you agree on your own failures
   c. if you agree on what action should be taken to correct the situation.
   If not, continue discussion, now or at another time, until you can agree on constructive action.

7. Having agreed on appropriate action, put your plan into motion. Pray for each other and for your parents and in-laws. (If your plan involves a confrontation with parents, it is usually best for the son or daughter to speak to his/her own parents rather than to in-laws.)

8. Be sure that you consider how your own behavior ought to change toward your in-laws and parents. Does your conversation and your behavior indicate that you "honor" them? Be honest. (Respect tends to beget respect.)

9. Do all that you do in kindness and firmness. Remember, your desire is to enhance the relationship, not to destroy it.

For the Unmarried:

1. If you are engaged or contemplating marriage, list the strengths and weaknesses of your prospective in-laws from what you have observed.

2. Make a similar list regarding your own parents.

3. Ask your fiancée/fiancé to do the same.

4. In a relaxed setting, discuss your lists with a view to increasing your understanding of your respective parents and prospective in-laws.

5. If you were get married, what potential problems do you see with regard to your parents or in-laws? Be honest and specific.

6. Are the potential problems of such a nature that an honest conversation with your parents before marriage would pave the way for more wholesome relationships after marriage? If so, exactly what should you say? Discuss this with your fiancé and decide upon a construc-

tive approach. (Dealing with a potential problem is often much easier than waiting until the problem erupts.)

7. As an individual before marriage, are you treating your parents with respect and honor? Make a list of the things you are doing for your parents that say "I love and appreciate you."

8. If your list is short, perhaps you have some premarital homework to do. What can you do that you are not now doing to enhance your relationship with your parents? What *will* you do?

9. Are you happy with the kind of relationship your fiancée /fiancé has with her/his parents? What would you like to see improved? Why not suggest such improvements? (The degree of openness to suggestions that you find before marriage is the degree of openness you can expect after marriage.)

10. Do everything within your power to have an open, growing relationship with both sets of parents before your marriage. This is a tremendous step toward a happy marriage.

11

"My Wife Thinks Money Grows on Trees"

Why has money become such a problem in American marriages? The poorest of couples in America have abundance compared to the masses of the world's population. I am convinced that the problem does not lie in the amount of money that a couple possesses but in their attitude toward money and the manner in which they handle it. This is in keeping with Paul's words in 1 Timothy 6:10: "For the *love* of money is a root of all kinds of evil. Some people, eager for money, have wandered from the faith and pierced themselves with many griefs" (italics added). Such sorrows are not the result of having money or not having money but of *loving* money. The root word for "love" in this verse is *phileō*, which means "to have a fondness for."

BIBLICAL PRINCIPLES

The error is in making the attaining of money an end in itself or in using it for the satisfaction of selfish desires. Such an attitude always ends in sorrow, for the truth is that "a man's life does not consist in the abundance of his possessions" (Luke 12:15). The files of counselors are filled with case studies that serve as examples of the truth of this statement.

As Jeanette Clift George has said, "The great tragedy in life is not in failing to get what you go after. The great tragedy in life is in getting it and finding out it wasn't worth the trouble!"[1]

Most couples assume that if only they made a hundred dollars more each month they could meet expenses. That is true whether they are presently making $1,500 dollars a month or $2,500. It is false reasoning. The problem is in the attitude toward money rather than in the amount available.

Real satisfaction is not found in money (any amount of it) but in "righteousness, godliness, faith, love, endurance, gentleness"—in short, living with God and according to His values (1 Timothy 6:11–12). Doing right, responding to others as God would respond, expressing love, being patient with imperfection, and having a realistic appraisal of yourself—these are the things that bring true fulfillment to a marriage.

Once I visited two contrasting homes. The first was a little three-room house. I walked into the living room to find a one-burner oil stove in the center. The baby in its bassinet was in one corner, the dog in another. The walls had only one picture, which accompanied a calendar. Two straight-backed wooden chairs and an ancient couch rested on a rough wooden floor. The doors that led to the kitchen on the left and the bedroom on the right were of the old handmade slat variety with the Z-frame and cracks between each slat.

It was a meager scene by twentieth-century-American standards, but the emotional warmth that I felt as I visited with the young couple was astounding. It was apparent that they loved each other, loved their baby, and loved God. They were happy. Life was exciting.

From there, I crossed to the other side of town and drove up a concrete drive to a beautiful, spacious, brick home. My feet sank into the carpet when I stepped inside. I saw beautiful portraits on the wall as I entered the living room. The fire in the fireplace had an inviting warmth (though the function was aesthetic), and the dog lay on the ultramodern couch.

I sat down to visit, but I had not been there long when I realized that about the only warmth in this family was in the fireplace. I sensed coldness and hostility wrapped in wealth. I drove home that night saying, "O God, if ever I must choose between those two, give me the three-room house with the emotional warmth of wife and family." Life does not consist in things, but in relationships: first with God and second with people.

"But I must have food for the children, clothes to wear, and shelter from the rain," someone persists. "These require money!" True, and these are promised by God to those who will put Him first in life: "But seek first [God's] kingdom and his righteousness, and all these things will be given to you as well" (Matthew 6:33). "These things" include food, clothing, and shelter (v. 25). Our physical provisions are the by-products of righteousness (right acts) and godliness (godly acts).

Is it right to work for wages? Indeed! "If anyone does not provide for his relatives, and especially for his immediate family, he has denied the faith and is worse than an unbeliever" (1 Timothy 5:8). Paul further states: "We gave you this rule: 'If a man will not work, he shall not eat'" (2 Thessalonians 3:10).

Working is a "righteous" act, and it is by this act that God normally provides our necessities. But work is only one "righteous act." There are many more, such as godliness, faith, love, patience, and meekness. We must not allow the pursuit of money to erode these more important areas, lest we miss life and find money useless.

Jesus warned against this danger when he said, "No one can serve two masters. Either he will hate the one and love the other, or he will be devoted to the one and despise the other. You cannot serve both God and Money" (Matthew 6:24). Money is an excellent servant, but a poor master; a useful means, but an empty end. When money becomes our god, we are bankrupt indeed.

The biblical pattern is that of stewardship. We are responsible for the wise use of all that God gives us (Matthew 25:14–30). The amount of our resources is relatively unimportant. The faithful use of our resources is all-important. The Lord said to the faithful steward, "Well done, good and faithful servant! You have been faithful with a few things; I will put you in charge of many things'" (v. 21). "From everyone who has been given much, much will be demanded" (Luke 12:48).

Financial resources have tremendous potential for good. As stewards, we are responsible to use in the very best manner all that is entrusted to us. Sound planning, buying, saving, investing, and giving are all a part of our stewardship.

Anxiety or worry over finances is condemned in Scripture. "Do not be anxious about anything" (Philippians 4:6). In Matthew 6, Jesus speaks again and again about the sin of worry.

> Therefore I tell you, do not worry about your life, what you will eat or drink; or about your body, what you will wear. Is not life more important than food, and the body more important than clothes? . . . Who of you by worrying can add a single hour to his life? . . . And why do you worry about clothes? See how the lilies of the field grow. They do not labor or spin. Yet I tell you that not even Solomon in all his splendor was dressed like one of these. . . . So do not worry, saying, 'What shall we eat?' or 'What shall we drink?' or 'What shall we wear?' . . . Therefore do not worry about tomorrow, for tomorrow will worry about itself. (vv. 25, 27–29, 31, 34)

We ought to confess worrying about finances as we would any other sin. It is right to pray, to work, to do any good thing to change our financial status, but it is never right to worry about it. Worry immobilizes us and makes us victims of our circumstances. This is never God's intention. You see, a poor man can be a slave to money just as easily as a rich man. When money or the lack of it pushes us to depression, unhappiness, resentment, and frustration, we are the servants of money. God's desire is for us to acknowledge Him as our sole master, and under His direction we are to be masters of our finances.

One aspect of faithful stewardship is giving to God through the church and other Christian organizations. The pattern for giving established in the Old Testament and commended in the New Testament is that of tithing, that is, giving one-tenth of one's income to the direct work of the Lord (Leviticus 27:30; Matthew 23:23).

The Scriptures indicate that our giving is to be done with a willing heart. Christian giving is an act of the will prompted by love to God, not a legalistic duty to be performed for merit. Paul speaks to this issue:

> Whoever sows sparingly will also reap sparingly, and whoever sows generously will also reap generously. Each man should give what he has decided in his heart to give, not reluctantly or under compulsion, for God loves a cheerful giver. And God is able to make all grace abound to you, so that in all things at all times, having all that you need, you will abound in every good work. (2 Corinthians 9:6–8)

Many like to claim God's grace and abundance, but they fail to recognize that this promise is made to the cheerful giver. The Scriptures say that one of the purposes of working for wages is that we may be able to give to those who are in need: "He who has been stealing must steal no longer, but must work, doing something useful with his own hands, that he may have something to share with those in need" (Ephesians 4:28). Any discussion of finances for the Christian must include provision for regular, proportionate, cheerful giving to the things of God.

Let me summarize and clarify the biblical principles discussed above before we look at the practical implications:

1. The Christian is never to allow money to become his master (Matthew 6:24).
2. Life does not consist of accumulating things (Luke 12:15).
3. Loving money as an end in itself is the root of all kinds of evil (1 Timothy 6:10).

4. God can be trusted to meet our needs if we place Him first in our lives (Matthew 6:33).
5. The Christian does have a responsibility to work for wages (1 Timothy 5:8; 2 Thessalonians 3:10).
6. Giving to the Lord's work is a vital part of our steward-ship (2 Corinthians 9:6–8; Ephesians 4:28).
7. As Christian stewards, we are responsible for making the best use of all the resources entrusted to us (Matthew 25:14–30)

PRACTICAL IMPLICATIONS

With these biblical principles in mind, I want to be as practical and helpful as I can. The application of the ideas I am about to present will keep you from the frustration and pain that so many have experienced regarding finances. The failure to come to grips with finances as a vital part of life will soon result in tremendous pressure being exerted upon an otherwise wonderful marriage. I hope that you will be as faithful in handling your financial resources as you are in handling your physical, intellectual, and spiritual resources. It is the responsible person who will be judged a "faithful steward."

One of the first implications of biblical principles in the area of finances is that in marriage it is no longer "my money" and "your money," but rather "our money." In the same manner, it is no longer "my debts" and "your debts," but rather "our debts." If you are about to marry a recent graduate who owes $5,000 on an educational loan and you owe $50 to the local dress shop, at the conclusion of the wed-ding ceremony you are collectively in debt $5,050. When you accept each other as a partner, you accept each other's liabili-ties as well as each other's assets.

A full disclosure of assets and liabilities should be made before marriage by both partners. It is not wrong to enter marriage with debts, but you ought to know what those debts are, and you ought to agree upon a plan and schedule of repayment. Since they are going to be "our" debts, then "we" need to discuss and agree upon a plan of action.

I have known couples who failed to discuss this area sufficiently before marriage and awakened after the wedding to realize that together they had a debt so large that already they felt a financial noose around their necks. What a tragedy to begin marriage with such a handicap. In my opinion, a large debt without a realistic means of repayment is sufficient cause to postpone the marriage. Financial irresponsibility before marriage is an indicator of financial irresponsibility after marriage. Most couples have some debts when they come to marriage, and a full disclosure by each will allow them to face marriage realistically.

Your assets, too, are now joint assets. She may have $6,000 in a savings account and he may have only $80, but when they choose marriage "they" have $6,080. If you do not feel comfortable with this "oneness," then you are not ready for marriage. Have we not established that the very motif of marriage is oneness? When it comes to finances you must move toward oneness.

There may be cases where, because of very large estates, the couple may be wise to retain individual ownership of certain properties or assets for tax purposes, but for most of us the principle of oneness implies joint savings accounts, checking accounts, property ownership, and so on. We are one, and so we want to express our oneness in finances as well as in other areas of life.

Since it is "our" money, then "we" ought to agree upon how it will be spent. The pattern for decision making discussed in chapter 8 should apply to financial decisions as well as to other decisions. Full and open discussion should precede any financial decision, and agreement should be the goal of all discussion. Remember: you are partners, not competitors. Marriage is enhanced by agreement in financial matters.

One practical principle that can prevent much tragedy is an agreement on the part of both partners that neither will make a major purchase without consulting the other. The purpose of consulting is to reach agreement regarding the purchase. The term *major purchase* should be clearly defined with a dollar value. For example, the couple might agree that neither would ever buy anything that cost more than fifty dollars without such agreement. It is true that many boats and lamps would still be in the showroom if couples followed this principle, but it is also true that many couples would be far happier. Happiness comes from relationships, not from things. Oneness between marriage partners is more important than any material purchase.

Further, a couple needs to agree upon a basic pattern for their spending. The word *budget* frightens many couples, but in reality all couples have a budget. A budget is simply a plan for handling money. Many couples do not have a written budget, and many do not have a very effective budget, but all couples have a plan.

Some couples' plan is to be certain that everything is spent on the same day it is received. On each payday they work frantically to see that it is all gone before the stores close. Others prefer to spend it before they get it; then on payday all they need to do is to write checks and put them in envelopes.

So the question is not "Should we have a budget?" but rather "How can we improve our budget?" We already have a plan, but could we have a better plan?

Budgeting need not be a burdensome bookkeeping procedure of laboriously recording every penny spent. Rather, a budget is a financial plan—simply an application of reason and willpower to the management of your income. You have the choice as to how your money will be spent. It is far better to make that decision based on reason in an open discussion with your mate, than based on emotion when you stand in front of the salesman.

It is beyond the purpose of this volume to give detailed help on budget making because such is readily available in other literature. One newly released financial workbook written by Larry Burkett especially for engaged couples is *Money Before Marriage*[2] (see Appendix). It offers help in budgeting, credit card use, buying insurance, and understanding each other's personality profile. Other helpful Burkett books include *The Family Budget Workbook*, *The Word on Finances*,

Debt-Free Living, The Financial Planning Organizer, Cash Organizer, and *The Financial Planning Workwork.*[3] Some of these are also available on audio. Other books to consider are *Money Sense,* by Judith Briles and written for women, and *The Financially Challenged,* by Wilson Humber.[4] Most couples could profit greatly from reading a few chapters from these or other books.

My objective here is to challenge you to rethink your present financial plan (budget). Could there be a better way to utilize the resources you have? As a steward, it is your responsibility to find out. Why should you continue doing things the same way year after year, when a little time and thought could generate improvement? If anyone should feel motivated to make the most of financial resources, it is the Christian. As a believer, you are under divine orders, and all that you possess has been entrusted to you by God, to whom you must give an account (Matthew 25:14–30). Improved financial planning is not only for your benefit but also for the kingdom of God (Matthew 6:33).[5]

In rethinking your financial plan, let me suggest some further implications of Scripture. First things should always be first, and for the Christian the kingdom of God should be first. The promise of Matthew 6:33 is practical. We tend to get our priorities out of line. We place food, clothing, shelter, and pleasure first, and if anything is left over we give an offering to the church. How contrary to the biblical pattern. It was the "firstfruits" that were to be given by Israel to the Lord, not the leftovers. Solomon was never more on target than when he said: "Honor the Lord with your wealth, with the firstfruits of all your crops; then your barns will be filled to overflowing, and your vats will brim over with new wine" (Proverbs 3:9–10). Ever wonder why the barn is empty? Could it be that you have concentrated on the barn instead of the kingdom of God?

The time to begin honoring God with your finances is before marriage. As individuals, you should already have the well-established habit of giving tithes and offerings. Before marriage, a couple should discuss their giving patterns and agree upon what they will follow in marriage. If you cannot agree on this practical expression of honoring God, what makes you think you can be one in other spiritual matters? One's relationship with God may best be judged by his check stubs, not his church attendance.

I would suggest that, from the very beginning of marriage, you set your budget to allocate the first 10 percent of your income for a thank offering to the Lord. After all, civil government insists that income tax be taken out even before you receive your check. Jesus was not opposed to such taxation but insisted that we should also "give to God what is God's" (Matthew 22:17–22). On occasion, you will wish to give offerings beyond the tithe, but the tithe should be considered a minimal standard of giving for those couples who take biblical principles seriously.

Another implication for biblical budget making is to plan for the future. "A prudent man foresees the difficulties ahead and prepares for them; the simpleton goes blindly on and suffers the consequences" (Proverbs 22:3 TLB). Throughout the Scriptures, the wise man is the one who plans ahead to meet the needs of his family, business, or other endeavor (Luke 14:28–30). Planning ahead financially involves savings and investments. Unexpected difficulties will arise. You can count on it. Therefore, the wise steward plans ahead by saving. To fail to save a part of one's income is poor planning.

Together, you should agree on the percentage that you would like to save, but something should be saved on a regular basis. Many Christian financial advisors suggest that 10 percent be allotted to savings and investments. You may choose more or less, but the choice is yours. If you save what is left after other matters are cared for, you will not save. Why not make yourself your "number-one creditor"? After tithing, pay yourself before you pay anyone else.

The couple who saves a percentage of their income regularly will have not only the reserve funds they need for emergencies but will also have the satisfied feeling that comes from being good stewards. Contrary to what some Christians seem to think, one is not more spiritual because he spends all that he makes. (According to some, this is supposed to exercise more faith in God to provide for emergency needs. In my opinion, it is simply a sign of poor stewardship.) Regular savings ought to be a part of your financial plan.

If you give 10 percent to the Lord's work and save 10 percent, that leaves 80 percent to be divided among mortgage payments (or rent), heat, electricity, telephone, water, insurance, furniture, food, medicines, clothes, transportation, education, recreation, newspapers, magazines, books, gifts, and so on. How this is distributed is your decision, but remember that you are a steward. You must give an account to God for 100 percent of your resources. The steward cannot afford the luxury of spending without thought. What is the best use of the 80 percent?

Quality does differ, and prices differ even for the same quality. Wise shopping does make a difference. In spite of the jokes we hear about the wife who spends five dollars on gas driving to the outlet store where she saves two dollars, the wise shopper can realize substantial savings. Such shopping takes time and energy. It is work and involves a great deal of insight, but the benefit will be revealed in extra money that may be applied to other needs or wants. My wife and I have a standard procedure when she comes home from a shopping spree. I never ask how much she spent, but how much she saved. It is more pleasant that way. Mastering he art of good shopping is worth the effort involved.

Before I leave the subject of planning your expenditures, I suggest that you include in your plans some money for each partner to use as he or she wishes without accountability for every penny. This does not have to be a large amount, but a husband needs to be able to buy a candy bar without having to ask his wife for a dollar.

One wife said, "Dr. Chapman, I'm ashamed to tell you this, but it illustrates the problem. Every time I need a pair of hose I have to go to my husband and ask, 'May I have five dollars to buy a pair of hose?' It's horrible! I feel like a child!" A financial plan that leaves either partner without money for incidentals is not a satisfactory plan.

Another extremely important matter that needs to be discussed by every couple is credit buying. If I had a red flag I would wave it here. The media scream from every corner, "Buy now, pay later." What is not stated is that if you buy now without cash you will pay much more later. Interest rates on charge accounts have a wide range. Some are 13, 15, or 16 percent, but many are 18 or 21 percent, or even higher. Couples need to read the small print. Credit is a privilege for which you must pay, and the cost is not the same on all plans.

If you must buy on credit, check several sources of credit and make the best purchase. Usually, your best buy is a personal loan from your local bank. A bank is in the lending business and, if you are in a position to afford credit, will be happy to make the loan. If the bank will not lend you the money, there is a high probability that you ought not to make the purchase.

The credit card has been for many the membership card to "The Society of the Financially Frustrated." It encourages impulse buying, and most of us have more impulses than we can afford to follow. My advice to young couples is that credit cards are best when burned. In a beautiful blue hue, the flames spell out "What we cannot afford, we will not purchase." I know that credit cards can aid in keeping records and that, if payments are made promptly, charges are minimal. Most couples, however, will spend more and stretch out payments longer if they have cards. The proliferation of credit cards by the business community is evidence of this fact.

Why do we use credit? Because we want *now* what we cannot pay for now. In the purchase of a house, that may be a wise financial move. We would have to pay rent anyway. If the house is well selected, it will appreciate in value. If we have money for the down payment and can afford the monthly payments, such a purchase is wise. On the other hand, most of our purchases do not appreciate in value. Their value begins to decrease the day we buy them. We buy them before we can afford them. We pay the purchase price plus the interest charges for credit, while the article itself continues to depreciate in value. Why? For the momentary pleasure that the item brings. I simply ask, Is this the sign of responsible stewardship?

I know that there are certain "necessities" in our society, but why should a young married couple think they must obtain in the first year of their marriage what it took their parents thirty years to accumulate? Why must you have the biggest and best now? With such a philosophy you destroy the joy of aspiration and attainment. You attain immediately. The joy is short-lived, and then you spend months in pain while you try to pay for it. Why saddle yourself with such unnecessary pressure?

The "necessities" of life are relatively few. They can be met on your present income. (If you are unemployed, then our society has help for you. The poorest in this country can have the necessities.) I am not opposed to aspiring for more and better "things," if these can be used for good, but I am suggesting that you live in the present rather than the future. Leave future joys for future accomplishments. Enjoy today what you have today.

For many years, my wife and I have played a little game that we have come to enjoy very much. It is called "Let's see how many things we can do without that everyone else thinks they must have." It all started in graduate school days out of necessity, but we got "hooked" and have continued to play it.

The game works like this. On Friday night or Saturday you go together to the department store and walk down the aisles, looking at whatever catches your eye. Read labels, talk about how fascinating each item is, and then turn to each other and say, "Isn't it great that we don't have to have that!" Then while others walk out with arms loaded, names duly signed, you walk out hand in hand, excited that you do not need "things" to be happy. I highly recommend this game to all young married couples.

Let me clarify. I am not suggesting that you never buy anything on credit. I am suggesting that such credit purchases ought to be preceded by prayer, discussion, and, if needed, advice from a trusted financial counselor. If these steps had been taken, many Christian couples who are today imprisoned in financial bondage would be walking our streets as free men and women. I do not believe that it is God's will for His children to be in bondage. Many in our day are in such bondage because of unwise credit purchases.

Another practical implication of biblical truth with regard to financial matters has to do with our creative ability. Man is instinctively a creator. The museums of art and industry located across our world bear silent but visual witness to man's creativity. We are made in the image of a God who creates, and we who bear His image have tremendous creative potential. The Christian couple who will channel this creativity toward financial needs will find significant assets. Sewing, refinishing used furniture, recycling others' discards, and so on can do wonders for the budget. Using special creative abilities may also lead you to the production of marketable items that may bring additional income.

Some time ago, I took a few college students to Chiapas, the southernmost state of Mexico, for a visit to Wycliffe Bible Translators' "Jungle Camp." Here we observed missionaries being trained in the technique of living in tropical environments. They learned how to build houses, ovens, chairs, beds, all out of materials available in the jungle. I have reflected upon that experience many times. If that same creativity could be used by the average Christian couple in America, what could be accomplished? I am not suggesting that you build your own house; I am suggesting that you use your creativity for good—your own and others'.

Now comes the question "Who will keep the books?" I do not believe that this need always be the task of the husband. I see no biblical support for such a conclusion. I do believe, however, that the couple should decide definitely who will write the checks, balance the check register, and see that the funds are spent according to the plan upon which you have agreed. It may be the husband or the wife. Since you are a team, why not use the one best qualified for the task? As a couple discusses financial details, it will usually be obvious which one is more adept at such matters.

This does not mean that the one chosen to keep the

books is in charge of making financial decisions. Such decisions are to be made as a team. The bookkeeper may not necessarily remain bookkeeper forever. For one reason or another you may agree after the first six months that it would be far wiser if the other partner became the bookkeeper. It is your marriage, and you are responsible for making the most of your resources.

Be certain, however, that the one who is not keeping the books knows how to do so and has full knowledge regarding various checking and savings accounts. This is wise stewardship in view of the fact that one of you will likely die before the other. Christian stewardship demands that you be realistic.

If you remember that you are a team and therefore work as a team—following the biblical guidelines discussed in this chapter, seeking practical help where needed, and agreeing upon financial decisions—you will find money to be your faithful servant. If, however, you disregard the biblical principles and "do what comes naturally," you will soon find yourself in the same financial crisis that has become a way of life to thousands of Christian couples. If you are presently feeling the pain of crisis, it is time for a radical change—*today*. There is a way out. If you cannot think clearly enough to solve the problem, then by all means seek the counsel of your local banker or a Christian friend who is adept in financial matters. Do not continue to allow finances to cripple your walk with God.

GROWTH ASSIGNMENTS

For the Married:

1. Evaluate your financial status. For one month keep detailed records of how you spend your money.

2. At the end of each month, list categories and amounts spent for each item. Add to this list the monthly portion of any semiannual or annual payments that you may have, such as auto insurance. This will give you a realis-

tic picture of your expenditures compared with your income (allow for incidentals).

3. Do you give at least 10 percent of your income to the Lord's work? Do you agree that you should?

4. Do you place at least 10 percent of your income into some savings or investment plan? Do you agree that you should?

5. Draw up a monthly plan that would give the first 10 percent of your income to the Lord, the second 10 percent to yourself (savings), and divide the remaining 80 percent among your other expenses. (If you are deeply in debt, this might require extending some of your debts or making a new loan with the bank to cover all existing debts so as to arrange smaller monthly payments.)

6. Discuss the above with your mate and seek agreement to follow such a plan. If you cannot work out such a plan alone, consult a local banker for assistance.

7. Discuss with your mate the role of credit cards in your financial plan. Seek to come to some agreement as to their function.

8. Can you agree that neither of you will ever again make a major purchase without consulting the partner? Agree upon the dollar value of a "major purchase" (for example, fifty dollars).

9. Do you feel financially liberated? If not, what will you do to change your situation? Discuss it with your mate and take action immediately.

For the Unmarried:

1. What is your present financial plan? Force yourself to write it down and ask your prospective mate to do the

same. (How do each of you presently use your financial resources? Be as detailed as possible.)

2. Do you give at least 10 percent of your income to the Lord's work? Do you agree that you should?

3. Do you place at least 10 percent of your income into some savings or investment plan? Do you agree that you should?

4. Discuss items 2 and 3 with your prospective mate and agree on what you will do after you are married.

5. Begin immediately to do whatever you plan to do after you are married. That is, if you agree to put 10 percent of your income into savings after marriage, begin immediately to do so while you are single. (What you do now is a good indicator of how well you will follow the plan after marriage.)

6. Declare your total assets and liabilities to your fiancé. Take a realistic look at your debts and resources.

7. Together work out a payment schedule for any debts that you will have when you get married.

8. Together work out a financial plan for spending your money after you are married. This will require information regarding housing and utility costs. (Allow for personal incidentals as discussed in the chapter.)

9. Discuss and seek agreement that neither of you will ever make a major purchase without consulting the other. No agreement—no purchase! (Agree upon the dollar value of a "major purchase.")

10. Who will keep the books? Why?

LOVING YOUR MARRIAGE ENOUGH TO PROTECT IT

A GIFT
OF LOVE

*One of the major causes of marital breakups in the
Christian community is the lack of protective hedges
that spouses should plant around their marriages, their
heads, their hearts, their eyes, and their hands.*

Writing "Of Scandals and Hedges" in my magazine column
bordered on being too personal. It concerned what we
must do to protect our marriages from infidelity, and I
worried that it might be more embarrassing than helpful—to the
reader and to me.

Here are some excerpts from that column:

I have a list of rather prudish rules that I used to be embarrassed to speak of except to my wife, to whom they are a gift of
love.

They are intended to protect my eyes, my heart, my hands,
and therefore, my marriage. I direct the rules toward appearances

and find that if you take care of how things look, you take care of how they are. In other words, if you are never alone with an unrelated female, because it might not look appropriate, you have eliminated the possibility that anything inappropriate will take place.

I say these rules appear prudish because my mentioning them when necessary has elicited squints, scowls, and not-so-hidden smiles of condescension. And in outlining them here, I risk implying that without following my list, I would immediately be plunged into all manner of affairs.

In enforcing my own rules I don't mean to insult the many virtuous women who might otherwise have very legitimate reasons to meet or dine with me without the slightest temptation to have designs on me.

Simply hedges, that's all these rules are. And much as people don't like to hear, read, or talk about it, the fact is that most Christian men do not have victory over lust. I have a theory about that. Scripture does not imply that we ever shall have victory over lust the way we are expected to win over worry or greed or malice. Rather, Paul instructs Timothy, and thus us, not to conquer or stand and fight, or pray about or resolve, but *to flee* lust.

I know he specifies youthful lust, but I don't believe he is limiting it to a certain age, but rather is describing it, regardless at what age it occurs. The little boy in me, and I have room for several, will have to flee lust until I flee life.

Moody Monthly, July/August 1987. Used by permission.

I then shared the six hedges I build around myself to protect me, my wife, my family, my employer, my church, and supremely, the reputation of Christ. I shared them not to boast, but to admit that I'm still fleeing and in the hope that there be some benefit to someone.

I was afraid I had been too open, too vulnerable, but that proved unfounded. I received more mail and comments about that column than anything I'd ever written. Clearly, the idea had struck a chord. People asked for more on the subject.

But I'm a layman, a writer—not a Bible scholar, psychologist, or counselor. That, some told me, was why I should expand on the subject.

"Be sure it's Bible-based, of course, but not heavily theological. And leave the psychology to the experts. Emphasize the practical. Provide handles, something to grab on to, something a person can *do* to protect a marriage."

This book is a result of that challenge and of the belief in the project on the part of the publishers.

Let me clarify one thing: my hedges may not be your hedges. You may need to plant some where I never dreamed they would be needed, and vice-versa. Resist the urge to get caught up in what a weak, paranoid guy I must be. Rather, if my hedge applies, plant it; if it doesn't, plant one of your own where you need it.

Your marriage, and the church, will be the better for it.

PART ONE

THE NEED
FOR HEDGES

*No one thinks he needs hedges
until it's too late.*

CHAPTER ONE

THE TANGLED WEB

Sexual immorality hits frighteningly close to home.
Without being aware of the need to protect ourselves
against it, we are vulnerable.

Sue was not the prettiest and certainly not the sexiest woman John had ever seen. In fact, she didn't hold a candle to his wife. But Sue worked for John. He spent a lot of time with her at the office. He could tell she admired him. He liked her, respected her, and thought she was bright, creative, and interesting. He liked being around her, liked her smile, enjoyed her wit. She was doe-eyed, had perfect teeth, and was married.

Was John romantically interested in her? The question would have offended him. They were both happily married. They didn't even think about an attraction between them. John told his wife about Sue from the day she was hired. His wife was eager to meet Sue and her husband, and the couples genuinely liked each other. The couples didn't socialize frequently because they lived too far from each other, but Sue kept John up-to-date on what was happening in her life, and John told his wife. Sue and John's wife talked on the phone occasionally. John wasn't starry-eyed about Sue, and John's wife had no reason to believe Sue held anything for John but respect.

Which was true.

Was Sue worth losing a home and family over? Now there was a question even more insulting than the first. No woman was worth that. In fact, John used to tease his wife, "If I ever throw you over, kid, at least I won't humiliate you by running off with a dog."

It was a joke, because it was the last thing on his mind. He was a Christian, active in church, a father of three, a baby boomer with a comfortable and happy life. He wasn't looking for anything more or different. He was challenged, motivated, and excited about his job and his career path. He was solid. John wasn't even going through a midlife crisis.

So he didn't worry when he first found himself missing Sue when she was out of town for a couple of days. He asked his secretary to be sure to let him know when she called, because he had "business to discuss with her." It was true. And when the business had been discussed, they talked a little more.

"We miss you around here, Sue." The emphasis was on "we."

"I miss you too," she said. "All of you. Look forward to seeing you when I get back."

"Me too."

Nice. Friendly. Innocent. Dangerous. But John didn't know that then.

When Sue returned, her relationship with John changed in subtle ways. In a meeting or a room full of people they could read each other's eyes in an instant. They weren't reading anything personal. They just knew what the other was thinking about the topic at hand. John could tell when Sue was hedging, being circumspect. Sue could tell when John was just being polite, when he didn't really like a proposal but was kind in how he responded to it.

John began to find reasons to be around Sue. He also found reasons to touch her in a brotherly or even fatherly way—a squeeze of the hand, a touch on the shoulder, a hug of greeting or farewell. He would not have described it as sexual or even sensual, any more than any man would enjoy physical contact with an attractive, young female.

John was waiting for a cab to the airport as Sue left the office for the day. "The airport's on my way home," she reminded him. "I'll give you a ride."

They talked business on the way. At the curb he looked into her eyes and thanked her warmly. "Any time," she said. "Anything for you." He held her gaze for a moment until the humor of her comment sank in. They both smiled. "You know what I mean," she added.

"Of course."

They both knew she meant she would do anything proper for such a good friend. But both also liked the intimate sound of words that could be taken a variety of ways. In the ensuing weeks and months, John and Sue began slowly to depend upon each other emotionally. He told her things no one else in the office knew: his dreams, plans, private ambitions, his assessments of others. They went from telling each other what good friends they were to making their conversation more personal, more meaningful. He called her his "favorite friend." She often told him he was "special."

Theirs wasn't a typical dual pity party, each badmouthing his own spouse and looking to the other for ingredients missing in the marriages. No, this was simply a case of two people who hit it off, liked each other, became special to each other, and eventually became enamored with each other. Suddenly, or so it seemed, the inevitable happened.

They justified a few lunches and even a working dinner. When their bodies touched while sitting in a cab or in a restaurant booth, neither pulled away. It was natural, familiar. Brotherly and sisterly. When he touched her arm while talking to her, he often left his hand there even after his point had been made.

At a convention out of town, even with six others from their office along, they found opportunities to be alone together. It wasn't easy, but though their relationship had not escalated to the declaring stage yet, they both knew. There was no one either would rather be with. After a late dinner with everyone from their office, she called his room and said she couldn't sleep.

"I'm not tired either," he lied. He had collapsed into bed after the long day. "What do you want to do?"

"I don't know. Just talk."

"So talk."

"You wanna go for a walk?"

"Sure."

They met in the lobby and strolled the deserted city streets. She thought her sweater would be enough, but the summer night grew chilly after midnight, and as they crossed a bridge over the river, he slipped his suit jacket over her shoulders. She smiled at him in the moonlight, and he put his arm around her. She slipped her hand around his waist. They walked silently for twenty minutes until they came to a dark spot between street lights.

John slowed to a stop, his emotions racing. Sue looked quizzically at him, but when he took her in his arms, they embraced so naturally, so perfectly that it seemed right. He could feel her heart pounding. "Dare I kiss you?" he whispered in her hair.

She held him tighter, as if stalling to decide. "It's your call," she said, mimicking his favorite expression to subordinates when insisting they make their own decisions. It was all he needed to hear.

Theirs was one long, soft, meaningful kiss that spoke volumes. They stared into each other's eyes for a slow moment, then headed back to the hotel, his hand gently on her arm. As the building came into sight, Sue stopped. "We have to talk," she said.

"I know."

"What are you thinking, John?"

"The same thing you're thinking."

"Don't be too sure."

"I'm sure, Sue. I'll be shocked if you're not thinking what I think you're thinking."

"You first, Boss."

"This will never work, Sue. It didn't happen. We go back to our respective rooms good friends, good associates, two people who happen to like each other very much."

Her eyes filled. "You know me too well."

"I'm relieved to hear you say that, Sue. I certainly didn't intend this, and I don't want to mislead you."

"The walk was my idea, but I didn't have this in mind either."

"Nothing happened, Sue. Deal?" He stuck out his hand.

She shook it but held on. "Why do I want to kiss you again, John? I agree we have to end this, but it seems so incomplete."

"I feel the same way. But we cannot. We must not."

"I know," she said, dropping his hand.

She thanked him for the use of his coat and smiled bravely at him as she left the elevator at her floor.

John stared at the ceiling until four in the morning, dredging up every negative detail of his marriage. In twelve years he and his wife had become known as a successful and happily married couple. By the time he gave up trying to sleep, however, he had convinced himself that he had never loved her, that the marriage was a mistake, and that he felt something for Sue he had never felt for any other woman, including—and especially—his wife.

His jaw set and his mind whirling, John strode to the window and gazed into the darkness. Was that a person sitting on the low concrete wall in the courtyard below? As John watched, the figure moved. It was a woman, and as he studied her, he knew it was Sue.

John freshened up and dressed quickly. He took the stairs all the way to the ground floor and exited a side door unnoticed. Sue started when she first saw him, then she sat still and stared ahead resignedly, as if this new meeting were somehow inevitable. John stood before her. "Sue, are you all right?"

She nodded and dabbed at her face with a tissue. "I just have to get over this," she said.

"Anything I can do?"

She shook her head. "It's not going to be easy working with you."

"It doesn't have to be difficult, Sue. We just need to back up a few months. We're good friends, and we can enjoy that, can't we?"

"You make the let's-be-friends routine sound easy, John. I can't."

"Why not?"

She took a deep, quavery breath and fought for composure. She hadn't looked at him since he first approached. "I'm in love with you, John. That's why."

He reached for her and she came to him. They embraced and kissed, and he told her he loved her, too. He led her back into the hotel the way he'd come, avoiding the lobby and the elevators. They trudged up the stairs to her room. He left there two hours later, in time to prepare for the day.

John and Sue shared a delicious, bleary-eyed secret for the rest of the convention. They spent most of every night together, and there was no more talk of how things would have to change when they traveled back home to reality.

John and Sue convinced themselves that their love was so perfect that God had to be in it. Neither was prepared for the vehement re-actions from their spouses and their extended families. The anger, the confusion, the accusations drove them closer to each other. With-in six months both divorces were final, and John and Sue were mar-ried. A year later, while Sue was pregnant with her first child, John announced that he had made a terrible mistake. He wanted his wife and family back, and he set upon such an impractical and obnox-ious approach that he lost his job and his new wife. In the process he permanently alienated himself from his former wife as well.

SURELY NOT THEM!

John and Sue's story is representative of several I've heard from friends, relatives, and acquaintances. It has become so common that I cringe when someone says, "Did you hear about so-and-so?" They may be informing me of a move or a new job or a new baby, but my first dreaded thought is, *Oh, no, please, not them too.* All too often, my worst fears are confirmed. No one is immune. The strongest mar-riage you know of is in danger today if hedges are not in place.

Not long ago I reminisced with several old friends. What a shock-ing disappointment to discover that every one of us knew personally of at least one painful marriage failure due to infidelity. Even more appalling, nearly all of us could point to incidents among our close relatives. Can anyone still doubt that the sexual revolution has brought about an epidemic of divorce?

In a strange way, the problem is exacerbated in the Christian com-munity because unfaithful spouses are generally not in danger—the way the secular community is—of contracting AIDS or herpes. The type of a person I'm writing about is not characteristically promis-cuous. John, in the above example, had never before slept with a woman other than his wife. Ironically, while the secular world is cleaning up its act due to fear of deadly disease, Christians blithely proceed, unaware they need hedges to keep them from surprise attacks in their areas of sexual weakness.

Try an informal survey on your own. Ask friends and relatives if they know people who have fallen to sexual temptation. Perhaps you don't need to ask. Maybe you know firsthand more such stories than you care to recount. And if the people involved were vulnerable, who else might be? Who will be the next one about whom you say, "I never would have dreamed he would do such a thing"? You know these people, and you have to wonder what made them fall. What made them vulnerable?

THE LITTLE FOXES

Just as it's the little foxes who spoil the vine, so the seemingly small indiscretions add up to major traps. John and Sue allowed themselves to admire, like, respect, and enjoy each other without giving a second thought to the progression of feelings, the danger of developing emotional feelings, the lure of infatuation. They never reminded themselves of their wedding vows because they had no intention of breaking them. Feelings and emotions sneaked up on them when they least expected it, and then it was too late.

Look at the biblical account of David's failure in 2 Samuel 11. Here was a man after God's own heart. Have you ever wondered why he didn't go to battle? Scripture doesn't provide a lot of detail about this incident, but the question arises: Was David too old, too tired, too successful, or too something to lead his army? Or was there some subconscious, or not so subconscious, maneuvering to get himself into a position where he could have an opportunity to get next to Uriah's wife?

Why did he take a walk on his veranda that day? Was Bathsheba not aware that her bath was within the line of sight from the king's palace? It's fair to say that an innocent walk and a bath in the open air could be considered nearly innocent indiscretions. Give Bathsheba the benefit of the doubt, and David should have turned away when he saw a naked woman. The fact that even a man after God's own heart was unable to do that lends credence to my theory that we are to flee rather than to try to conquer lust.

Inviting the wife of your commanding officer over after seeing her bathe must be considered more than a small indiscretion. Even in my respect for a man of God, I have to suspect David's motives. Could he simply have wanted to get better acquainted? Indeed! He knew this woman. Surely she was known in the social circles of the government, being married to a high-ranking soldier and living within sight of the palace. Did David know when he invited her that he would sleep with her that night? Surely he wasn't testing his resolve to remain pure before God. What Bathsheba knew or didn't know we can scarcely guess. In that time, a summons from the king was disobeyed only under the threat of death, so from the time she received his invitation, her fate was sealed.

Safe to say, had it not been for the initial indiscretions, adultery may never have resulted. And look at what happened after that. Bathsheba became pregnant. David called Uriah home from battle in the hope that he would sleep with his wife and believe the child was his own. Uriah, a man of honor (how that must have made David feel!), refused to enjoy the comforts of his home and his wife while his men were engaged in battle. Had Uriah slept with his wife, David would have fostered deceit. As it turned out, Uriah's sense of duty drove David to have him killed. Scripture tells how David sent the Hittite back to war with his own death notice in his hand (2 Samuel 11:14–17).

ENCOUNTERS OF THE TOO-CLOSE KIND

How close have you come to being burned? Have you found yourself impressed with someone and then attracted to them? Maybe it seemed innocent and safe, but then you said or did things you never thought you would say or do. Maybe on a business trip you hung around with a colleague of the opposite sex, and upon reflection you know you wouldn't have wanted your spouse to do the same thing. It could be that nothing improper was said or done, but simply investing the emotional energy and time was inappropriate. Maybe, looking back, you can see that you were living dangerously. When friends fall right and left, you see that perhaps you were lucky you weren't snared.

Or maybe you did become emotionally or even physically involved and fell just short of actually committing adultery. Perhaps you live with guilt because you never confided that to anyone, including —and especially—your spouse.

If so many of your friends and acquaintances have fallen—people you never would have suspected—how will you avoid being a casualty?

CHAPTER TWO

THE CHANGING CLIMATE

There's a new openness to interaction between the sexes in the workplace, in the neighborhood, in counseling— even in the church. Christians touch more, speak more intimately, are closer to one another. There are advantages to this but also grave dangers. Fear can be good. Fear is as good a motivator as any to maintain fidelity.

In a survey conducted by Christianity Today, Inc. researchers, of one thousand readers (nonpastors) of *Christianity Today,* fully 23 percent indicated they had engaged in sexual intercourse with someone other than their wives. Twenty-eight percent indicated they had involved themselves in other forms of sexual contact outside their marriages. In a separate survey of pastors, 23 percent said they had done something sexually inappropriate outside their marriages, 12 percent indicating adulterous intercourse.[1]

What could John and Sue have done to insure against the misery they brought upon themselves? Such second marriages seldom work; but, make no mistake, had their marriage been idyllic, it would still have been disastrous for their previous spouses, John's children, and both extended families.

First, both should have been aware of the potential danger and recognized the infatuation for what it was. This is basic, though not admitted to by most Christians. It simply is not uncommon in the workplace to meet someone with whom there seems an immediate bonding. You like them, they like you, you hit it off. That is the time to deal with the problem, because it can become a serious dilemma.

You can be married ten years and still develop a crush on someone. You think about them, find yourself talking about them, quoting them (even to your spouse), and generally becoming enamored with them. The Christianity Today, Inc. survey showed clearly that the major factor contributing to extramarital relationships is physical and emotional attraction (78 percent), far outdistancing marital dissatisfaction (41 percent).[2]

That is the time to remind yourself that this is nothing more than an adult version of adolescent puppy love, and it will pass. It really will. The person is off limits, and you should run from the situation as from a contagious disease.

You may still see the person in the work setting, and you may still enjoy proper interaction with them. But ground rules need to be set. Never tell the person that you are attracted to them. Talk about your spouse frequently in front of them. Tell your spouse about the person, but use your own judgment as to how fully to explain your dilemma. I have a friend who seems to delight in telling his wife about all the women upon whom he develops such instant and fleeting crushes. He encourages her to do the same, but while she admits she is susceptible to similar experiences, she prefers not to talk about them or to hear about his. My own wife is fully aware of my hedges, and thus she is not threatened by my extolling the appropriate virtues of an associate. Of course, I don't rhapsodize about someone's looks or say stupid things like, "If I had met her before I met you. . . ."

When you first become aware of the impact the other person has on you, that is the time to move into action. You should be able to determine the extent of the danger a person represents to you by your own body language, how you sit or stand when talking with them, how much eye contact seems acceptable, whether you seem magnetized by them, and how much you look forward to seeing them.

Don't treat your new friend the way you treat an old, respected friend. Refrain from touching them, being alone with them, flirting with them (even in jest), or saying anything to them you wouldn't say if your spouse were there. (While you may not be so rigid in your conduct with a long-time friend of the opposite sex, beware. Certain guidelines must be enforced. Friendships, especially with long-admired associates, can turn into something more intimate even more quickly than new alliances.)

So, what could John and Sue have done? Had either realized they were becoming enamored with each other, they could have shifted gears, gone into a protective mode, and saved themselves from ruining many lives.

If hedges are constructed early enough, preferably well in advance of even meeting someone else, they can be painless and can nip marriage-threatening relationships before they get started. That's the reason we so desperately need practical suggestions on ways to build impenetrable hedges around our marriages.

If you can believe *The Hite Report on Male Sexuality*,[3] which I don't recommend reading or believing, nearly three-fourths of married men cheat on their wives. Admittedly, the responses are from people with enough interest in the subject to answer a multipage questionnaire that gave them the opportunity to discuss sex in the most pedestrian and vulgar terms, generally robbing it of any sacred mystery. In fact, the monumental report itself (1,129 pages in hardback) could be enlisted as a masturbatory aid, if one was so inclined. A huge percentage of the respondents appear so inclined, as evidenced in their comments.

On the subject of adultery, the author summarizes:

The great majority of married men were not monogamous. Seventy-two percent of men married two years or more had had sex outside of marriage; the overwhelming majority did not tell their wives, at least at the time [of the incidents].[4]

Given the unscientific, nonrepresentative nature of the research, the above quotation can be taken with a healthy dose of sodium, but it should be pointed out that a significant number of respondents referred to themselves as born-again Christians. Putting this body of research with the Christianity Today, Inc. survey provides a rough idea where the Christian community fits in the overall scheme of marital faithfulness.

When a famous television evangelist announced he was stepping aside from his ministry because of an affair, I shook my head. I had never been a follower of the man, but I had been bemused by what appeared to be a confused set of values. Sadly, the news of his moral failure was thus not a surprise. Further revelations included gross financial mismanagement, empire building, and even homosexuality.

Another Christian television personality's moral failure included a lifelong fascination with pornography and an apparent attempt to get as close as possible to extramarital sex without actually committing it.

Hearing the stories of the ruined ministries of television evangelists due to sexual immorality is one thing. Seeing the same thing happen to your neighbor, your friend, or a family member is something else altogether. It may be hard to identify with the man who has everything—a ministry, wealth, status, popularity, a beautiful family—and risks it all for a season of pleasure, but it is not hard to identify with the man next door.

When your assistant pastor, brother-in-law, or best friend from college falls, that's too close to home. Then you get to see at close range the tumble of dominoes set in motion by infidelity.

THE PRICE OF INFIDELITY

Infidelity. What a genteel word for the act it describes. Such a word goes down easier than violating one's trust, breaking one's marriage vows, being unfaithful, sleeping around, fornicating, committing adultery. But using a mild word for sin doesn't change a thing.

I was twelve years old when I was first affected by the ravages of immorality. Something was wrong in the only church I had ever known, and no one would tell me what was going on. There were meetings, public and private, charges, accusations, arguments, tears, factions. I badgered and bugged and bothered until I forced my mother to tell me what I really didn't want to know.

"You're too young to deal with it."

"No I'm not, Mom. I'm twelve!" How old that sounded at the time!

"You'll wish you hadn't asked."

"Just tell me! Please!"

"You wouldn't believe it."

"Yes, I will! Tell me!"

"Would you believe me if I told you that our pastor doesn't love his wife anymore?"

"No!"

"See?"

It couldn't be true. The pastor and his wife were perfect! They had four of their own children and had adopted another. I had looked up to and admired and respected them for as long as I could remember. A young married woman in the church had been the center of the rumors. Was there an affair? Had someone seen them embrace? Could the stories be true of the pastor berating his wife? My head swam as the rumors flew around our church.

The pastor's final sermon was a not-so-veiled admission of a mistake he had made years before—his choice of a wife. The church was ravaged by a near-split soon after his departure. Then came the news of the divorce. His ministry was over. That little church was left in pieces, and it took years to pull itself back together.

I thought no such trauma had ever before hit a wonderful church like ours, nor could it ever happen again. Since then I have heard countless such stories about pastors—including both a senior pastor and an assistant pastor I had sat under. One left notes for his trusted friends and associates, praising God for "this new, divine love that is so wonderful that He had to author it." Another friend tried to convince me that the relationship that broke up both his and his girl-friend's marriages was "in the center of God's will."

THE UNDERLYING ROOT

What seemed an aberration more than twenty-five years ago in a small town was merely a harbinger for the marital devastation that has hit the Christian community today.

Marriages are breaking up at such an alarming rate that it's hard to find someone who has not been affected by divorce in his imme-diate family. How many divorces can you count in your own family, including grandparents on both sides, aunts, uncles, and your own siblings?

You may not know how many of those divorces were the result of immorality, but half is a fair assumption. Women leave their husbands for a variety of complex reasons, the most minor of which—according to marriage counselors—is their own lust. Rarely do you hear of a woman who simply fell for someone who, by his sexual appeal alone, turned her head and heart from her own husband.

But men—yes, even those who would blame their frumpy, crabby, boring wives for their own roving eyes—don't really need an ex-cuse. They will point to myriad reasons for having to leave, but it near-ly always can be traced to lust, pride, and a false sense of their own strength. Remember that the major factors leading to the illicit re-lationships in the Christianity Today, Inc. survey showed 78 percent of respondents citing physical and emotional attraction while only 41 percent cited marital dissatisfaction. [5]

Think of the men you know and the reasons they gave for find-ing someone new. Did some of them have incredibly attractive, even sexy wives? Can all those men complain of their wives' frigidity?

A strange aspect of infidelity is that a man usually has to invent reasons after the fact. The man who once taught marriage seminars, raved about his wife, treated her right, was proud of her, now must say:

"We hid the truth. Our marriage was never good."

"In private she was not what she appeared to be in public."

"I never loved her."

"She didn't understand me" (the oldest saw in the tool kit).

NO EXCUSE

We all know the adage that every broken marriage has two sides and that there's no such thing as a completely innocent party. How-ever, those statements need examination. No, none of us knows what went on behind closed doors, and we all know how base we can be in private, compared to the image we like to project in public.

But if you know divorced couples, you know of examples where, if she was not innocent, the wife was certainly not guilty of anything that justified her husband's leaving her for another woman. I've been acquainted with enough such offending men to see their defenses coming a mile away. Suddenly this woman we all know as a wonderful person—not perfect, maybe a bit dull, maybe harried and overworked, maybe not as dazzling as she was when they first married— is painted as a monster. This from the man who is no prize himself, yet he has justified breaking the laws of God, breaking his promises to his wife, violating their union, and blaming it on her! I once knew a denominational leader in his sixties who carried on a year-long affair with a younger woman. When he was exposed and defrocked and called before his superiors, he brought along his wife, who took full responsibility. No confession. No apology. It was her fault, he said. She said it herself.

Call it what you will, but a man with as perfect a wife as he could ever want is still capable of lust, of a senseless seeking of that which would destroy him and his family. If he does not fear his own potential and build a hedge around himself and his marriage, he heads for disaster.

A HEALTHY FEAR

Shall we all run scared? Yes! Fear is essential. "There are several good protections against temptation," Mark Twain said, "but the surest is cowardice."[6]

Look around. Let your guard down, don't remind yourself that you made a vow before God and men, don't set up barriers for your eyes, your mind, your hands, your emotions, and see how quickly you become a statistic.

A man may say, "It could never happen to me. I love my wife. We know each other inside out by now. We've left the emotional infatuation stage that ruled our courtship and honeymoon, and we love God's way: unconditionally and by the act of our wills. We each know the other is not perfect and we accept and love each other anyway. We're invulnerable to attack, especially by lust that leads to immorality."

But when—because he has not planted hedges to protect himself —he falls, his tune changes. Then his excuse is that he fell out of love, the old magic was no longer there, the wife was too busy with the house and kids, his needs were not fulfilled at home.

Worse, the Christian deserter becomes so infatuated with his new love that he often gives God the credit. Know a counseling pastor or a Christian psychologist? Ask him how many times he's heard a man say, "This new relationship is so beautiful, God has to be behind it." Never mind that it goes against all sense and every tenet of Scripture, not to mention everything the man has ever believed in and stood for.

What is happening? When we baby boomers were in elementary school we knew one, maybe two kids from broken homes. Divorce among church people was almost nonexistent. Now the solid, happy marriage is the exception. From people we never dreamed would have problems come stories of affairs, adultery, separation, and divorce.

This is not the forum in which to debate the issue of divorce. Scripture is clear that God hates divorce (Malachi 2:16), but opinions vary as to whether He forbids it altogether or allows it in only one or two circumstances, and whether remarriage is allowed regardless of the reason for the divorce.

No matter where you stand on those issues, you must agree that no one marries intending or wanting to divorce. Some, no doubt, from the beginning consider divorce a convenient option and vow to stay together for as long as we both shall *love*. But even the Christian with the most liberal position possible on divorce says and means at his wedding that he is pledging himself to his wife forever. He may later forget it or decide that it was merely archaic formality, but there's no way around it. His vows were legal, sacred, and moral. When he commits adultery, he breaks his promise.

One of the most effective ways to deal with a friend who is trying to justify his adultery is to say, "Bill, don't forget that I was there. I heard you say it. I heard you promise that you would take no one but Jane unto yourself for as long as you both shall live."

"Yeah, but—"

"You can 'yeah, but' all you want, but the fact is, you broke your promise."

"But she—"

"Regardless of what *she* did or didn't do, you broke your promise, didn't you?"

That can take the wind out of any sail made of excuses.

RUN, DON'T WALK

A complex litany of events takes place between the vows and the adultery, and it behooves those of us who want to remain pure to examine those events, expose them for what they are, and either avoid letting them happen or avoid letting Satan use them to trick us into justifying our sin.

Once we have identified them, what will we do about them? Will we pray over them? Resolve to conquer them? Turn over new leaves? Ironically, the answer is easier than that. We are not to win, not to gain the victory, not to succeed by the sheer force of our wills, our consciences, or our determination.

> Flee the evil desires of youth, and pursue righteousness, faith, love and peace, along with those who call on the Lord out of a pure heart. (2 Timothy 2:22, NIV)

We are to run. To flee. To get out. To get away. Why? Does this admonition to flee somehow serve as an admission on God's part that He did not even equip us with the ability to subdue our natures in this area? The question is valid. Of adultery, in the Old Testament God tells us, "You shall not" (Exodus 20:14), and in the New Testament He says that if we so much as look upon a woman to lust after her, we have already committed adultery with her in our hearts (Matthew 5:28).

In other areas, God grants us victory. We can win over jealousy, a bad temper, greed, and even pride. We can train our consciences to avoid theft, bad mouthing, and lying. But who do you know who could avoid a peek at pornography if convinced no one would find out?

Clearly there are times when we are stronger than at other times. So what is the solution when temptation rages? If we are weak and have not taken precautions, if we have not applied preventive medicine, we have already failed. The only answer is to plan, to anticipate danger, to plot the way of escape.

The time to build hedges is before the enemy attacks.

NOTES

1. "How Common is Pastoral Indiscretion?" *Leadership* (Winter 1988), 12–13.
2. Ibid., 13.
3. See Shere Hite, *The Hite Report on Male Sexuality* (New York: Alfred Knopf, 1981).
4. Ibid.
5. "How Common Is Pastoral Indiscretion?" 13.
6. Mark Twain, *Following the Equator,* vol. 1, "Pudd'nhead Wilson's New Calendar," chap. 36.

CHAPTER THREE

DON'T BLAME GOD

*One of the most fascinating and misunderstood
differences between men and women is in their thought
processes and sexual triggers.*

I was in the eighth grade when short skirts became popular. I thought I'd died and gone to heaven. Our school went through ninth grade, so to me, ninth-grade girls were women. Of course, in 1962–63, what I considered short skirts were just an inch or two above the knee. Lord, have mercy! The trend would escalate to micro minis by the time I reached college, so I spent my entire adolescence with my eyes open.

I suppose that era made me a leg man, though it would be a lie to say that any other female physical attribute is far down my appreciation list. Lest I sound like a wolf-whistling lecher, please know that this was a private sport. While we junior high boys might nudge someone so he could follow our eyes to a choice target, for some reason we didn't admit to each other how deeply we felt about looking at girls.

Indeed, I thought I was probably the only Christian boy attracted to the female figure. From childhood on I had read in a denominational magazine letters from teenagers lamenting having gone too far in their relationships and pleading for advice on how to control themselves. That turned out to be a good foundation for me when I began dating and facing temptation. I credit that early input— along with dating virtuous women—for coming to my wedding night as virginal as my bride: wholly.

Yet in junior high and high school I feared I would wind up as one of those letter writers. I was so enamored with women and their sensual beauty that I was convinced I had the potential to become a fiend. When I realized that even more exciting to me than any sports drama was watching a girl cross her legs and catching a glimpse of thigh, I knew I had it bad.

Had I only known this was normal! That I was not alone! That such attraction to women, yes, even to their sexuality, was God's idea! Is that heresy? It's not now, and it wasn't then. Though I can't recall having purely lustful thoughts in junior high, I carried a deep sense of guilt about even *wanting* to look at girls. As best I can recall, I had no thoughts of illicit sex. Still, I felt guilty. Something seemed wrong with thinking about this all the time. What a relief it would have been to discover that (depending on which expert you read) the typical American adolescent male thinks about sex no fewer than four times every minute!

Of course, as I graduated from puberty and went on for a master's degree in girl watching, it became more and more difficult to separate looking and appreciating from lusting. It was of only small comfort to me when I heard a Christian youth leader say that 99 percent of all heterosexual boys have a problem with lust and that the other 1 percent are liars. I was devout in my faith and knew right from wrong, yet I seemed to have no control, no resolve, no victory in this area. I regret not having had an adult perspective that would have allowed me to enjoy those years with wonder and without guilt.

With my own three boys, two of whom are teenagers, I already allow for the natural attraction to and preoccupation with females, and we talk about it rather than pretend there's something wrong with it. I sometimes caution them about thoughts, and we discuss openly the priceless value of their goal to reach marriage without having fallen into sexual sin.

Beyond that I don't pretend that they should chastise themselves for appreciating a form designed by God to attract them. Without being crude, we discuss which girl in an ad or on a television program is most attractive and why I admit that women are still fun to look at, even at my ripe age (I'm in my forties). They probably get tired of my cautioning to be careful about dwelling on the sexual and to simply admire, delight in, enjoy, and respect God's beautiful creativity.

Drs. Miriam and Otto Ehrenberg classify parents in four categories according to their views of sex in raising their children: Sex Repressive (sex is bad and should be discussed or dealt with only in that light), Sex Avoidant (sex is OK but is best not talked about), Sex Obsessive (sex is everything, no taboos, even young children should be conversant about it), Sex Expressive (sex is good and healthy and should be discussed appropriately).

They write:

> The aim of Sex Repressive parents is very specific: to curb sexual behavior and keep their children, especially their daughters, away from sexual entanglements before they are married. The impact of Sex Repressive parents, however, goes way beyond this goal. They instill a sense of shame in children about their innate sexuality which alienates children from their parents and interferes with their later capacity to form satisfying relationships with the opposite sex.... Children in these circumstances grow up feeling bad about the sexual stirrings which are an essential part of their nature, and resentful towards their parents for disapproving of this very basic aspect of their being.[1]

Any conscientious parent would want to be Sex Expressive, but for Christians, there is a major problem with this secular view of sexuality. While it is almost always positive and healthy to be Sex Expressive, we must also instill in our children the biblical admonition that sex before or outside of marriage is wrong, is sin, and has consequences. In other words, during the time of our children's peak sexual awareness—adolescence—we might be labeled Sex Repressive by the experts, even though we assure our children that sex is good and healthy and fun and was, in fact, God's idea.

I know some people may laugh at my notion of looking at women to appreciate God's creativity and would accuse me of inventing a spiritual reason to leer. I maintain that, after years of steeling myself to avert my eyes from something made attractive by God, developing an appreciation for it is far healthier. Clearly it would be wrong to gawk and dwell upon some stranger's beauty, especially when I have vowed before God and man to put my wife ahead of all others. Dianna knows I am attracted to pretty women (she is one, after all). She also knows that I know they are off-limits and that even entertaining a lustful thought is wrong. The point is, I don't pretend before my wife that I no longer look at other women. My gaze doesn't linger and my thoughts stay in check (not easily and not always), but how much worse it would be if I pretended to have been blind since our wedding and she caught me sneaking a peek. Her standard line is, "When he quits looking, he quits cooking."

Don't get the idea that my eyes are always roving and that my poor wife can't keep my attention. (Anyone who has seen her knows otherwise.) It doesn't take a lingering look to appreciate beauty, and there are more than enough reasons not to stare at other women. First, it would threaten Dianna and jeopardize my covenant with her. It would be dangerous to my thought life, because past a casual observance of God's handiwork (go ahead, laugh!), my eyes and mind have no right to dwell there. Even if the woman doesn't belong to anyone else, I do!

It's interesting, the double standard that comes into play here. My glance at a nice-looking woman is even quicker when she's escorted. I know how I feel when men stare at my wife. I watch their eyes. I'm possessive and jealous. I have a right to be. If their gaze lingers, I assume they're trying to catch her eye, and they probably are. No fair. Out of bounds. Off limits. She's mine. It gives me a great sense of security that Dianna is largely unaware how many heads she turns and that, even if she were aware, she's not one to return another man's gaze. Still, I resent it when I see someone stare at her, and I want to practice the golden rule when the shoe is on the other foot.

I'm quick to point out to my son that the rush of feeling he might experience for a beautiful woman should never be mistaken for true love. Such a rush is mere infatuation, physical and sensual attraction, a path to a dead end. A relationship may begin with physical attraction, but to build on that alone leads to disaster. It's also important to differentiate here between beauty and cheap sexuality. Almost any woman—within reason—can dress or make herself up in such a way that she looks sexy and available. I maintain that, unless a man is looking for thrills, he won't find such a creature attractive. Focusing on a hooker-type is selfish and fleshly, perverting the natural attraction between the sexes that was God's idea.

I realize that women may shake their heads in disgust at my obvious male perspective. Guilty. I was born this way. My friend Lois Mowday covers much the same territory from the female viewpoint in her excellent book, *The Snare,*[2] but neither of us could have written the other's book. Men and women think and act and are different, and no amount of modern talk can convince me otherwise.

Another high school youth leader first impressed upon me that girls don't think at all like guys do. I didn't believe him at first. Even the minor exposure to pornography a sheltered evangelical male gets tells him that women can be vamps, tramps, teases, flirts, come-ons, hookers, you name it. Therefore, the male assumes that innocent, young Christian girls who dress, act, walk, or talk provocatively know exactly what they are doing. Unless the girls are asking for trouble, which I found difficult to accept, they are playing a dangerous and contemptuous game with us guys. They know we are turned on by hair-trigger switches through the mind and all five senses, so unless they mean business, they are cruel.

This idea that they were, on the whole, ignorant of their effect or unaware how males react was so revelatory and revolutionary that I couldn't accept it. I'm not saying there aren't women base enough to fit precisely the description in the above paragraph, but just that most of those who turn men on would be shocked to know how they are viewed.

I tested that theory as a high school senior and as a college freshman. I dated a Christian girl who was careful and virtuous and could not be described as a flirt. I discussed with her the actions and dress of mutual friends and found that she agreed with our youth leader. The girls in question were ignorant or naive. They were not sinister or on the prowl. I mustered my courage and began to ask them.

My freshman year at a Christian college allowed me to meet many beautiful women students, a whole range of personalities, modes of dress, and behavior. Our school policy stipulated that skirts could be no shorter than the top of the knee. Some of my best friends, women I respected and admired and enjoyed looking at, seemed to push the rule to the limit. How does one determine the top of the knee? (My friends and I volunteered to help!) Depending on the skirt, the material, and the woman, a skirt that was legal while she was standing might be four inches above the knee when she sat. Even the most modest skirt that touched the top of the knee was a problem for men and women when she wanted to cross her legs.

Not wanting to appear an oddball, I waited until I felt a woman was my friend before I popped my question.

"Can I ask you something, just out of curiosity?"

"Sure."

"How would you feel if you thought that the way you dressed caused men to lust?"

I asked at least six college women, ages ranging from eighteen to twenty-one. Every one of them responded with some variation on this answer:

"Oh, I'm sure we don't have any guys that perverted around here."

Remember, I was not on a crusade to get the rule changed or even to get the skirts lengthened. I was just testing a theory, and I was stunned by the response. They actually didn't know. They dressed for fashion, for comfort, and for their own taste. Had they realized they were causing problems for male students, I have no doubt they'd have made adjustments. In fact, things have somehow changed in the ensuing twenty years. I recently read in a Christian college newspaper an editorial by a woman student who said she and her sisters had gotten the point. They felt a responsibility not to lead their brothers into sin. She took it a step further and said some of the guys could take a lesson in how to wear their jeans.

That's a new concept: men turning women on by what they wear and how they wear it. What has contributed to this shift? Some would say novels—written by men that portray women triggered sexually by the same stimuli that affect men, plus the advent of male strippers and magazines like *Playgirl,* which depict male nudity. It is generally accepted that women are aroused by environment, atmosphere, tenderness, romance, and touch. The idea of men baring themselves has been considered repulsive to women. Today you can even see television commercials in which girls on the beach rate the various body parts of the men that walk by. Women friends and relatives tell me, however, that while the occasional broad shoulder or narrow hip might be a mild turn-on, most women are still not sexually aroused in the same way men are. There is no longer any question that women can be aroused to a similar state of excitement and eroticism, but the route is different.[3]

These differences in attraction actually compete with each other. A man is turned on by the mere thought of a beautiful woman—imagining, fantasizing about the possibilities. When he meets a woman, the scenario has already been played out in his mind. She might like his voice, his smile, his manner. Meanwhile, he's light-years ahead. She smiles at his interest, then he says or does something inappropriate. Immediate disaster. She's turned off, he's offended, and neither understands what went wrong. She thinks he's a typical male. He thinks she's a typical female. Both are right. Some like to blame God for this seeming inequity ("I can't help myself; He made me this way"). Others say our makeup justifies aggressiveness, that men are to be the leaders, planners, visionaries. Women are to be submissive, supportive, reactive. Neither view is wholly acceptable, of course. Sure, there are times, especially as teenagers, when we men might wish we hadn't been equipped with an engine that idles like a rocket but which isn't supposed to be launched for years. But to hide behind nature to justify aggression and chauvinism is cowardly. Theologians and psychologists can work out the reasons why we're made this way. Our task is to channel our drives into something positive and to glorify God in the process.

NOTES

1. Miriam Ehrenberg, Ph.D., and Otto Ehrenberg, Ph.D., *The Intimate Circle* (New York: Simon and Schuster, 1988), 47–48.

2. See Lois Mowday, *The Snare* (Colorado Springs: NavPress, 1988).

3. William H. Masters and Virginia E. Johnson, *Human Sexual Response* (Boston: Little, Brown and Co., 1966), 301–2.

CHAPTER FOUR

THE
DYNAMICS
OF FLIRTATION

*Flirting is fun and usually begins in innocence. It's a
hard habit to break, even after marriage. Yet it causes
jealousy. Worse, it puts us into situations we never
intended to fall into, and it creates misunderstandings
that can lead to infidelity.*

Apart from sex, what could be more fun than flirting? If you say
softball, you're reading the wrong book.

Flirting is so much fun because the rushes, emotions, and
pleasures are sexual. It's foreplay with no payoff. It makes the heart
race, the face flush, and a feeling of well-being wash over the body.
It seems harmless, but it's not.

If you want to flirt, flirt with your wife. She may not look, feel,
or sound the way she did when you first flirted with her years ago,
but she still wants you to flirt with her. Try it. Wink at her across the
room. Blow her a kiss no one else sees. Play footsie with her under
the table. Give her a squeeze, a pinch, a tickle no one else notices.

Are you afraid she'll think you're crazy? Well, you are crazy, aren't
you? Put yourself in her place. Would you like to be flirted with by

someone who loves you, someone who can tease about what she might do with you later and then deliver? Do you, or would you, appreciate your wife making a pass at you, making a suggestive comment, giving you a knowing look? I do, and she does, and I love it.

Married couples do not commonly flirt with each other, and it may have to be relearned. Marital flirting is really no different than adolescent flirting. You can do the same things, only everything you're thinking about and hoping will come of it is legal, normal, acceptable, and beautiful. Marital flirting is fun and safe.

But! Who do we usually flirt with? Who would we *like* to flirt with? Good friends from work? From church? Relatives? Young people? Wives of friends?

We don't mean anything by it. It's innocent. They're safe. It's a way of having a good time at no one's expense. Right?

Then why does it bother us so much when we detect someone trying to flirt with our wives? A wink, a smile, a "Hey-why-don't-you-dump-this-guy-and-run-off-with-me-ha-ha," a touch, and the hair on our necks bristles. Who does this guy think he is? He thinks this is funny?

We're also extremely interested in how our wives react to such an approach. Can she bob and weave with the best of them, return the barbs, keep it alive? We trust her. She's faithful. It's all a game, a diversion.

Then why does it bother us so much?

Because the flirter has no right to the emotions, the inappropriate attention, the sexual/recreational lives of our spouses. I don't flirt with other women, even in jest, because I wouldn't want my wife to be offended or hurt or to wonder or be embarrassed. And I certainly would not want her to do the same.

My wife doesn't flirt because something deep within her knows it is basically wrong. She doesn't have to fight the urge, and when someone tries to flirt with her, her unpracticed reactions cool his heels. She doesn't try to be mean or cold—though she could be if someone actually came on to her—but extramarital flirtation is so far from her *modus operandi* that she usually doesn't recognize it. Thus her reaction is either puzzlement or seriousness, and a flirt needs a target that flexes, that gives, that bounces back.

Because I enjoy having fun and being funny, and because my mind tends to find humor in words and unusual combinations of ideas, I could easily flirt with anyone I thought was receptive. Much flirting is funny. If someone says something flirtatious to me, my first impulse is to expand on it, play with it, see how quick and funny I can be. But I resist that. It isn't fair. It's mental and emotional unfaithfulness. I would be exercising a portion of my brain and soul reserved for my exclusive lover.

That seems a little rigid, and I am careful not to chastise, put down, or otherwise embarrass or insult a woman who might flatter me by flirting with me. It is flattering, of course, even if it does somehow lower my esteem for her. I usually respond with humor that changes the subject or ends the conversation, in the hope that she will later realize that I deflected the approach without embarrassing her.

The reason I don't scowl at flirters or lecture them is that I believe most flirting is well-intentioned. It's meant to be a compliment, a friendly gesture, a you-and-me kind of a thing that separates those of us with certain kinds of minds and attitudes from everyone else in the room. It's elitist. It's subtle. It marks you as smart and clever.

But, as usual, we find ourselves confronted by the age-old difference between men and women. A friend of mine, a woman, says something grossly inappropriate to me almost every time I see her. She does it to bug me, and she has absolutely no ulterior motives. Even my wife thinks she's a scream.

Women mean something entirely different by flirting than men do. Most women I have discussed this with tell me that they agree flirting with someone else's husband is not right, and often they feel guilty later. But initiating the flirting or responding to someone else's approach is fun and exciting because of the attention.

"Usually it surprises me," a friend says. "Often a meeting of the eyes or a smile or a flirtatious joke makes me realize for the first time that a man is even aware of me in a group. Then, I admit, I encourage it, but with no thought of actually leading him on."

I'm not saying that men intend anything serious at first either, but if a flirtatious advance is returned, it tends to escalate. I know two men who have left their wives for other men's wives, and it all began with what each party thought and intended to be harmless flirting.

In one case, the process took a year; in the other, only a little over a month. In both cases, the same thing happened. The man started it. The woman responded. They teased each other on several occasions until the man grew bold enough to think that maybe she meant something by her encouraging responses. In the first case, he made a move on her; she was stunned and hurt; and in the apologizing and reconciling process, they fell in love. In the second, she was surprised but pleased at his interest, but in the throes of a bad marriage, she jumped ship, and two marriages sank.

As with any other innocent activity that eventually gets out of hand, flirting can be a good and natural part of a person's progression toward true love. God made us able to respond emotionally and physically to attention from the opposite sex, and that is the initial aim of flirting. But like any of His gifts, this is one that can be cheapened and counterfeited and used for evil as well as for good.

I was twelve when I first experienced the euphoric surge of excitement at knowing that a girl and I had locked eyes on purpose. What began as an accident became an anticipated activity. What a revelation! It happened like this:

I helped a friend deliver papers on his route every day. We traded off, from one day to the next, handling the two halves of the territory. One day I tossed a paper onto the big front porch of a house, then moved on to the next home. I had just dropped that paper on the steps when I heard the door of the first house open and saw a girl about my age come out to retrieve the paper.

I recognized her from school, though I didn't know her—not even her name. She was probably a year ahead of me. As she bent to pick up the paper, her long brown hair cascaded over her face, and as she stood up, she flipped it back into place with a turn of her head. And she looked right at me.

I had been idly watching her as I moved along, but I was embarrassed that she saw me, so I quickly looked elsewhere. But what was that out of the corner of my eye? Had I turned too quickly? Had she smiled at me? I shot a fast double take her way; she had already turned back toward the door. But out of the corner of her eye she must have seen me looking back at her, so she turned back.

We smiled shyly at each other and said nothing. I don't know what she was thinking. Probably nothing. To a twelve-year-old, a thirteen-year-old is almost an adult, and I was very much on the young side of twelve. I probably had a ball glove in my newspaper bag, maybe even a pocketful of marbles. My hair would have been flying.

She was more sophisticated. Grown up. She was probably just smiling at some dumb paperboy, I decided, but I sure liked it when she smiled at me. The next day I pleaded with my friend to let me deliver on the same end of the route again. Nothing doing. I would have to wait another twenty-four hours to see that smile. I never considered that it was probably a fluke. Why hadn't I ever seen her before? Did I think she would wait at the window for me next time?

Two days later my hair was combed, my cleanest jeans were on, and I wore new tennies. I imagined her watching me from halfway down the block, so I did my best to look older, more conscientious, important, in a hurry, doing a good job. A couple of times I walked past a house without dropping a paper, only to nonchalantly flip one behind my back to the precise spot. I was hot.

At the house before hers I had to mount the steps and put the paper in the rungs under the mailbox. I casually bounded up the stairs two at a time, slipped the paper in, and jumped all the way to the ground. No problem. I don't know what I would have done if I had wound up with a face full of dirt. I never thought about that. I imagined her eyes on me, smiling, and I could do anything. Down deep I was hoping against hope that she was home and would come out to get the paper again.

I approached her porch. Slowly. Dropped the paper in front of the door. Turned. More slowly. Then moved resolutely to the next house. No action. No movement. No noise. I looked back several times, hoping. Nothing. Maybe that's why I was doing only one side of the street at a time. When I crossed at the corner and delivered papers to the other side of the same street, I could see her porch for half a block. I worked ever so deliberately.

The house directly across from hers was not that of a paper subscriber, but it sat on a wide expanse of lawn. I delivered the paper to the house before it, then traversed the entire distance to the next subscriber with my head turned, staring at the magic porch. Had someone planted a tree in my path the day before, I'd have worn it home.

The trail I blazed was as circuitous as you can imagine for one without his eye on where he's going.

But my persistence paid off. She appeared. And she was dressed up in a fluffy, red dress. She stepped out, picked up the paper, went to the edge of the porch, leaned on the railing, and smiled at me across the street. Her smile and her eyes followed me until I had to look away or careen into the street. This had been no accident. I couldn't swear she had dressed up just for me—clearly she had somewhere to go early that evening—but she had looked for me, found me, smiled at me, and made it obvious she was pleased to have done so. I began wondering where we might raise our family.

You can't imagine the thrill, unless you remember similar experiences on the threshold of puberty. We continued that ritual every other day for a little over a week, until I found out she was doing the same to my friend, the other delivery boy. I hadn't even said hello to my intended, and she had already cheated on me. I wasn't even motivated to fight for her. My interest cooled overnight.

As a freshman in high school I enjoyed another silent flirting season with a girl in my algebra class. She was a fresh-faced blond with glasses and a turned-up nose, and for some reason, I loved to look at her. We sat on opposite sides of the room. To see her, I had to lean back and look past all the heads in my row. One day she caught me looking, so I turned back. But when I sneaked another peek, she was staring right at me.

It seemed my heart skipped a beat. Was it obvious to everyone in the class that we were in love? I didn't even know her name, yet my pulse quickened and I was short of breath when I caught her gaze, me leaning back and her leaning forward. We didn't even smile at each other. This was too intense. Occasionally I tried to tell myself I was imagining this, and then we would settle into our desks, the teacher would begin his lecture, and I would zero in on that pair of eyes.

For a week we stared at each other, sometimes for twenty minutes at a time. I was stunned the teacher did not call us down for it, or at least one of us. He would not have been able to see both of us staring at the same time, but he could have followed one's gaze to the other. Either he didn't notice or he had already given up on my algebra potential.

One day, when I had finally learned her name, I mustered the courage to send a note across to her. Everybody looked at her and then at me as she read it. "See you after class?" it read. She looked up at me, still unsmiling, and nodded. Has there ever been a longer forty-minute wait? I couldn't even look at her that day. I just studied the clock.

After class she went out the door, turned right, stood with her back against the wall and her books embraced in front of her and waited expectantly. "Hi," I said.

"Hi," she said.

I wanted so badly to say something cool like, "You know, I've really enjoyed studying you these last several days, and I thought it was time we got better acquainted."

But I didn't. I said, "Um, I was wonderin' if you wouldn't mind if I walked you to your next class."

"No problem," she said, in a voice too hard, too sharp for such a pretty face. "'Cept it's like right here." She nodded to the study hall next to the algebra room.

"Oh, yeah, well, I guess you can make it there by yourself all right."

"Yeah," she said, and walked away.

I saw her again, but I never looked at her, if you know what I mean. I was learning valuable lessons in illusion versus reality.

My point in these two anecdotes, however, is that the same surge of ecstasy is available to me—or to any man—today. If you work at it, you can catch a woman's eye and see if she wants to play the game. The problem is that it's short of adultery only in the physical sense, and it can lead to that.

I'm sometimes embarrassed in public, maybe in a restaurant, when I happen to catch the gaze of a woman, look away, and then we look back at the same moment. Neither of us is looking for anything; each is embarrassed and wonders what the other thinks. I usually smile apologetically and then fight the urge to look once more.

I'm not looking for other women's eyes, and I don't want them or anyone, especially my wife, to think that I am. There is a comfort, a sensuality, a sexuality, a bonding deeper than with anyone else when I look deeply into Dianna's eyes. I know her, I can read her, and we can communicate that way.

I also communicate with her by flirting, touching, caressing, yes, even playing footsie. We consider these fun and funny ways of communicating to be personal and private. They make up a part of our sexual language of love, and every one of them, even the looks, smiles, and suggestive comments—are off-limits for anyone else.

I don't flirt with anyone but my wife, and vice versa.

CHAPTER FIVE

THE BIBLICAL BASIS FOR HEDGES

People will tell you to beware of legalism, even in the area of sexual purity. It's true that a balanced, appropriate view makes our stand attractive rather than shrill, but Scripture is clear. There's a price to pay.

W e're far enough along in this book now that the following should be no revelation: I am making the assumption that you care what God thinks about your life. If you don't care, you're reading the wrong book. I believe in God, and I accept the Bible as the basis of authority for my life. If you don't, this has all long since appeared foolish to you anyway.

Perhaps you're in the middle on these issues. Maybe you aren't sure about a personal God and are very unsure whether the Bible is relevant. That puts you in the same category, sadly, as many who call themselves Christians. They are smorgasbord church people who sample what looks good to them and leave what doesn't. And a God who cares about our sexual conduct and even has rules regarding it doesn't seem to fit our contemporary "me first" society.

The problem with that view is that it assumes that God has rules for rules' sake. He's just a spoil sport, trying to make a goody-two-shoes out of everybody. If we can't find practical reasons for following His rules, we justify ignoring them.

My simple mind cries out for a God who is personal, orderly, and logical. I believe that a God who created everything and loved us enough to make the supreme sacrifice for us has reasons for His prohibitions and would rather see us happy and fulfilled than miserable and confined.

If I'm right, there must be sense and logic behind His rules. Let's look at them briefly to determine what they are, and then let me make an amateur's—or at least a layman's attempt at making them fit with my view of God as a fulfiller, not a taskmaster.

HERE COMES THE JUDGE

Jesus talks about the law most extensively in Matthew 5:17–19:

> "Do not think that I came to destroy the Law or the Prophets. I did not come to destroy but to fulfill. For assuredly, I say to you, till heaven and earth pass away, one jot or one tittle will by no means pass from the law till all is fulfilled. Whoever therefore breaks one of the least of these commandments, and teaches men so, shall be called least in the kingdom of heaven; but whoever does and teaches them, he shall be called great in the kingdom of heaven."

The law He's talking about, of course, is the Ten Commandments. Most people, even nonchurchgoers, can remember a few of them. Don't lie, don't murder, don't commit adultery, don't steal. We can see the obvious problems with lying, stealing, and murdering, but if sex is so good and beautiful and fun, what's wrong with a little adultery among friends?

And what is Jesus talking about when He says He's fulfilling, not replacing, the law? This is the wrong forum from which to get into Jesus' claims of deity, but suffice it to say He was establishing Himself as one with God, the Son of God, the fulfillment of God's law. The embodiment of perfection, the personification of sinlessness, was

Jesus Christ. Now—lest anyone else claim to also qualify as the righteous king—Jesus, in essence, changes all the rules.

Later in the same discourse He says,

> "Unless your righteousness exceeds the righteousness of the scribes and Pharisees, you will by no means enter the kingdom of heaven. You have heard that it was said to those of old, You shall not murder, and whoever murders will be in danger of the judgment. But I say to you that whoever is angry with his brother without a cause shall be in danger of the judgment." (Matthew 5:20–22)

Murder is worthy of judgment, but now even anger with a brother is just as bad! Who can live up to that standard? Only Jesus. Then He gets down to the toughest part. "You have heard that it was said to those of old, 'You shall not commit adultery.' But I say to you that whoever looks at a woman to lust for her has already committed adultery with her in his heart" (Matthew 5:27–28).

What is the point of all that? Wasn't the original law hard enough? Wasn't it a good enough standard by which to be judged? Why would Jesus rewrite it and make it impossible? Let me speculate, as a layman. Jesus, the God/Man who died for us, could take no pleasure in making life difficult or unachievable for us. Clearly He was setting a standard here to make a point. The point was that if someone was somehow able to keep from lying, murdering, even coveting for an entire lifetime, there was no way to ever dream of following this new standard. Hatred, anger, is murder. Lust is adultery. We're all guilty.

Only Jesus could meet and fulfill that standard, so we are forced to rely upon Him for our standing before God. He takes the penalty for our sin; He becomes our advocate before a Holy God. God looks at us and sees not our sin but the perfection of Jesus, and we who would otherwise be unqualified to be in His presence are assured of a place with Him for eternity. The apostle Paul said it this way in 2 Corinthians 5:21: "For He made Him who knew no sin to be sin for us, that we might become the righteousness of God in Him."

BETWEEN OUR EARS

When my friend Robert Wolgemuth teaches from Matthew, he

makes the point that what Jesus was really talking about was not murder or adultery but attitudes, what goes on between our ears. He's
talking about the things most people can't see. Jesus is saying that
the law is not something you do or don't do; it's something you are.

The question then arises as to why Jesus puts adultery in the same
category as murder. Leviticus 20:10 says, "'The man who commits
adultery with another man's wife, he who commits adultery with
his neighbor's wife, the adulterer and the adulteress, shall surely be put
to death.'" Murderers and adulterers deserve death according to the
law, and Jesus has made the law impossible to obey. What's going on?

A lot of this, I admit, will not be comprehensible this side of
heaven, but we had better find out why these two sins are considered equally reprehensible before we start building our lives on our
own principles. Why was it so important that people not commit
adultery? I submit that the reasons, whatever they are, are the same
reasons we need to build hedges around our hearts, eyes, hands, spouses,
and marriages. If adultery is in the same class as murder, it is a threat
not only to our marriages but to our very lives.

Some have said that only a crazy person can commit murder. A
man or woman has to lose contact with reality to become so angry
or distraught or jealous that he or she can take another's life. I've found
that adulterers suffer from this same malady. They'll violate a vow they
made years before, drag their wife and family through torture and disgrace, and set aside or reformat their entire set of values. How else
could a man justify the chaos wrought by his actions?

A friend of mine once found himself pulled into a situation in
which he was to officiate at a family meeting where an adulterous
father tried to explain to his children, in front of his wife, why he
was leaving her for another woman. One of this man's first asser-
tions was that he had never really loved his wife. (To a person who
believes that love is a feeling rather than an act of the will, falling
out of love or deciding you never loved someone is a convenient
rationalization.)

The young teenaged son admitted to his father that he didn't
understand. "How, after all these years, can you say you don't love
Mom? After all we've done together . . ."

The only way the man could live with himself was to tell himself lies, to reorder his standards. He asked his younger daughter, "Honey, tell me what you're thinking."

She looked up at him, fighting for composure. "I'm thinking I'm sad," she said.

ADULTERY CAUSES CHAOS

Adulterers are liars, and they are as good at it as alcoholics are. Another friend of mine was awakened in the middle of the night by a call informing him of the infidelity of a good buddy. He didn't believe it, so he went to see his buddy. "Dave," he said, "what's the story about you and this woman?"

Dave played dumb. "It's not true," he said, looking my friend squarely in the eye. "No way. Not me. Never have, never will."

"Wait a minute," my friend said. "What about all these allegations?" He proceeded with a litany of charges, names, dates, places.

"Someone's trying to frame me," Dave said. "Never happened."

What a relief! My friend wouldn't have to see this man confess to his wife, disappointing her, breaking her heart, ruining their marriage. It was good news.

Good news until two months later, when my friend's wife got a call from Dave's wife. She was frantic, nearly hysterical. My friend and his wife raced to her home while Dave was away on business. She had discovered the affair and had a pile of evidence to prove it. My friend was assigned to meet Dave at the airport upon his return. Rather than being met by his family as usual, Dave was puzzled to see my friend standing there solemnly. "It's over," my friend told him. "Your wife knows and I know."

He led him out to the parking lot where his car was jammed floor to ceiling with his belongings. There was barely room for the two men. Dave drove my friend home and then set out to look for a place to live. My friend watched him pull out of sight in the darkness and he knew: Adultery causes chaos.

I had an acquaintance once tell me that, yes, he had been seeing another woman, but that, no, he was not interested in her romantically and didn't think she was interested in him either. They were just friends. Middle of the night, sometimes all-night friends. He liked her baby daughter. Yeah, that was it. They had a lot in common, talked easily, liked each other's company. I told him he didn't have the right to have a woman as a close friend when he was married and that it was slowly killing his wife.

He seemed to see the light, said he would break it off that night, and I returned to his wife with the wonderful news. That night he met the woman after work. I saw them embrace and kiss before they left the state in her car. By the time he really came to his senses and pleaded for his wife to take him back—he missed his four boys terribly—the divorce was final.

Adultery causes chaos.

ARE YOU GUILTY?

As much as television, movies, and videos try to convince us otherwise, adultery is not funny. The media has convinced too many people that adultery is no more serious than exceeding the speed limit. Everybody does it. This is a new age. Don't be so old-fashioned. Get with the program!

If the Bible deals with this modern issue, it had better do it in a sophisticated, up-to-date way or no one will pay any attention. What could a musty old religious tome have to say about life as we know it today?

Remember Leviticus 20:10? Adulterers are put to death. Remember Matthew 5:27–28? Lust is adultery. Are you guilty? You may be guilty of more than lust. You may be guilty of adultery itself, and more than once. Be glad Jesus fulfilled the law for you, because even if your offense was the attitude and not the act, you were still guilty.

There is forgiveness. There is starting over. There is a future for you. John 8:3–11 tells this story:

> Then the scribes and Pharisees brought to Him a woman caught in adultery. And when they had set her in the midst, they said to Him, "Teacher, this woman was caught in adultery, in the very act. Now Moses, in the law, commanded us that such should be stoned. But what do You say?" This they said, testing Him, that they might have something of which to accuse Him.
>
> But Jesus stooped down and wrote on the ground with His finger, as though He did not hear. So when they continued ask-

ing Him, He raised Himself up and said to them, "He who is without sin among you, let him throw a stone at her first." And again He stooped down and wrote on the ground.

Then those who heard it, being convicted by their conscience, went out one by one, beginning with the oldest even to the last. And Jesus was left alone, and the woman standing in the midst. When Jesus had raised Himself up and saw no one but the woman, He said to her, "Woman, where are those accusers of yours? Has no one condemned you?"

She said, "No one, Lord."

And Jesus said to her, "Neither do I condemn you; go and sin no more."

Don't make the mistake of assuming that Jesus was condoning adultery. He called her adultery sin and told her to sin no more. I've always appreciated the irony in this story. Jesus says that the one "among you" without sin should cast the first stone. Have you ever thought about the fact that there was one among them who was without sin? It was Jesus Himself. And He chose not to cast a stone. His point was to label the accusers as adulterers, because indeed we all are—even if we have never committed the act. We may not have murdered, but we have hated; and we may not have committed adultery, but we have lusted. And Jesus says to us with the voice of loving forgiveness that rings through the ages: "Neither do I condemn you; go and sin no more."

Out of pure thanks and appreciation and wonder at that freeing compassion, we should want to obey.

BUT WHAT ABOUT TEMPTATION?

First Corinthians 10:13 says, "No temptation has overtaken you except such as is common to man; but God is faithful, who will not allow you to be tempted beyond what you are able, but with the temptation will also make the way of escape, that you may be able to bear it."

The problem with lust and its result is that it is difficult to resist and that people try everything to win over it. They pray, they stand

and fight, they resolve, when all the while our plan of attack is clear—and it's not a plan of attack at all. We are to retreat! Paul wrote to his young friend in 2 Timothy 2:22, "Flee also youthful lusts; but pursue righteousness, faith, love, peace with those who call on the Lord out of a pure heart."

The problem with the temptation verse (1 Corinthians 10:13) is that people apply it too late. Ten minutes into foreplay with the wrong partner, they're ready to seek that way of escape that was supposed to have come with the temptation. That's just it: The escape comes with the temptation. It's preventive medicine, not first aid after you've already set your course on a path toward injury.

MORE BIBLICAL BASES FOR HEDGES

Need any more evidence that there are biblical bases for planting hedges around your marriage? Psalm 89:40 implies that strongholds are brought to ruin when hedges are broken down. Job 1:10 implies that Job was so richly blessed—before God allowed him to be tested—because God had made a hedge around him, his household, "and around all that he has on every side."

Jesus told parables about landowners who planted vineyards and protected them with hedges. When those hedges were trampled or removed, ruin came to the precious possessions of the landowners.

We hold people and relationships much more precious than land or holdings. If we can keep from deceiving ourselves about our own resolve and inner strength, we will see the necessity for a healthy row of blossoming hedges that keep love in and infidelity out.

CHAPTER SIX

THE POWER OF SELF-DECEPTION

Knowing our own weakness is one way to begin tilling the soil for the seeds of the hedges that will protect us.

Before I get into my own list of hedges, which evidences also my own weaknesses, I need to ask you: What are yours?

A friend of mine has planted two hedges for his business life. First, he stays away from pornography, which is becoming more difficult all the time. Rather than pretend to be disgusted and turned off by it, he admits it can be seductive. It can be tantalizing. Although looking at pornography may result in his feeling disgusted with himself and wondering how he could ever be attracted to such a cheapening of God's gift of sexuality, he is more successful in fending it off by acknowledging in *advance* that it's something he wants to avoid. So, if it's pumped into his hotel room via television, he tells the front desk to lock it out. Sometimes the clerk will act surprised or wonder aloud if he has children with him in spite of his reservation as a single. My friend doesn't let this daunt him. He clarifies he is alone and insists on the lock-out service. As part of this hedge he often travels with his business partner, and they keep each other honest.

What if my friend told himself that since he had gone many years without succumbing to the temptation of pornography, he could surely travel on his own and not have to embarrass himself by asking a desk clerk half his age to lock out the adult movies? A sexy show on regular television might whet his appetite for something racier, something he might not even consider if he did not know it was available. But with the seemingly innocuous touch of a button, with the first five minutes not even billed to his room, he might convince himself he's mature enough to satisfy his curiosity.

The key is preventive maintenance. Once that first step has been taken down the road of self-deceit and rationalization, there is no turning back. Each excuse sounds more plausible, and, before he knows it, the typical male has satisfied every curiosity, every urge. Regardless of the remorse, the self-loathing, and the pledges for the future, the pattern will repeat itself for as long as he refuses to flee. There is no other defense.

My friend's second hedge comes in the form of pictures he carries in his wallet of his wife and his two daughters. These pictures serve the usual function of reminding him of his loved ones and allowing him to brag about his beautiful family. But they also serve as a safety net, which he used several years ago when he found himself next to a beautiful, young, single woman on an airplane.

Normally he feigns fatigue and isn't interested in conversing during a long flight, but this woman was fun to look at and more fun to talk to. He asked her about herself. She sounded more interesting and exciting every minute. She was staying in the same city for which he was headed. She had a car and could give him a ride to his hotel. And why not? Each seemed nice enough to the other.

WE'RE NOT ALL THE SAME

To illustrate differences in styles and personalities, I must say that I would have hid behind a hedge I planted years ago that does not allow me to accept a ride alone with an unrelated woman. I wouldn't trust my weak, self-deceiving, rationalizing mind once I was alone with a beautiful, willing female. My friend, however, used a different hedge and was able to accept the ride. When she asked about him, he pulled out his wallet. Before he showed her the photos of his wife and daughters, he looked at them himself.

"It was as if they spoke to me right out of that wallet," he says. "They said, 'Thanks, Daddy, for being faithful to Mom and to us.'"

He smiled as he showed her the pictures and spoke lovingly of his family, especially of his wife, Jackie. The conversation mellowed and became friendly in a different sort of way than before. My friend rode with the woman to his hotel, shook her hand, and heard her say in farewell, "Say hi to Jackie for me."

"If you think I didn't want to spend the night with her," he admits, "you're crazy."

But it sure wasn't worth his spiritual, mental, and family life. He used a hedge, one that wouldn't have worked for me, but an effective one for him and his personality.

CUSTOM-MAKE YOUR HEDGES

Just as my friend used a different hedge than I would have, so there are also temptations difficult for some and not for others. For instance, the temptation to frequent prostitutes happens to be one I can only write about and not identify with. I know it's a very real temptation and that it has been the ruin "of many a poor boy." I know this temptation is one that has been the ruin of Christians, even preachers, and that the book of Proverbs is replete with admonitions about and against it. It just happens, though, that this is an area in which I have never been tempted—although I was propositioned once.

I was on business in Cleveland and had innocently booked a hotel room in the seediest part of town. The hotel chain was a large, well-known one, so I was stunned when I went out for a walk and found myself in the red-light district. While I might have been young and curious enough to be tempted to slip into an adult movie theater, my fear of a fire bomb or a raid was sufficient defense. "Christian Writer Among Dead in Adult Theater Fire" would have been a nice final page for my wife's scrapbook, huh? I know that fear of detection is not the highest motive for avoiding such temptations, but you tend to use whatever works at the point of weakness and develop the proper spiritual discipline and reasoning later.

It was dark out and the area seemed overrun with potential muggers. I was hurrying back to my hotel when a teenaged hooker made me an offer I'm sure she thought I couldn't refuse. I was nearly paralyzed. I had always wondered what I would say. This girl was not unattractive, but I had not the slightest second thought. The question was what I would say.

I could have ignored her and kept walking, which is what I would do today. I could have looked shocked and disgusted and told her off. I could have witnessed to her. (I have friends who do that, but I don't recommend it unless you're with your wife or a group. Say the wrong thing while witnessing to an undercover cop and you'll find yourself, and your ministry, in the overnight lockup. Or, if you're alone, try explaining to someone who recognizes you just what you were saying to the hooker on the corner.)

Well, I was in my early twenties, and all my upbringing and training came to the fore. I was polite, maddeningly, and as I think about it, hilariously polite. I said, "No, thanks."

She acted disappointed and asked, "Are you sure?"

"Yes, but thanks, anyway."

"Whatcha wanna be alone for tonight when you can be indulgin' yourself?"

"That's all right," I said. "I hope you won't be offended if I pass."

As she shrugged and trudged on, I thought, *I hope you won't be offended! What a stupid thing to say!* That girl was threatening my moral and spiritual health, trying to get me to jeopardize my marriage, encouraging me to go against everything I had ever been taught or believed, and I was polite!

ARE YOU LONESOME TONIGHT?

I was with an older colleague in a top-flight hotel in Detroit several years ago when we smelled perfume and heard a spraying sound near the door. He tiptoed over in stocking feet to discover that indeed someone was spraying perfume under the door. He swung the door open to see a middle-aged woman in a miniskirt leaning seductively in the frame.

"You lonely, hon?" she asked.

"I'll never be that lonely," he said, and shut the door. I wish I'd thought of that.

On the other hand, I heard a prominent preacher say that he got on an elevator in a hotel in a big city and was greeted warmly by two beautiful young women. A glib, social type, he engaged them in friendly banter for a few seconds before they boldly asked him to join them in their room. "In the space of less than a minute, I had to make a decision," he says. "I was far from home. I could get away with this, in one sense." He knew it would be wrong, silently prayed for the strength to resist, and left the elevator on his own floor.

I know it can be disappointing to hear that a man of God would even have to talk himself out of something like that, but each man carries with him his own weaknesses and temptations. Whereas I have never been able even to imagine being attracted to or turned on by a woman who has had sex with others all day, I need to plant hedges against being alone or working too closely with women I simply admire or like. That, to me, is more dangerous. I could see myself becoming attached to or enamored with someone I worked with if I didn't emphasize keeping everything on a professional basis.

A WORD OF CAUTION

Just because I cannot imagine ever being tempted by a prostitute doesn't mean I am cavalier or naive about their areas and haunts. There are other forms of illegal activity that don't tempt me either, but I don't hang around their headquarters.

In other words, if you're tempted to cruise prostitution row, the way of escape is to do something else. Go somewhere else. While you have your wits about you—before you're at the edge of the abyss —make a rule for yourself that you won't drive within a certain number of blocks of the area for any reason.

Some hedges may appear ridiculous to you because they are unnecessary in your life—just like the one above is for me. I used to drive home right through an area where hookers frequented the corners. I knew enough not to look interested, because I truly wasn't. I was curious, sure, wondering about these sad girls with wasted bodies and faces, clearly addicted to drugs, waving at cars and trying to avoid detection by police. But tempting it was not.

A man I used to work with told me he drove through that area and that as he was looking at a hooker while at a stoplight, she approached his car. She asked if he wanted a date. He said no, but she seemed friendly and so he asked her what the going rate was for a date. She told him, he smiled at her, waved, and drove off. I knew him. He would not have been any more attracted to a prostitute than I was, but he had been stupid. Somehow, even with the spate of documentaries and dramas about the world of prostitution, he had missed the fact that negotiating the price is the operative offense that can get you locked up. Had his hooker been an undercover cop, he would have been arrested for negotiating with a prostitute.

STUPIDITY

Too many men are stupid in other ways. They think they can handle any temptation. Their resolve, their marriage, their spirituality will carry the day. These men are self-deceived, and we all know too many of them.

No one wants to admit he has a problem or a weakness. I confess it bothered me when I heard the minister in the hotel elevator story above give that account. I wondered why he didn't admit to some other, less offensive temptation, like maybe the urge to spend more on a car than he should have. For some reason we don't want our spiritual heroes to be human. Wives don't want their husbands to be human. Kids don't want their dads to be human. We'd all like to know someone who is so spiritual, so wise, so disciplined that he could ignore or throw away a men's magazine left in his hotel room by the previous guest. I'll tell you, if I didn't throw it out upon first discovering it, ignoring it would be a chore.

No one likes to admit that. I can hear people saying, "How disgusting! Who would want to poison his mind with that trash?"

Certainly not I. Or would I? All I know to do, according to Paul's letter to Timothy, is to flee. Why? Because of what Paul also says in his letter to the Romans:

For what I am doing, I do not understand. For what I will to do, that I do not practice; but what I hate, that I do. If, then, I do what I will not to do, I agree with the law that it is good. But now, it is no longer I who do it, but sin that dwells in me. For I know that in me (that is, in my flesh) nothing good dwells; for to will is present with me, but how to perform what is good I do not find. (Romans 7:15–18)

And in Romans 7:22–25:

For I delight in the law of God according to the inward man. But I see another law in my members, warring against the law of my mind, and bringing me into captivity to the law of sin which is in my members. O wretched man that I am! Who will deliver me from this body of death? I thank God—through Jesus Christ our Lord! So then, with the mind I myself serve the law of God, but with the flesh the law of sin.

The only future in self-deceit is ruin. Let's quit kidding ourselves. No, we don't have to broadcast every base thought and urge to the public, but in our heart of hearts, let's avoid denial. If the greatest missionary in the history of Christendom could make himself vulnerable by admitting that in his flesh dwells no good thing, who are we to think we should be above carnal drives and desires?

The only regret I have since going on my hedges campaign a few years ago is that occasionally some wonderful woman colleague or new friend will say, "I don't know how to act around you, whether I can touch you or not, or just shake your hand."

The last thing I want is a reputation as a guy who is desperately trying to contain his lustful thoughts for everything in a skirt. As you'll see later, I do trust myself to touch and even embrace women I'm not related to. But I have strict guidelines and hedges, because I do not want to fall to my own self-deceit.

Let's start planting some practical hedges.

PART TWO

HOW TO START PLANTING

Here are pragmatic ways to guard ourselves against our weaknesses. We can plant hedges only after we have determined where they must grow.

CHAPTER SEVEN

TWO'S COMPANY; THREE'S SECURITY

Hedge No. 1—Whenever I need to meet or dine or travel with an unrelated woman, I make it a threesome. Should an unavoidable last-minute complication make this impossible, my wife hears it from me first.

This hedge is about pure logic. Scripture is clear that Christians should "abstain from sexual immorality" (1 Thessalonians 4:3), for "this is the will of God."

So, you ask, what is sexually immoral about meeting, dining, or traveling with an unrelated woman? Nothing. But it is also true that, unless I am alone with a woman, I will not engage in immorality.

But, you're still wondering, what does one necessarily have to do with the other? In other words, if it is true that I won't commit adultery if I'm not alone with a woman, is it also true that if I am alone with her, I will? No, that is not logical. Logic says that if I am following the biblical injunction to abstain from even the appearance of evil (1 Thessalonians 5:22), I will also abstain from the evil itself.

My philosophy is, if you take care of how things look, you take care of how they are.

Where I work we have a tiny window in every office door. When these were installed forty or fifty years ago, they were not intended to make immorality difficult. They were intended to eliminate suspicion and protect reputations. As long as that little eye to the outside world is uncovered, no one feels free to attempt anything untoward, and, just as importantly, no one else is suspicious about what goes on behind closed doors. Were it not for those little windows, I would feel obligated to invite my secretary to every brief meeting I might have with a woman, or to keep my door open.

Why? Am I really that weak or dangerous? Or are those with whom I might meet? No, I don't think so. But I don't want the reputations of the woman, my employer, my wife, or my Lord—not to mention myself—even to be questioned.

RISKY BUSINESS

One of the saddest and scariest stories I've ever heard on this subject was about a young evangelist. He was just barely twenty-one, on fire for God, effective in his preaching and soul-winning, and in great demand from local churches. He had preached several large crusades and was soon invited to an area-wide effort at which he would be the main speaker.

Though he was not yet even out of college, he was a protégé of international evangelist Sammy Tippit and was admired and considered wise. Though he didn't have a steady girlfriend, he dated regularly at Bible college. Spiritually he was alert and mature. He was, however, naive. The first night of the crusade he headed up the counseling ministry in a large room near the pastor's study. A beautiful teenager asked if she could speak with him personally. He tried to assign her to someone else, but, when she persisted, he agreed for her to wait until he was finished with the others.

More than an hour after the meeting had ended, the rest of the counselors and counselees had left, and he was alone with the young girl. A few minutes later she burst from the room, screaming, "He made a pass at me! He wanted to make love to me!"

That very night the pastor of the host church and a small group of the crusade planners confronted the young preacher and demanded an explanation. He denied the girl's charge but had no witnesses. The girl had seemed an upstanding young woman in the church, and there was no reason to disbelieve her story.

"What did happen in that room?" the pastor demanded.

"To tell you that would be to make an accusation behind someone's back," he said. "Which is what happened to me. I ask only that I be allowed to face my accuser." The pastor and the others canceled the rest of the crusade and agreed that the young woman should be asked to face the preacher in their presence. Two nights later she showed up with her parents at a private board meeting. The pastor asked if she would care to speak about her charges against the preacher.

"She has already said all she has to say," her father said sternly, her mother nodding and glaring at the accused.

"Would you, son, care to share your version of what happened in that room the other night?"

"No, sir," the evangelist said. "I see no future in that. Only she and I know the truth, and I cannot defend myself. I'd just like to say this to her. Cindy, you know what happened and what didn't happen in that room. If you don't tell the truth, I will be branded and may never preach again. This will damage my reputation and that of this church and even that of God. If I did what you say I did, I deserve no better, but we both know that is not the truth. I'm begging you in the name of Christ to set the record straight."

The silence hung heavy as the board and her parents watched her face contort into a grimace before the tears began to flow. "I lied," she said quietly. "I'm sorry. I lied. He didn't make a pass at me; I made a pass at him. When he turned me down I was so embarrassed and ashamed and angry that I made up that story. I'm so sorry!"

Had that young evangelist not had the wisdom to face his accuser in just that manner, his ministry might have been ruined forever. And had not God worked in that young girl's heart, she might have sat there silently, refusing to change her story.

That preacher is no longer young. He has never again allowed himself to be alone in a room with a female to whom he is not related. Along with his spiritual wisdom came a painful, almost fatal, farewell to naïveté. He might have been embarrassed that night, early in his ministry, if he'd had to ask someone to stay with him while he counseled the young woman, or if he'd had to tell her that he could see her only in the sanctuary. But now he sees embarrassment, or sometimes even the risk of offending, as a small price to pay for the protection of all those reputations.

A MOVABLE FEAST

You may have noticed that I included dining alone with my meeting and traveling prohibitions. I don't know why, but there is something very personal and even intimate about eating with someone. If that weren't true, why are so many dates centered on food?

My embargo against dining alone with an unrelated woman is also for my wife's sake. Dianna is not the jealous type, but this way I don't have to keep track of every lunch partner so I can tell her about each one before someone else does. People love to say, "Oh, I saw your husband having lunch with so-and-so the other day," with that lilt in their voice that begs to know if anything is going on.

My intention is that if someone told Dianna that I had been seen with someone alone, she would immediately say, "No, he wasn't," because she knows if that were to happen, she would have known about it first. Once my secretary and I invited a friend of hers to have lunch with us. At the last minute the friend was unable to go. We just changed our plans, had the lunch delivered, and enjoyed it in the office with the door open. I mentioned it to my wife in advance, just as a courtesy.

The first few times my secretary and I changed our plans because a third party was unavailable, she may have thought I was being a bit ridiculous. She had no designs on me, and vice versa, though we are friends. I'm sure I seemed to be straining at a gnat. But over the years, as we have seen marriage after marriage fail and family after family suffer, my prudish rules seem to have made more sense.

There will always be times, of course, when rules cannot be followed to the letter. During the years when I was headquartered ten miles north of our campus, I occasionally found it necessary to drop a woman off at one location or another. Sometimes this came up when it was inconvenient or impossible to let my wife know in advance. It would have been silly to wait until I could either tell her or appear to ask permission. I told her later and, though she never demanded it, she always appreciated it. On those rare occasions when I do question the reputation of one with whom I might have to meet or dine or travel alone, I don't think twice. I don't call to inform Dianna or to ask her permission. I just don't go.

ON THE ROAD

Travel is chock-full of dangerous possibilities for appearances and behavior. Assume that every motive is pure. How does it look for a man and a woman who don't belong to each other to be on a long trip together, in a car, on a plane, in a cab, at the same hotel, even if in separate rooms?

I had to travel to a distant city with a woman manager who reported to me, so I asked her to select someone to go with us. The young woman she chose woke up ill on departure day, and I didn't learn about it until I arrived at the airport. My manager was also a friend of our family, which helped, and though she was single and close to my age, our relationship was such that we didn't worry about anything happening. We worried most about how the trip would look.

Because originally she had planned to room with the younger woman, we had thought nothing of booking our seats together on the plane and sharing a ride to—and staying at—the same hotel. All those arrangements had been made, but I was willing to absorb the cost of canceling them if necessary. My first query was to the manager herself. She expressed her knowledge of, trust in, and respect for me; she said she had no problem traveling with me, but that she would understand if I chose not to go.

I then called my boss. An unwritten rule in our ministry forbids unrelated men and women traveling together without a third party, but under the circumstances my boss left it up to me. With a phone call from the airport, I passed the buck to my wife. She nearly laughed. The fact that I had called her and had made a practice of keeping her informed of such seeming improprieties for years gave her the confidence to immediately agree.

ADVICE FROM ONE WHO KNOWS

In the July 1985 issue of *Advance* magazine,[1] evangelist Robert

M. Abbott writes that, just as the fact that "a certain percentage of people die annually through traffic accidents does not mean we stop searching for ways to remedy the situation," neither should we be ready to shrug off moral impurity among our leaders.

Abbott continues, "None of us plan[s] to have moral accidents, but we must also plan not to! Danger rides with us all the time." He compares the moral danger to that of a driver pulling several tons of equipment behind his car. "[This] requires more braking power and a longer stopping time.... Brakes! Thank God for brakes!"

Abbott writes that "[we] must learn to keep plenty of space between us and sinful acts, so we can start braking soon enough to stop before it is too late." He offers a list of twenty-eight times when we might "need to put on the brakes early and well." Among them:

- When you are so busy there is no time to be alone with God.
- When you are too busy to spend at least one relaxed evening a week with your wife and family.
- When you feel you deserve more attention than you are getting at home.
- When you wouldn't want your wife or colleagues to see what you are reading or looking at.
- When the romance in your marriage is fading.
- When your charisma, appearance, and personality are attractive to women and you are tempted to make the most of it.
- When you enjoy fantasizing about an illicit relationship.
- When a woman makes herself available by her behavior.
- When some woman tells you how wonderful you are and how much she loves you.
- When Scriptures concerning adultery are for others, not you.
- When you start feeling sorry for yourself.
- When you hope God isn't looking or listening.

Sadly, so many pastors and other Christian leaders fall into sexual temptation because of a common problem. They have planted no hedges and find themselves counseling weeping, exasperated women who seem to have a lot to offer but are frustrated in bad marriages. They wish their husbands were more spiritual, more popular, had more leadership qualities, were more authoritative, more patient, better listeners, men of the Word, men of prayer.

And guess what? The pastor fits the bill on every point. The woman may be surprised to find herself falling for him, but, once she has, she'll find the fact difficult to hide. And the pastor may at first innocently enjoy being so revered by a woman who needs him. If his wife is nagging him for spending too much time at church, he may begin looking forward to private counseling sessions with a woman who worships him, eats out of his hand, and gives him her full attention.

Pastors and other Christian leaders need hedges as much, if not more, than the rest of us. If they counsel women at all—and they would, in most cases, do better to assign them to some wise, older women in the church— they should counsel with the door open and the secretary close by. Meetings with any female staff member or parishioner should take place only in public or with at least one other person there.

The dining and traveling hedges should never be trampled when it comes to pastors being with unrelated women. And the only reason their standards are stricter than for us rank-and-file types is that, in most cases, more is at stake.

For all of us, however, the price of suspicion is high, and the price of infidelity is even higher. There are more hedges to plant.

NOTE

1. Robert M. Abbott, "Thank God for Brakes," *Advance,* July 1985.

CHAPTER EIGHT

TOUCHY, TOUCHY!

Hedge No. 2—I am careful about touching. While I might shake hands or squeeze an arm or a shoulder in greeting, I embrace only dear friends or relatives, and only in front of others.

I don't know when touching returned to vogue in the United States, but I recall clearly when the encounter group, get-in-touch-with-yourself philosophy finally reached the church. I was in high school in the midsixties, and somewhere around that time something new began happening.

Worship became more expressive. People became more emotional. And maybe because there was a significant Jesus People movement heading east from California, and that movement had originated among street people and hippies accustomed to more openness than the rest of society, certain things became more acceptable in the church.

It wasn't all bad. I was visiting a camp when I was about fifteen or sixteen, and after a particularly moving evening of testimonies, singing, and speaking, people were weeping and swaying—as they sang with arms around each others' shoulders. And they finished by giving God an ovation.

That was kind of interesting and different, but what really impressed me was the freedom everyone felt after that to hug each other. I had a girlfriend I didn't mind hugging, but I wasn't crazy about anyone else hugging her. I was shocked to see high school girls hugging camp leaders I knew were married, but it didn't seem to bother anyone else.

That was at a time in my life when I would have enjoyed hugging any female, but still it didn't seem right. When you're that age, you wonder if you can literally control yourself if given the opportunity to embrace a beautiful girl. Suddenly, it seemed OK to hug anybody who was as happy as you were because we were brother and sister in Christ.

I was slow to catch onto the joy of it, and it was hard to keep emotions and feelings in check when you could embrace an adult woman, plus all the girls your own age. It happened all of a sudden, this new freedom, and there was something vaguely spiritual about it.

The rub (pardon the pun) was that—unless I was the only pervert around—I had a good idea that most of the guys my age were less spiritual and more sensual and physical about all this, regardless of their highest ideals. And we all did have high ideals. As I mentioned in chapter 2, one of my deepest desires was to remain sexually pure— celibate, virginal—before marriage. This I did, with God's (and a chaste girlfriend's) help, but, I confess, this new wrinkle in social behavior was of little assistance.

Say I was a hot-blooded teenager if you want, but this new openness to embrace was both a dream come true and a nightmare for the two sides of my nature. Christian psychologist James Dobson says that outside of hunger, the most powerful of all the human urges and drives is the sexual appetite. He adds that Christians have the same biochemical forces within their bodies that non-Christians do, and I can add from experience that teenagers, especially males, are bursting with erotic yearnings.

Remember, we're talking about a scant twenty-five years ago. This wasn't the Dark Ages. But how far we've come as a society and as a church since then is staggering. We might not want to admit that maybe things were better before the sexual revolution even in the church—but we have to ask ourselves: Were infidelity, divorce, and scandal as rampant then?

No, I'm not blaming it all on a new openness to touching and hugging, but I know stories of people who fell in love because they enjoyed and looked forward to what began as a spiritual expression of brotherly and sisterly love.

The irony here is that I saw this totally from my own narrow, adolescent viewpoint back then. I told myself that women weren't as interested in sex as men were, and that adults certainly weren't as sexually on fire as teens. I was way too young to know the difference between the sexual responses of males and females.

I knew I could be turned on by the very thought of something sensual. Seeing it was even better. Touching, embracing—well that was just short of making love, wasn't it? What I didn't know then, and what statistics, studies, and experts have proven repeatedly since, is that women are not turned on sexually in the same way men are. They are less likely to be aroused by thought or even sight. They are aroused more slowly, more subtly, but touch plays a major role.

How could I have known then that embracing a woman who belonged to someone else might be almost the culmination of lust on my part, while it might be the beginning of arousal for her? Am I saying that this new freedom to express ourselves to each other is wrong, sinful, dirty, inappropriate?

No.

I admit that the church needed some thawing, some warming to each other. Men and women particularly needed to loosen up around each other, talk more, get to know each other better, and, yes, maybe even touch each other once in awhile.

Remember that back then, except for the healthy exception of certain ethnic groups, men did not touch each other either—except for a formal or macho handshake, back slap, or thump on the rump during a ball game. I can't speak to the effect this new unpretentiousness might have had on men tormented by a bent toward homosexuality, but one such suffering friend of mine admitted it was a terrible temptation.

As I've grown older, I've realized more of the good that has come from the new style. I'm much more comfortable around women, and because it is now appropriate to greet them with a squeeze on the arm or even a warm but proper embrace, I feel better about my relationships. There can be a certain friendly and even spiritual intimacy that doesn't cross the line to impropriety or sensuality. Part of that is due to my own maturity (praise the Lord the testosterone season of youth is pretty much past!), but it is also because of the hedge I'm discussing here.

If I embrace only dear friends or relatives and only in the presence of others, I am not even tempted to make the embrace longer or more impassioned than is appropriate. I like hugging women. It's fun, and it can be friendly. But if I allowed myself to embrace just anyone, even dear friends, in private, I would be less confident of my motives and my subsequent actions.

For instance, what would happen if I just lingered an instant to see what kind of reaction I might get? And let's say that reaction was encouraging. We might both pretend it didn't happen, but what about next time? Would we not be carefully checking each other out to see if what we thought we felt the first time was accurate? And what if it was? At what point would we overtly embrace passionately, silently declaring our feelings for each other?

I don't know, and I don't want to know. That's why I keep such activity public, ensuring its appropriateness.

A FUNNY MEMORY

I have a cousin a few years younger than I. She's married and has kids. We've been long-distance buddies for years. Once I was in her state at a writers' conference, and she and her husband invited me for dinner. I waited for her while chatting with a woman from the conference, having idly said my cousin was coming to pick me up.

Oddly, we happened to be discussing this very subject of building hedges around marriages. The woman had read my *Moody Monthly* column on the subject and was telling me some of the hedges she and her husband had planted that fit their careers and lifestyles.

A car slowly pulled up outside, and I thought I recognized my cousin behind the wheel. I said my good-byes, but, as I hurried out, my cousin left the car and headed toward me. Youthful, tanned, and in shorts, she was striking and attractive. "Your cousin, huh?" the woman said, laughing. "I'll bet!"

My cousin had a child sleeping in a baby seat in the back, and I was tempted to drag him out and display him to prove we had a chaperone! My cousin was normally a person I would embrace after not having seen her for a long time, but I decided against it for the sake of appearances. She got a good laugh out of the incident.

A NOT-SO-FUNNY MEMORY

Early in my journalism career a young friend of mine went through a trauma. His brother was a wild kind of a guy. The brother lived in Oregon, and though he had had both a drug and alcohol problem in the past, he somehow landed a job as a security guard. One night after work, while at a party, he scuffled with someone, drew his gun, and shot the man, killing him.

My friend, as you can imagine, was distraught. He worried constantly about his brother. Would he be sentenced? Would he commit suicide? Would he get the death penalty? My friend could hardly work, though his job as a copy boy on the midnight shift was important to our paper.

He was a good friend of the managing editor, a man twenty years his senior. The editor and his wife had taken a liking to the young man and encouraged him in his career. Both had been very sympathetic to his worries over his brother and even helped him financially so he could travel to visit him once.

Upon returning from that visit, my friend was convinced that his brother was in worse shape emotionally and psychologically than ever. Rather than help calm his fears, the trip had only upset my friend more. He visited the managing editor's home one night, looking for consolation and advice. The editor was gone. The editor's wife embraced my friend and rocked him as he wept for almost a half hour.

This went on for two more nights in a row before my friend came back with the shocking story that this woman, almost a mother figure to him, had made what he considered a pass at him. We scoffed, assuming he was bragging at best, lying at worst. The next night he said he had "made out" with her for twenty minutes.

She was a woman with a husband who had other priorities. She was a woman who, upon marrying (as Helen Rowland was quoted in *Reader's Digest* in January of 1955), "exchange[d] the attention of all other men she knew for the inattention of one."[1] She was starved for passion, and she found it where she could.

My friend was the victim. He was not without fault, but he was weak and vulnerable. Once she had taken advantage of him, there was no turning back. A marriage ended and an affair began. There was no future in it for either of them, but they still played it out.

It all started as an innocent, sympathetic embrace, an act of compassion that turned to passion.

DIFFERENT STROKES FOR DIFFERENT FOLKS

I realize that this entire subject of hugging and touching may present no problem for some and a very serious problem for others. If you have never been turned on by the embrace of a friend, you may think this is ridiculous. For you, perhaps it is. But if a person you embrace or who embraces you has a problem, beware.

There are times, places, and situations where physical touch is the only appropriate response. It's therapeutic, loving, and kind. There are other instances where the same response is overkill.

A dear friend of ours recently suffered a terrible tragedy, losing the two people closest to her in the world in an accident in which she also was severely injured. This friend is close enough that I feel free to embrace her in public regularly. Now that she was in the deepest physical and emotional agony a person could endure, I didn't think twice about holding her hand as we talked or even resting my hand on her head as I would with a child in pain. My wife was also there, and this seemed the most logical and normal behavior.

In another context, at another time, a different set of actions would be appropriate. I love this woman in the purest nonromantic sense. I felt deeply for her and wanted her to know it. In another situation or circumstance I would want to guard appearances by responding differently.

The matter of touching and being touched, embracing and being embraced, is as much a matter of common sense and decency as it is of ethnic background and custom. Because of the way I was raised, I tread carefully in this area. If it doesn't happen to be an issue with you, I recommend only that you be sensitive to the attitudes and interpretations of those you choose to touch.

NOTE

1. See *The Reader's Digest Treasury of Modern Quotations* (New York: Reader's Digest, 1975), 82.

CHAPTER NINE

SOME COMPLIMENTS DON'T PAY

Hedge No. 3—If I pay a compliment, it is on clothes or hairstyle, not on the person herself. Commenting on a pretty outfit is much different, in my opinion, than telling a woman that she herself looks pretty.

Am I dealing here only with semantics? I think not. I still remember the first time, in the eighth grade, I mustered the courage to tell a girl, "You look sharp today." I was so nervous, and gushing that compliment was so disabling, that I never thought to study her reaction.

She thanked me, but clearly I had made her feel uncomfortable, too. Was she as affected as I was? I mean, I was a person so afraid of girls at that point that even adding, "How are ya?" at the end of a greeting was too much to consider.

Girls might call me by name and say hi. I would say, "Hi." They would add, "How are ya?" I'd say, "Fine," and keep moving. Why didn't I add, "How are you?"

Conversation, my mother always told me, was like a tennis match. "Someone lobs one to you; you lob it back."

But I was in high school before I marshaled the courage to do that. The results were amazing. A girl I thought was gorgeous greeted me and asked how I was. I said fine and asked her how she was. She assured me she was great and that she was glad I was fine. And she smiled at me. That alone was enough of a payoff. I had a limited enough self-image to know there was no future in a relationship with her. After all, I hardly knew her, but having a normal, polite, albeit empty, conversation with her provided its own euphoric rush.

So you can see what an accomplishment it had been in junior high to have summoned the fortitude to actually tell a girl she looked sharp. I lived on that high for days, realizing only after a week or so that the girl was carefully avoiding me. Had I upset her? Scared her? Made her think I was interested in her? Nothing was worse at that age than having someone after you in whom you were not interested. I wasn't cool or "in," wasn't a sharp dresser, and didn't have money. I was invisible. The only girls I attracted were those who knew they couldn't land someone impressive. When they chased me, I ran. And now I knew how they felt. I even sent that girl a valentine card, one my brother had dreamed up. It included several small slips of paper with various flowers drawn on them. The card itself was a poem, instructing the recipient to send back to me one of the flowers as a message. For instance, "If I am the one you chose, send me back the big, red rose." There were flowers that would tell me to be patient, to wait, to keep trying, and there was even a dandelion with the verse, "If I waste my time in tryin', send me back the dandelion."

I waited and waited for some response. I was being ignored and even avoided at school, and it got to the point where I would have been happy even to get the dandelion back. I merely wanted to know if she was aware of my existence. Maybe she had never received the card. The worst possible reaction was no reaction, and that's what I got. Valerie, if you're out there, I need to tell you I'm happily married, and it's too late. If the rose merely got lost in the mail and you thought I had ignored you after that, what can I say except I'm sorry. (I wish I could remember her last name. She sure looked sharp that day.)

LESSONS

In retrospect, I realize what I did wrong there. Had Valerie been pining away for me, perhaps my compliment on how sharp she looked would have thrilled her. But since my approach was clearly a surprise, I should have emphasized the clothes and not the person. I should have been just slightly less personal, which is what I need to do now. I don't have the right to tell a woman how she looks, though it might be nice and appropriate to comment on her clothes or hair.

I base part of this hedge on my own reaction to how men talk to my wife. Dianna is tall, dark, and stunning—a head turner. It makes me proud to see men do a double take when they see her. If they keep staring, though, I stare right back until they notice that she's with me.

Dianna is one of those typical beautiful women who is unaware of her beauty and its impact. If I thought she was looking for compliments it might bother me, but I'm used to the fact that she gets many. And I know she is truly beautiful as opposed to merely sexy, because she gets just as many compliments from women as from men. (In my experience, women compliment each other only on their beauty, not on their seductivity.)

For some reason, it does not bother me if a man comments on my wife's hair or makeup or clothes. But if he should say that she looks pretty or is gorgeous or beautiful, that is too personal. Interestingly, either kind of compliment makes her uncomfortable, but she agrees that the personal approach is worse.

As a hedge, I stop short of the purely personal compliment, because you can never be sure of the reaction. Some women would be offended at such familiarity, and men who talk to women that way tend to get reputations for it. I know a man who is known not only for talking to and about women that way, but also for hanging around them whenever he gets the chance. He always chats with the best-looking woman at work, church, or at a party. At conventions, he spends most of his time at the swimming pool, talking to the best-looking women. I don't know him well enough to know whether his marriage is strong, but you can imagine what people will think if a rumor of infidelity ever begins making the rounds. Innocent or not, he won't have a chance to survive it.

I don't get complimented about my looks, but occasionally I'll wear something that people like, and they say so. If a woman tells me she likes my tie, jacket, hat, or even my beard, I don't wonder if she's on the prowl or frustrated by a bad marriage. I merely feel complimented about my taste.

HEARING VOICES

On the rare occasion when a woman compliments me on the way I look, I confess I'm uncomfortable. Like anyone else, I have certain needs in my life, and among those are what Dr. James Dobson calls emotional requirements: love, acceptance, belonging, caring, and tenderness. My goal is to seek the fulfillment of those needs within the context of my own marriage.

Dr. Dobson says there are certain voices that would lure a person away from the straight life—the life of giving yourself to your spouse and children, working, paying the bills—toward infidelity. These are pleasure ("Come on, have fun, life is passing you by!"), romanticism (someone who cares, someone interested in you as a person, someone who wants to love you), sex (the pure pleasure of the physical act), and ego needs (someone finds you attractive for your mind, tastes, or talents).

Dr. Dobson ranks sex at the low end of the scale of these reasons and puts ego needs at the top for both men and women. For women, he says, romanticism may be a close second, depending on the health of the marriage, and sex may be more important to men than to women because of the differences in biological makeup. The late James L. Johnson, on the flyleaf of his book *What Every Woman Should Know About a Man,* called sex "the strange and mysterious drive of the God-given chemistry that has shaped nations, destroyed kingdoms, and brought ruin or ecstasy to millions from the beginning of time."[1]

The problem with these voices that would lure us away from the straight life is that they are lying voices. They promise something other than simply another straight life, but that is not possible. If we run off with another spouse—even if we do find more pleasure, more romance, more sex, and more of our ego needs fulfilled—there is still a straight life that has to be dealt with. In fact, it may be more burdensome than the one we left because of the alimony and child-care expenses from the previous marriage. As Dr. Dobson says, "The grass may be greener on the other side of the fence, but it still has to be mowed."

GO AHEAD, MAKE HER DAY

The problem with ego needs and the need for romance, especially in a woman's life, is that they are hidden, unseen factors that men need to take into consideration when talking to women. We may innocently think it'll make a woman's day if we pay her a compliment that borders on the personal. So, rather than telling her that her sweater is beautiful and asking if she made it (implying that if she made it she's incredible and if she bought it she has great taste), we tell her she looks great in it.

How do we know that perhaps the pleasure and romance and even the sex and ego strokes haven't long since evaporated from her marriage? How do we know that she hasn't been longing for just this sort of attention from her husband? How do we know she hasn't given up on ever getting any more strokes from him, and that this very personal approach from us may reach deep needs of which she is hardly aware?

I want to be careful not to make women in bad marriages sound so weak and dependent that they live and die for any personal interest on the part of other men. But in individual cases, we don't know, do we? It never ceases to amaze me when I hear about the latest wife-abuse victim or wife who has been cheated on.

Several years ago a visiting preacher friend counseled the middle-aged wife of a pillar in our church. Her husband, a leading evangelical, had been in the ministry more than forty years.

The story she told the evangelist was incredible. She had been a psychological prisoner in her own home for decades and had been physically abused every few weeks during her entire marriage. She was nearly suicidal, but she had heard something in the evangelist's sermon that gave her a glimmer of hope. My friend told her there was nothing he could do for her until she was prepared to tell someone in authority—her pastor, her husband's superiors, or the police—about her husband. She was unwilling to do that.

Her husband is dead now, and I have lost track of her. Sadly, however, her daughter must have suffered all those years, too. A few years after seemingly marrying happily and starting a family—and several years before her father died—she disappeared for a few days and committed suicide a hundred miles from home.

I share that sordid story to make the point that we never know what kinds of wounds and pains a person carries to church every Sunday. The woman in the account above would probably not have been vulnerable to an approach by any man except for an extremely kind, gentle, godly person. But what about the others? What about those we know just as little about?

No doubt a case could be made for the fact that some women wouldn't know the difference between a compliment of their hair or dress and of themselves as persons. However, there is a difference, even if it registers only subliminally. Planting a hedge that allows you to compliment only a woman's taste in styles and clothes frees you to be friendly, outgoing, and encouraging to women without being suspected of anything worse.

BEST FRIENDS

Years ago I had a boss who told me a story that illustrates the dangers I've been discussing in this chapter. A friend of his was suspected of taking too much interest in a female teacher at the school where he coached. Bill insisted there was nothing going on, but, as rumor after rumor persisted, my friend felt obligated to confront him.

"If there's nothing going on between you and Nancy," my friend said, "why don't you quit spending so much time with her?"

"I like her," Bill said. "And she likes me. Is there anything wrong with having a friend of the opposite sex?"

"It depends on how your wife feels about it," my boss said.

"She hates it, but she's never been a friend to me."

My boss counseled him to break off the relationship. Within six months Bill and Nancy had divorced their spouses and married each other. Bill finally confessed to my boss that they had been intimate almost from the beginning of their relationship. "It all started with my telling her how pretty she looked every day," he said. "She said she had been starved for that kind of attention, because she worked so hard at looking good and no one, she emphasized no one, ever seemed to notice."

"Except you," my boss said.

"Except me," Bill said smiling. He was thrilled. He had found the girl of his dreams. No matter that two marriages and five children had been caught in the whirlwind. And neither Bill nor Nancy pledged that they would be truer to each other than to their first spouses. Bill never said he would quit complimenting women personally, and Nancy never said she would quit looking for the same from men other than her husband. For Bill to have kept the second marriage intact, he would have had to realize he was competing with anyone who thought his wife looked good and had the guts to tell her.

Apparently, he couldn't keep up with the competition. The marriage lasted fewer than four years, and it was she who left him for an older man. (How long would you give that relationship?)

There was something about being dumped that brought Bill to his senses. He realized what he had done to his wife, and he seemed remorseful. He pleaded with his first wife to take him back. Even though she felt that, as a divorced woman, she was not free to marry anyone else, she didn't trust him. She was still in such pain over what he did to her that she asked for time to think it over before taking him back.

He couldn't wait, and he married again. Chaos.

THERE IS A WAY

Sometimes it feels great to compliment a woman other than your wife in a personal way, and you sense it would be a good thing to do. In cases like that, I talk it over with Dianna first. We had a friend who was dumped by her husband, and he tried to justify taking up with another married woman by telling anyone who would listen that, despite her image, his wife was a shrew—cold, mean, unattractive, and dull.

Maybe behind closed doors she was all that, but my wife and I felt we knew her well enough and had seen her in enough situations to know that she was sweet, spiritual, a good mother, and a loyal and loving wife. She may not have been the hottest thing in town or the most fashionable dresser, but she had certainly done nothing that would justify her husband's adultery.

After planning and almost scripting our approach, Dianna and I made sure we ran into her after church one Sunday night. With my arm around my own wife but looking directly into that suffering woman's eyes, I said, "You're not going to let what Benny says convince you that you're not pretty or attractive or exciting, are you?"

She blushed and shook her head. I would not have felt free to say that to her without my wife at my side, nodding her assent. And Dianna added, "We know how much you have to offer, and if Benny can't see that, he's just wrong. If he follows through with this, it'll be his loss, not yours."

As a rule we make it a point not to take sides in separations and divorces, but when there is flagrant adultery, we feel little loyalty to the offending party, friend or not.

To quote James Dobson once more, "Marriage is an institution designed to meet individual needs."[2] The key is for husband and wife to meet each other's needs and for other people to mind their own business. Let me meet my own wife's need for pleasure, romance, sex, and ego strokes, and I'll let you meet your wife's.

NOTES

1. James L. Johnson, *What Every Woman Should Know About a Man*, Grand Rapids: Zondervan, 1977.
2. James Dobson, "The Lure of Infidelity," audio cassette from Focus on the Family (1978).

CHAPTER TEN

LOOKING DOWN THE BARREL OF A LOADED GUN

Hedge No. 4—I avoid flirtation or suggestive conversation, even in jest.

y dad, a police chief, firearms expert, and marksman, once told me that prayer is like looking down the barrel of a loaded gun. "You're likely to get what you're asking for."

I put flirtation and suggestive conversation in the same category as a loaded gun. Maybe that's because I believe in the power of words, written and spoken. Have you ever noticed that compliments and flattery are always heard? People have reminded me of compliments I have given years before and almost forgotten. They remember criticism too, but flattery all the more.

Idle flirting gets people in trouble because the other person needs and wants attention so badly. Not many years ago I slipped from behind this hedge, not intending to flirt but rather to be funny. It didn't get me in serious trouble, but I was certainly reminded of the reason for my hedge.

On a business trip a woman colleague and I were going to go out to dinner with a male associate of ours. When she came to pick me up, she was dressed and made up in flashy, coordinated colors that demanded some comment. I should have just said something about her clothes, but instead—since she is always a good audience for my humor—I said the first funny thing that popped into my mind: "My, don't you look delicious."

She laughed, and I hoped she knew I meant that her colors reminded me of fruit, and not that I wished to devour her. As soon as our third party arrived, she told him what I had said. He gave me a look that would have put a wart on a gravestone, but what could I say? I couldn't deny it, and it was too late to explain.

Men, of course, are just as susceptible to flattery as women. Most people think that the man in Proverbs heading down the road of destruction to the harlot's bed had followed his lust for sex. Surely that was part of it, but the text indicates that he also was seduced by her words. Proverbs 7:4–5 says, "Say to wisdom, 'You are my sister' and call understanding your nearest kin, that they may keep you from the immoral woman, from the seductress *who flatters with her words*" (emphasis mine). And Proverbs 7:10 and 21 say, "There a woman met him, with the attire of a harlot, and a crafty heart. . . . With her *enticing speech* she caused him to yield, with her *flattering lips* she seduced him" (emphasis mine).

KEEP HUMOR IN ITS PLACE

Everyone knows that funny people speak the truth through humor. They may exaggerate how upset they are that someone is late by looking at their watch and saying, "Oh, glad you could make it!" But beneath the joke is a barb of truth. The jokester has slipped in a little lecture without having had to embarrass anyone by saying, "Hey, pal, we agreed on six o'clock and now here you come at six-thirty! What's the deal? Get your act together!"

But the same thing happens when someone tries to be funny in a flirting manner. A man tells a woman, "Why don't we run off together? Tell that good-for-nothing husband of yours you got a better offer, huh?"

How's a woman supposed to react to that? The first time she may think it's funny because it's so far out of the realm of possibility. Each succeeding time Mr. Comedian says something like that, it gets a little more irritating. That is, unless the woman has always been attracted to him and has problems at home. Then she might hope there's some truth behind the humor.

Often, there is. The only time a funny flirter is totally putting someone on is when he throws his arm around a particularly old or homely woman and tries to give her a thrill by saying something she's probably never heard before. "Gorgeous! Where have you been all my life?"

Women like that know better than to believe such drivel, but they may long to hear it anyway. A colleague of mine once toyed with just such a woman by caressing her cheek with his hand. "I'm melting," she said, and I sensed that she meant it.

The real danger comes when the man is pretending to be teasing, but he'd really love to flirt in just the way he's exaggerating. A woman may not suspect the truth behind his humor, and, if she responds in kind, there is the opportunity for misunderstanding. Or worse, she may indeed suspect that he means it, and then there is the opportunity for real understanding.

Such a tragedy occurred at a church in Michigan where a couple flirted humorously for almost ten years. They did this in front of everybody, including their spouses, who laughed right along with them. The flirters were never seen alone together, because they never *were* alone together.

Then came the day when the woman's husband was sick and in the hospital. She needed rides back and forth, and her friend and his wife provided them. No one suspected anything, but on one of those rare occasions when it was just the man doing the driving, the wife of the sick man told him how difficult and cold her husband had been for years.

The flirters began to see each other on the sly until the day came when she told him she had always hoped he'd meant what he said when he had teased her about how wonderful she was, how good she looked, and how he wished he'd met her before she was married. Whether he really meant it was irrelevant now that she had declared herself. The fact was, he admitted later, that this was what he had unquestionably wanted all along. He would never have made the first move, however. He had hidden his true desires behind a cloak of humor. A little crisis, a little honesty, and suddenly years of innocent flirting had blossomed into an affair.

INNOCENT HUMOR

I worked at a camp one summer during my high school years. One week one of the women counselors, about a year older than I, shared my last name. We were not related and had never seen each other before. When we were introduced, we had not even made much of an issue over the name duplication. While Jenkins is not as common as Smith or Jones, neither is it as unique as Higginbottham or Szczepanik.

One night after the campers were in bed a bunch of us staffers and a few of the counselors, Miss Jenkins included, were watching a football game on television. A couple of the guys started kidding Miss Jenkins and me about being married. We were both so young and naive and insecure that we just blushed and hoped the running gag would run out of gas.

For some reason I had to leave the impromptu party before the game was over, and as I headed for the door, someone said, "Hey, Jenkins, aren't you takin' yer wife with ya?"

I got this urge to show the crowd that I could be just as funny as they and that I was a good sport, so I turned and pointed at her. "No, but I want you home in bed in fifteen minutes."

I was out the door and ten feet from the TV cabin when I heard the hooting and hollering. I had not intended even to imply anything risqué. I had merely been trying to go along with the joke, and instead of speaking to the girl the way a husband would to a wife, I had spoken to her as father to daughter. Of course, everyone took my wanting her home in bed the wrong way, and with my reputation for enjoying a funny line, I knew I would never live it down. In fact, if I tried to go back and explain, no one would even believe me. They would wonder why I didn't want to take the credit for such a great joke.

The girl was as sweet and chaste as most counselors would be at a camp like that, and the last thing I wanted her to think was that I had been inappropriate and had gotten a cheap laugh at her expense. A hundred feet from the cabin, still hearing the laughter, I knew I had to go back.

When I opened the door, no one even noticed me. Something had happened on the game that had everyone's attention. I was glad to see that Miss Jenkins wasn't sitting there weeping with her head in her hands. When I called her name and she looked up so did everyone else, and the snickering began again. I wished they had been laughing at me for saying such a stupid thing, but I knew they were laughing because I had gotten away with such a saucy line.

"Could I see you for a minute?" I asked, and the room fell deathly silent.

I'll never forget her response as long as I live. "I'm not too sure," she said. It was the funniest comeback I could imagine in that situation, and I wish I'd anticipated it. If my original line had been intentional, I would still have always thought hers was better, especially on the spur of the moment.

The place erupted again, and I winced self-consciously, knowing that I appeared to deserve that. I was grateful when she bounced to her feet and followed me out into the darkness. I had the impression she knew what I was going to say.

"You need to know that I didn't mean that the way it sounded," I said.

"I know," she said.

"You do?"

"Uh-huh."

"I don't think anyone else understands that."

"Maybe not, but I do. I've seen you around, heard you be funny. That's not your style. At first I was embarrassed and disappointed, but I caught a glimpse of your face as you hurried out, and I knew."

"Your comeback in there was priceless," I said.

"I couldn't pass it up. But I knew you were back to apologize, so I figured I could say something and apologize for it at the same time."

"I'm sorry," I said. "I didn't mean to embarrass you."

"Accepted," she said. "I know. And I'm sorry too, though I admit I *did* mean to embarrass you."

I laughed and she added, "We Jenkinses have to stick together, you know."

Strangely, we didn't see any more of each other after that than we would have otherwise. She was older and was not on staff, so she had her crowd and I had mine. I had learned a lesson, though. I knew to be more careful about teasing in a flirting manner. I also learned how wonderful and forgiving and insightful some women can be. Funny, too.

BY THE SAME TOKEN

Along these same lines, I have made it a practice—and can probably list this among my hedges—of not making my wife the butt of jokes. There are enough things to make fun of and enough funny topics without going for easy laughs at the expense of your spouse.

One of the reasons for this, besides my memory of how bad I felt about unintentionally ribbing my teenaged camp "wife," is that I would never want Dianna to think I was trying to tell her something serious under the guise of humor. We have made it a policy to speak honestly and forthrightly with each other about anything that bothers us.

We give the lie to that pontification that married couples who never fight are probably as miserable and phony as those who fight all the time. We love each other. We don't always agree, and we get on each other's nerves occasionally, but neither of us likes tension in the air. We compete to see who can apologize first and get things talked out. We follow the biblical injunction to never let the sun go down upon our wrath (Ephesians 4:26).

When a group of adult Christians decides it would be healthy to be honest and to share some of their most embarrassing or petty fights, we always confess that we'll either have to pass or make one up. Slammed doors, cold shoulders, silent treatments, and walking out just are not part of our routine. I think this comes as a result of being careful with our tongues.

Just as I don't want to make the mistake of flirting in jest or being suggestive in conversation with anyone but my wife, I want to watch what I say to her, too. Scripture has a lot to say about the power of the tongue and the spoken word. Proverbs 18:21 says that death and life "are in the power of the tongue," and Proverbs 21:23 says, "Whoever guards his mouth and tongue keeps his soul from troubles."

Proverbs 28:23 says that "he who rebukes a man will find more favor afterward than he who flatters with the tongue." In the New Testament, James says that the tongue is a little member but that it boasts great things. "See how great a forest a little fire kindles!" (James 3:5).

Flattery, flirtation, suggestive jesting, and what we say to our own spouses are all shades of the same color. Beware the power of the tongue.

CHAPTER ELEVEN

MEMORIES

Hedge No. 5—I remind my wife often—in writing and orally—that I remember my wedding vows: "Keeping you only unto me for as long as we both shall live." Dianna is not the jealous type, nor has she ever demanded such assurances from me. She does, however, appreciate my rules and my observance of them.

People seem to make their wedding vows so cavalierly nowadays that you have to wonder if they have any idea what they're saying. Census figures show that one of every four marriages performed in 1931–33 ended in divorce. By the midfifties the rate had jumped to one in three. By 1971 it had hit 41 percent.[1] Everybody knows that the figure passed the 50 percent mark early in the 1980s.

It may be naive to think that people would remain true to their vows just by repeating them frequently, but who knows? At least couples might come to understand what they said in a ceremony before God, friends, and spouse.

PRACTICAL SUGGESTIONS

There are many creative ways to remind your spouse and yourself of your wedding vows, and they can be adapted to any budget. Try surprising your wife with a progressive search that culminates in a trip somewhere special. If you can afford it, take her out of the country. If you can't, drive to the next town for a weekend at a hotel. Or even just to McDonald's.

Set it up this way:

Write out slips that contain your wedding vows, particularly those that refer to remaining sexually faithful, in a rhyme or even a little story format. At the end of each slip, leave a clue for where your wife can find the next one. Then hide them around the house and in the garage.

Mail the first one home. It might say, "Keeping you—" and then "Look for another message in the freezer."

When she looks in the freezer, she finds another slip that reads, "—only unto me—" and "Look for another message in the car."

In the car is a slip that reads, "—for as long—" and points her to the mantel over the fireplace. There she finds a note that says, "—as we both—" and "Look for another message in the junk drawer." There is a message that reads, "—shall live." There you might also plant her plane ticket or hotel reservation or baby-sitting certificate or McDonald's gift certificate.

It can be just as effective, though maybe not as much fun, simply to call her at home or at work, and tell her, "I made this vow _____ years/months/days ago, and I still mean it: 'I will keep you only unto myself for as long as we both shall live, or until Christ, who has saved us by His grace, returns to take us unto Himself forever.'"

Sending your vows in a telegram or mailgram can be effective. You might even have someone do it in calligraphy or have it printed so you can decoupage it. I've heard of people having their vows written in icing on a cake, chiseled into a rock, burned into wood, even written in moist dirt in the front yard. A friend of mine spent a couple of hours forming the letters to his vows in tiny bits of twig, then set them up on the cement slab in front of the door of his house, only to see his wife miss their significance and sweep them off the porch onto the grass.

Sometimes I like to just tell Dianna that I remember my vows and that she is the only woman I have ever slept with, and the only one

I ever wish to sleep with. I usually add my own sentiments on anniversary, valentine, and birthday cards, too. I don't think she ever tires of hearing me reiterate my vows. I know I never get tired of hearing or saying them.

WHAT'S GOOD FOR THE GOOSE

The sad fact is that there is simply not enough emphasis on wedding vows any more. We need to face it: this is one of the most significant problems in modern marriage. I've never understood the long-standing double standard that seems to wink at males' infidelity while holding women in contempt for the same offense. Of course, the breaking of a sacred vow should not be tolerated for either sex, but there is a boys-will-be-boys mentality that allows some men— even Christians—to have occasional or long-standing mistresses their entire married lives.

As we've seen countless marriages break up during our nearly twenty years together, Dianna and I have talked seriously about this issue. Divorce is not in our vocabulary, but we have discussed whether either of us could forgive the other for the ultimate in unfaithfulness and betrayal.

Early in our marriage Dianna told me she didn't think she was capable of forgiving sexual unfaithfulness. Though I had, of course, never considered violating my vows, it was impressive to hear that. I tried to imagine the shoe on the other foot and decided the same. The thought of sleeping with my wife after she had been unfaithful was inconceivable. It still is, but both of our views have grown on this subject.

We have seen friends' and relatives' marriages shattered by adultery, and yet we have also counseled wives to forgive husbands and take them back. Regaining trust after adultery still seems impossible, and neither of us has come to the point where we will say unequivocally that we could take back the other after unfaithfulness. We admit, though, that there are other things to consider.

For instance, we have seen that adultery is usually not the major problem in bad marriages. It is a result of a bad marriage or a symptom of a bad marriage. It may be the worst thing that can happen to a marriage, but it is rarely the basic problem. We hope and trust and believe and pray that any of our discussions about this subject are academic in our own marriage because we work so hard at it, but adultery does occasionally invade even seemingly solid marriages.

Take the case of a Christian leader who stepped down from an executive position with a mission organization ten years ago after his adultery was revealed. His wife, his pastor, and a couple of close relatives already knew of his sin and also of his repentance. When it came to light, however, he realized that resigning was the only way to protect the reputation of the mission and keep it from extended controversy.

Anyone who knew this man knew he had been a model husband and father. Even his wife and children said so. Thus the shocking moral lapse was clearly not the result of a pattern in his life or of a bad marriage. He admitted that during a period of burnout and extreme fatigue, he allowed a friendship to become immoral, and he apparently sincerely repented.

Most interesting was that his wife not only forgave him but has also said that she would not dwell on his short period of unfaithfulness. To their credit, neither discounted that he had sinned, that his actions were unacceptable, or that he needed to repent and ask forgiveness of God and all parties affected. There are those who feel he has forever disqualified himself from the ministry, but my purpose here is to deal with the forgiveness aspect.

If he was truly repentant, did his wife have a choice as a Christian to do anything but forgive him and welcome him back? Whereas many believe that adultery is biblical grounds for divorce, surely divorce is not mandated when the offending party is remorseful and wants to reconcile.

Therefore, even though both Dianna and I cannot imagine finding within ourselves the wherewithal to forgive the other should adultery ever disgrace and defile our marriage, clearly the biblical, Christian response to a repentant sinner is forgiveness. In ourselves, in our flesh, this would probably not be possible. Only through Christ can divine, unconditional love find forgiveness for a spouse who has foisted the filthiest pollution on a marriage.

Even as Dianna and I continue to struggle with the proper response—and, as I say, continue also to pray against such a problem and work toward a marriage that will not allow it—we counsel those who have been victimized to forgive the offending spouse if he or she is willing to reconcile. We can only pray that we could be as charitable to each other, as inconceivable as that is to us now.

One thing is certain. Marriages in which the ultimate loss of trust has been suffered can never be the same. We can only imagine what a wife who has taken back a husband who slept with another woman, or vice versa, must go through when that offending spouse wants to enjoy the marriage bed again. How long would it be—if ever—before either could forget that the vows had been broken, that one of them had not kept the other only unto himself or herself? Could deep, abiding trust ever be fully regained? No wonder few marriages survive such an onslaught.

Although I would probably want more than anything to reconcile with my wife after such a failure, I certainly wouldn't be able to blame her if she simply was not able to forgive that outrage, that transgression of her trust. And whereas, if I was the offended party I cannot fathom being able to put her sin out of my mind, I'd like to think I would not turn away my truly repentant wife whom I love.

Even considering that jumble of horrifying emotions is so distasteful that all it does is make me want to emphasize again the whole reason for this book. Again I need to say that adultery is usually a result or symptom of a marriage with weaknesses throughout. If it takes occasionally just running through your mind's eye being caught or having to confess to your wife that you have been unfaithful, then I recommend that exercise.

You won't find it pleasant. Imagine breaking down as you tell her, hoping she'll understand, seeing her turn cold and hurt and dark, not wanting to be touched or to hear anymore. My guess is that the typical woman won't want to see her husband's tears of grief and remorse right away. He will tumble off whatever pedestal he may have been on, and should she ever find it within herself, by the grace of God, to forgive him and take him back, it will not be without deep pain and suffering.

Imagine, just imagine, what that would do to your wife. Plant hedges wide and deep and tall against any weakness you may have. Remind yourself what price you would have to pay for a brief sea-

son of carnal fun. Study what is wrong with you or your relationship with your wife that would allow you even to consider such a
drastic breach of her trust.

Dianna and I had college friends who were married ten years and
had two sons when we first got wind that there was trouble. The
wife suspected her husband was seeing another woman. We stood
by her, helped her find out, confronted him, heard the denials, and
then learned the awful truth: It was true.

He was unrepentant, hostile, and flagrant. He had complaints
about his wife, but none justified this complete setting aside of his
morals and values. She kept fighting for him, wanting him back. We
warned her that until he gave up the other woman and—in essence—
came back on his knees, she should be slow to open her arms. Maybe
we were intruding rather than helping at that point, but she received
similar counsel from others.

Still, she was desperate. She couldn't stand the thought of losing
him to someone else. No, she was not the woman he had married.
She had given birth to both sons within a year of each other, and
she had grown weary and harried trying to keep up with them.
Maybe she had become shrill, and maybe she had neglected him a bit,
but he had never grown up either. Now he played most of the time
and was gone more than he was home. And now this. Another
woman.

She moved in with her aunt and took the boys with her. He
begged her to come back, promising to change his ways. It was all
she wanted to hear. She set conditions: Give up the other woman,
spend time at home, don't expect Olympic sex after this rupture of
my trust, and grow up.

The first night they spent together, he got a call from the other
woman. "Take that call and I'm out of here," his wife told him.

"Just some loose ends," he assured her, and he talked on the phone
for a half hour. Then he left. "Just getting some stuff, settling accounts.
Don't worry. It's over."

He was gone all night and still tried to tell her nothing had happened. But he had pushed his wife past the brink. She packed up
the boys and all her belongings and moved out. Even while he was
again trying to plead with her to take him back, a friend saw his car

in front of his girlfriend's house all night. The friend left a note, berating him for living a lie. That finally brought him to his senses.

From what we could tell, he had finally truly repented. He'd come back to God, cut off the relationship, and done everything he could to win back his wife.

But do you know what? It was too late. If she had been Jesus, she might have forgiven him seventy times seven, and there were those who felt she was being cold and unforgiving and even unchristian. Sadly, he had pushed her too far. I'm not saying she was right, but she got to the place of rage, and suddenly she could believe nothing he said and could trust nothing he promised. She could only suspect everything he did.

The story is ten years old now and both partners have been married again. She has divorced for the second time. We're talking about Christian people here. Adultery creates hags. Adulterers lie. Victims get angry. There are human limits to forgiveness, even among Christians.

Somehow, some way, we who have remained true to our spouses need to do something to ensure that we continue that way. That means working on our weaknesses, shoring up our strengths, pouring our lives into each other, and planting hedges. We must avoid the mess of adultery and divorce and the besmirching of the reputation of Christ. The time is long past for us to worry about people snickering at us for being prudish or Victorian or puritanical.

Treat this blight on marriage as the epidemic that it is. Flee. Plant a hedge. Do something. Anything. Don't become a sad statistic.

NOTE

1. *The Reader's Digest Treasury of Modern Quotations* (New York: Reader's Digest, 1975), 83.

CHAPTER TWELVE

QUALITY TIME VS. QUANTITY TIME

Hedge No. 6—From the time I get home from work until the children go to bed, I do no writing or office work. This gives me lots of time with the family and for my wife and me to continue to court and date.

Something subtle but unusual happened to me after Dianna and I had been married for about a year. I had recently left the field of secular journalism and begun working for Scripture Press. Among my duties was the responsibility to interview people for stories for the Sunday school papers.

Coincidentally, several of my interviews during a short span were with middle-aged men. Their stories were all different, but eventually we got around to the subjects of home and marriage and family. Five or six of these men shared with me their regrets about those areas of their lives. Their marriages had been fine and their children had turned out OK, but every one of them regretted not having spent more time at home. They had a lot of "if onlys."

"If only I'd realized that my daughter's recital was more important than the big real estate deal . . ."

"If only I could have proved to my son how proud I was of his
athletic ability by showing up at his games . . ."

"If only my wife had known before she died how much I enjoyed
talking with her and traveling with her . . ."

Someone has said that no one has ever been heard to say on his
deathbed, "I wish I'd spent more time at the office."

These discussions of regret over misplaced priorities during the
sunny years of their careers—which always seem to coincide with the
growing up years of a man's family—had little to do with their stories and didn't wind up in the pages of Scripture Press's Sunday school
papers. But I sensed God had put me in contact with these men for
a reason: They were all sending me the same message. I was barely
twenty-two years old, but I caught the drift.

I remember lengthy discussions with Dianna about it. We wouldn't
have our first child until we'd been married four-and-a-half years,
and that gave us lots of time to set goals, policies, and priorities. We
wanted to be good parents and avoid regrets.

We decided that once the children came along, regardless of their
ages, I would do no writing and no office business between the time
I got home from work and the time the kids went to bed. (I've been
accused of putting them to bed at four-thirty!)

In the beginning the biggest benefit was to Dianna, who had
someone to take over feeding and changing and entertaining a baby
while she finally had time to fix dinner. Sometimes baby Dallas was
sleeping when I got home, but that didn't count; he had to be down
for the night before I felt free to get into my own projects.

As Dallas got older and Chad came along (two-and-a-half years
later), he learned to take for granted that I would be around during
that time of the day. I didn't insist that the boys take advantage of
me or even play with me. I just wanted them to get used to the fact
that I was theirs to talk to, to play with, or even to ignore.

During that period I learned that the idea of *quality time* was an
evil lie. Some experts pushed the idea that successful overachievers,
those we call Yuppies today, could have children and be guilt-free
about the little time they were able to devote to them. The remedy

was *quality time*. Sort of like one-minute parenting. It went like this: Be sure to make what little time you are able to spend with your child *quality time.*

What garbage. I've seen the results of kids who were given only *quality time*. The problem is that kids don't know the difference. What they need is time—all they can get. Quantity time is *quality time,* whether you're discussing the meaning of the cosmos or just climbing on dad.

There are times I wish my kids knew how wonderful I was being about all this. I don't know too many fathers who give their kids at least two-and-a-half hours a day—and there certainly aren't any other fathers who play ball with the whole neighborhood every summer afternoon.

I confess that this is not all just for the kids' benefit. I can't imagine missing out on some of their growth experiences, the funny and touching things they say, and even being there in times of crisis when I could easily be somewhere else.

There came a point in our lives when Dallas, at about age four, told me he wished he had a new dad. Like who? I asked him. Like the man down the street, he told me. I knew exactly who he was talking about and why.

The man down the street came home so infrequently that he got a royal welcome every time he did. And he was usually feeling so guilty about his drinking or topless-bar hopping or compulsive spending that he brought gifts for everyone. What a guy! What a dad! He must be super to get that kind of reception and be so generous!

I couldn't explain the distinctions to Dallas until he was old enough to understand why the man down the street left his wife a note for breakfast one morning, telling her she would find him in the garage with the car running. He had committed suicide.

SO WHAT?

What does all this have to do with marital hedges? Hedges can do wonders for a family, and this policy of spending megablocks of time with the kids each day has turned into rich benefits for Dianna and me, too. Our time together is more relaxed, less hurried, less pressured, less obligatory. We have learned to just be with each other, to be used to having each other around. We don't have to talk, plan, schedule, or make appointments with each other. We know each other's schedules, and we count on when the other will be available. Dianna adds that she enjoys a tremendous sense of satisfaction and well-being when I am devoting time to the kids. She has never felt left out or jealous of the time, especially since she and I also spend a lot of time together.

At the time of this writing our boys are fourteen, almost twelve, and seven. They are old enough to figure out that their relationship with their parents is out of the ordinary, at least as it relates to the amount of time spent. We hardly ever miss one of their school or sports-related events, and we will not be gone from home more than a certain number of days without taking them with us. Our trip to Africa this past summer was one of the richest family times we've ever had.

More important, the kids can see a difference in our marriage, too. They know we're still affectionate and in love and demonstrative about it even after all these years. The older two boys especially are at ages where they want to know the whys and wherefores of all our ideas and behavior, so I've been able to tell them about our hedges and why we feel they're so important.

They're intrigued by it all, even though it probably won't make total sense to them until they are in love or married. But having my sons know of my hedges serves almost as another hedge. Just like my friend who carries pictures of his wife and daughters as a hedge on business trips, I carry the knowledge that my kids are aware of my concern for our marriage. They would be front-line victims if I let my guard down.

Another of our unwritten traditions is that, until our kids are teenagers, I will put them to bed every night possible. We talk, read, sing, and pray together. Following a tradition set by my own father, I take that opportunity, too, to say nice things about their mother. "Don't we have a great mom? Isn't she good to us? Do you have any idea how much she loves you? Do you know she works at least twice as hard as Daddy? Aren't you proud that she always looks so nice?"

A ROSE BY ANY OTHER NAME

I thought of how important the strength of a marriage is to children when I saw a quote by Pete Rose, Jr. The betting scandal his father was in meant little to Petey. He still dwelt on his parents' years-old divorce. His father was remarried with a new child and another on the way. His mother was tending bar in Cincinnati.

Petey is a better-than-average big-league prospect himself, and athletes at that stage in their careers are usually single-minded and driven. Yet Petey said something like this: "I would trade whatever future I have in big league baseball to see my parents get back together."[1]

It was as if he hadn't read the papers, didn't know the truth about his parents' marriage. Pete, Sr., had such an incredible reputation for chasing women and such nasty, impossible-to-take-back things had been said by each about the other, that no one would give two cents for the possibility of any civility, let alone a reconciliation. And with Pete, Sr. remarried, there's no chance.

Yet that comment from little Pete, if he were my son, would haunt me to my grave.

LOVE ME, LOVE MY MOM

The following statement has been attributed to everybody from Howard Hendricks and Josh McDowell to James Dobson. It probably preceded all three, but it remains a truism: The most important thing a father can do for his children is to love their mother. When we know that one of the great fears of childhood is abandonment, we can only imagine the impact of a broken marriage on a child.

MAY "THE VORCE" NOT BE WITH YOU

Several years ago *Campus Life* magazine ran a story about "the vorce," which was a child's misunderstanding of the word *divorce*. A child in the story said that sometimes people even talk about "the the vorce," which she couldn't understand at all. All she knew was that anytime anyone ever talked about "the vorce" or "the the vorce," it was sad and bad news. It had something to do with Mommy and Daddy, and she didn't like the vorce.[2]

It reminded me of a little girl I knew when I was seven. I thought she was the sweetest, cutest four-year-old I had ever seen. Because of our difference in age I didn't see much of her during the next few years, but by the time she was nine she was a sad little creature with a drawn face and red eyes. The only thing she would tell her Sunday school teacher was that she was afraid of the vorce. Her teacher thought she meant some kind of force, but soon the truth came out.

Her parents were leaders in the church and seemed to have an idyllic family with several children, including a couple of adoptees. More than once, however, the children had been awakened in the night to their parents' arguing, even yelling and screaming. That was when this pretty little girl had first heard about the vorce. Her mother was pleading with her father not to get the vorce. Whatever it was, the little girl knew it was bad.

Divorcees will tell you that children are resilient, that a divorce is better for a child than a bad marriage. But experts in child psychology tell a different story. Some kids who bottle up their emotions and pretend it's all right to be shuttled back and forth between parents and cities, sometimes by air, grow up emotional wrecks. They're unable to trust or fully love anyone. They fear rejection, suffer low self-esteem, career in and out of doomed marriages, and leave in their wakes children just like themselves.

This is the generation that is growing up now. What will family reunions and family trees look like at the turn of the century? What kinds of adults will be running our corporations, leading our government, pioneering technological progress?

We can grow paranoid, I guess, but with more than half of all new marriages ending in divorce and wreaking havoc on the minds and emotions of that many children, mayhem seems the only prognosis. The only way to ensure a future with stable marriages and home lives is to begin strengthening our families now. Give kids a model of love and caring and interdependence. Show them what it means to make and keep a commitment, to set your course on a lifetime of love with no wavering, no excuses, and no me-first philosophies.

Don't fall prey to the Quality Time trap or to the myth that kids are resilient and will be better off in two halves of a broken home. Most children of divorce are just like Pete Rose, Jr. They'd give up everything else important in their lives if only their parents would get back together. Make a decision. Set a course. Carve out the time it takes to devote yourself to your wife and children, and plant a hedge that will protect you and her and them from the devastation of a broken home.

NOTES

1. Mike Bass, *Cincinnati Post,* as printed in the *Chicago Tribune.*
2. M.J. Amft, "The Vorce and Other Questions," *Campus Life,* January 1978, 43.

PART THREE

WHAT HEDGES CAN DO FOR YOUR FAMILY

*Verbalizing the hedges in your marriage
will give your spouse and your children a
deep sense of love and security.*

CHAPTER THIRTEEN

EVERYBODY LOVES A LOVE STORY

It's important to share with our spouses and children the memories of our own courtship, marriage, and honeymoon.

It's never too late to try to recall the memories of your early love, but the longer you go without doing it, the easier it is to forget important details. By telling our stories over and over through the years, we solidify in our minds the things that attracted us to our mates in the first place. Just as important, our children learn the history of the relationship. I was always fascinated by the stories my parents told about how they met, fell in love, and stayed true to each other during their engagement, although World War II kept them apart for thirty-four months.

There are various ways of reminding one another and your children of your own love story. Obviously, it's not a good idea to force the story on casual acquaintances or neighbors—unless they ask— but you'd be surprised at how many people are indeed interested:

old friends, close relatives, people from church you know well. Trade stories with them. Everybody loves a love story.

I share my own story here only to show you the types of memories you can ferret out to share with your mate. I call it my own, rather than our own, because every courtship is really two stories, yours and your spouse's. Dianna's story contains parallel elements, of course, but the emphases are her own, and her perspective makes for an account with its own unique interest.

Every time we tell our stories, we remind each other of incidents we hadn't thought of since they occurred in the early 1970s. Every birthday, anniversary, holiday, or-no-reason-I-just-felt-like-sending-a-card occasion provides an opportunity for a note or a comment, maybe just a sentence from our wedding vows to share with each other. Repeat a wedding vow in your spouse's ear the next time you kiss hello or good-bye. There's no reason not to celebrate your wedding anniversary every day in some small way. If you have a good marriage, build a hedge around it by celebrating it. Think how unique a gift you have been blessed with in this generation of divorce.

MY STORY

I had not dated for a year when a friend and his fiancée began telling me of a girl I just had to meet, a classmate of theirs at Fort Wayne (Indiana) Bible College. She was tall and beautiful, they told me. *Oh, sure,* I thought. That's why she has to resort to blind dates.

I got a look at her from afar when I visited the campus and saw her in the homecoming court. They were right. She was gorgeous. So much so that I was intimidated. No way I would have dreamed she had a night free, let alone that she would accept a date with me. I figured I'd be wasting my time and pride by asking her out.

"But we've told her about you," my friends said. "She's open to a blind date."

I told them to forget it.

"I've seen her," I said. "She hasn't seen me."

But my interest was piqued. Maybe someday.

Someday came a few months later. They talked me into driving over from Chicago for a double date. Ever the romantic, I started building up the possibilities in my mind. I decided that if anything was to come from this encounter, I would know immediately and would be smitten with her.

The blind date on a Friday night in May 1970 was fine. She was lovely, refined, soft-spoken, smart, likable, and easy to talk to. No whistles, bells, or fireworks. As soon as he got me alone, my friend wanted to know what I thought.

"Fine," I said.

"Just fine?" he asked.

I nodded. "Could you get interested? Try to build something?"

"Nah. I don't know. I don't think so."

"Why not? Something wrong?"

"No. We just didn't click."

"You've had all of one date!"

"Yeah, but I'd know."

"You're crazy."

"Maybe I am."

The next night we doubled again and my reaction was the same. Dianna and I promised to write, and I said maybe I would come back again, feeling polite and benevolent. We corresponded occasionally over the next few weeks, and I sensed Dianna was more interested than I was. In fact, if she had not gently pressed the fact that I had said I would come back sometime, I probably wouldn't have.

Dianna told me later that at the wedding of the friends who had introduced us, she sensed my lack of enthusiasm. I was busy in the wedding party and only really spoke to her as she was leaving. For some reason, just before she got into her car, I reached out and touched the tip of her nose. I meant it as a friendly gesture. She took it as the only bit of encouragement she had.

Before I finally drove back to Fort Wayne on July 18, I had the audacity to tell my friend that if everything went the same as before, I was not going to pursue the relationship. "You're crazy," he said again.

This time it would not be a double date. She was going to cook dinner for us at her place and then we would walk around The Landing, an old section of Fort Wayne. I pulled in the driveway and went to the front door. As I rang the bell I could see Dianna through the screen door, heading for the kitchen.

"Come on in," she said. "I have to catch something on the stove."

She flashed a smile as she hurried past, and something happened to me. After two double dates and a brief chat at our friends' wedding, it was love at fourth sight. Dianna says the only difference since I had seen her last was her tan. I don't know what clicked. All I knew was that it was the most dramatic emotion I have ever felt, before or since.

I hardly knew the woman, but I knew beyond a doubt that I would marry her. I don't know how I knew, but I knew it as surely as I knew my own name. I followed her into the kitchen, and I was speechless. I literally couldn't say a word. If she had asked me how the drive was, I would have been able to manage only a nod.

Anyone who knows me knows that being speechless is not one of my common maladies. And Dianna is the opposite. She's most comfortable when someone else is carrying the ball in a conversation. That was one of the things she liked about me—that I enjoyed talking, drawing people out, discussing whatever anyone was interested in.

She acted as if she didn't notice anything unusual, and she uncharacteristically chattered about the chicken, the vegetables, the salad. I watched her slice carrots, thinking, *She is going to do this in our home someday. I'll watch her do this for the rest of my life.* I can't explain it. I just *knew* and I never wavered.

When I finally spoke, my voice cracked, and I noticed her double take. I recovered quickly, but what an ordeal that meal was! Dianna grew up on a farm and was a 4-H champion cook, so the food was wonderful. But there I sat trying to make small talk on our third date, all the while hiding my delicious secret: I was going to marry this girl. She had been more interested in me than I in her, and now I had shot past her by light-years.

Dianna and I were impressed by different little things that night. I remember I was impressed that a basically shy girl felt comfortable enough to put her feet up on a chair during the meal. Later, as we strolled The Landing, holding hands for the first time, she was impressed that I wouldn't let her run to the car when it began to rain. She worried about how her hair would look. To me, she would have looked good bald that night.

Later we drove to a park in the center of the city where we walked in the rain. It was one of those nights that nearly every couple has at one time or another in their relationship. We talked of everything, learned of childhood memories, quizzed each other on favorite colors, foods, tastes in clothes, books—anything that came to mind. I was in paradise.

I could hardly contain my secret. I wanted to tell her something, anything, that would alert her that to me this was much, much more than a typical date or even a new relationship. I knew it didn't make any sense, but I also knew to the core of my being that this was it. She would be my wife, and there didn't seem to be anything anyone could do to stop it.

Before I left her for the two-hour drive back to Chicago at midnight, I pretended to be kidding and told her I thought I was falling in love. She thought that was funny, and I was glad I hadn't seriously revealed my heart. By the time I got in the car, sense or not, I was helplessly, haplessly, wholly in love. I thought I had been in love before, but now I knew better.

All the way to Chicago I sang, whistled, talked to myself, and tried to think of someone I could tell. One of my friends worked in an all-night gas station in my home town. I arrived there at two in the morning, grinning from the waist up. I went into the station and sat on a fifty-five gallon oil drum.

"I want you to be in my wedding," I told him, beginning a three-and-a-half hour rhapsody.

My friend had never seen me like that. He shook his head.

"You've got it bad," he said.

I didn't know how right he was until I climbed down off that oil drum at 5:30 in the morning and realized I'd been sitting in a quarter inch of motor oil the whole time! It had soaked through my seat and down my pant legs, even into my socks, and I hadn't had a clue!

With the morning newspaper between me and my car seat, I arrived home at six o'clock in the morning and peeked into my parents' bedroom. My mother opened one eye.

"You're in love," she said.

She couldn't have paid me a higher compliment. I couldn't get over the fact that it showed, and she hadn't even seen the oil yet.

I didn't sleep for a couple of days, but I did get started on what would become astronomical phone bills over the next several months. I tried as hard as I could not to let my temporary insanity show through, but I was not successful. Dianna didn't know what to make of it, and when she visited Chicago for a weekend, my secret was out. For the next several months, I tried not to make a fool of myself, and she carefully considered this new friend who had started with such ambivalence and was now running ahead of her own feelings.

It was during that period that I discovered the depth of the woman I was already convinced would be my wife. Before long, my infatuation had matured to true love. By September, Dianna shared my feelings and we began to think seriously about the future. In November she suggested a brief moratorium on the relationship. We had known each other such a short time and were talking so seriously of marriage that she wanted to back off for a couple of weeks and sort out her feelings.

I was devastated.

I didn't tell Dianna, but I was convinced she was doing this only because it was the type of thing her friends had done. Worse, I was in dread that she would come to her senses and realize she could do so much better. I believed that if I ever heard from her again it would be in the form of a Dear John letter or a phone call suggesting that we could be just friends.

This was, of course, years before Dr. James Dobson's excellent *Tough Love,* which advises the waiting party in such a relationship to maintain dignity. Part of me wanted to beg and plead and cry and ask how Dianna could do such a thing to a person willing to crawl in front of her for the rest of her life, licking up dirt so she wouldn't have to step in it. Wouldn't that have been a nice example of the kind of man a woman wants as a husband?

I resisted the urge to grovel, but I did do a lot of tearful walking and praying. In retrospect, I see myself as a sniveling weakling who had enough foresight to keep it to himself. But at the time, I was truly in turmoil. I felt that Dianna was meant only for me, that only she could make me happy. I held to the conviction from our fourth meeting that we were meant to be married.

But I had to come to the point with God where I was willing to give her up. I had to get to the place where I conceded that if I truly loved her, then I would want what was best for her. If what was best for Dianna was not me, then that was what I wanted for her. Otherwise, my love was selfish. It was not easy, but after four days in the pits I made that concession in my own mind. I didn't feel much better, and I wouldn't like it if it turned out that way, but I knew I had done the right thing by being willing to accept it.

That night she called.

"Enough of this nonsense," she said. "I miss you. Come when you can."

I was tempted to let her wait a few days, but I drove two hours to see her for half an hour, then drove back home. We married within three months.

I don't begrudge her the four days she needed. I am glad, however, that she didn't need the entire two weeks. I would have been a basket case. Whatever she settled in her mind during those few days has lasted our entire marriage. For whatever grief it caused me then, it has afforded me a wife with no second thoughts.

PEORIA?

Clearly, that story is personal and is of real interest only to those involved—a group that includes our children. If we go several months without sharing our story, our sons insist on hearing it. They like to hear of the wedding, too, giggling over the account of my father pushing the play button rather than the *record* button on his tape recorder at the worst possible moment. While the pastor exhorted us, we were also treated to ten seconds of a business seminar Dad was trying to tape over.

We wrote our own vows, borrowing some ideas from the friends who had introduced us. We promised each other that we would "keep you only unto me," and rather than the morbid "till death do us part," we used the more upbeat "for as long as we both shall live, or until Christ, who has saved us by His grace, returns to take us unto Himself forever."

I also vowed to make Dianna laugh, which I have tried to do daily for nearly two decades. (If I've failed by the end of the day, I sometimes resort to swinging from the chandelier.)

We were married in downstate Illinois and left the next day to drive across the country for a job in Washington state, so we spent our first honeymoon night at the Holiday Inn in Peoria. It didn't seem at all funny then, but that gets the biggest smile today when we re-count our story.

Tell your story. Tell it to your kids, your friends, your brothers and sisters, but especially to each other. The more your story is im-planted in your brain, the more it serves as a hedge against the myr-iad forces that seek to destroy your marriage. Make your story so familiar that it becomes part of the fabric of your being. It should become a legend that is shared through the generations as you grow a family tree that defies all odds and boasts marriage after marriage of stability, strength, and longevity.

CHAPTER FOURTEEN

WHEN VICTORY COMES

Something wonderful happens in a relationship when hedges begin to grow.

It's crucial to understand that the hedges I've discussed have been my own, tailor-made for an over-sexed, gregarious, fun-loving, busy person who might otherwise follow his lusts, say things he shouldn't, flirt, forget the most important person in his life, and not spend as much time with his family as he should.

Your weaknesses may be different. Some of them would make me laugh or think you're a nut, as some of mine may have done to you. The important thing is to know yourself, understand the dangers in your weak areas, and do something practical and concrete about them.

The case studies that follow are of two couples who have learned the hard way to plant their own hedges. Their hedges bear little resemblance to mine. That's the point.

Except in the case of the first couple, names and insignificant details have been changed to protect identities.

PAT AND JILL WILLIAMS

I was privileged to work with Pat and Jill Williams on a book about their marriage. I met Pat in the early 1970s when he was general manager of the Chicago Bulls professional basketball team and I was a young writer interviewing him for a story. I eventually wrote his biography and then a motivational book with him, but the most significant project we ever hooked up on was *Rekindled,* which became a surprise best-seller and still sells in hardback at this writing, several years after its release.

The Williamses still receive an average of a letter a day from some distraught spouse, lamenting the state of his or her marriage, informing Pat and Jill how similar their stories are, and pleading for help. Pat sends me a copy of every letter, and I need to tell you, such correspondence provides one depressing look at the state of Christian marriage in this country.

Pat and Jill and I have often remarked on the sadness and desperation and also on the remarkable similarity among the letters. They have received hundreds and hundreds of letters, and they are nearly all the same. The husband has ignored the wife, busied himself in his career, and become a cold, uncommunicating partner. The wife has tried everything to get his attention until finally she was ripe for the attentions of someone else and is now involved in an affair.

Sometimes these stories happen the other way around, but that is the typical scenario. The letter to Pat and Jill comes either from a frantic husband who has seen the error of his ways and is willing to do anything to win his wife back, or it comes from the wife who says she knows it's wrong to be having an affair and she feels sorry for her pitiful, blubbering husband, but she has lost her love for him.

Pat and Jill's story is similar, but Jill did not resort to finding someone else. There is a depth of spirituality and character in her that precluded her looking for another man and even eliminated from her mind the possibility of divorcing Pat. She admits, however, that she was terribly vulnerable during the crisis and can't say with certainty that she could have fought off the urge to look to someone else if the circumstances had been just so.

At the time of the predicament, Pat was general manager of the Philadelphia 76ers, one of the premier organizations in the National Basketball Association. He was at the top of his profession—admired, sought after, a speaker, a jogger, a Bible memory freak—in short, the envy of many other wives. Only Jill knew the truth. He was invisible at home, wrapped up in his work, speaking engagements, devotions, and his physical fitness. "Jilly" was the little woman who was to handle the home and provide the ideal environment for him so he could remain at the top of his game.

Pat thought he had a good marriage. His wife was beautiful and talented and a good mother. She was a creative decorator, a good cook, a singer, a violinist—in short, everything a man like Pat could want in a wife.

For years Jill had tried to get Pat's attention. Her methods became more and more drastic as his solutions to her tantrums became more and more predictable. If she crabbed about his lack of attention or demanded to know why he ignored her in public, if she complained about his curtness to her or his condescension, or if she wanted to know why he never touched her except in bed or didn't have time to talk to her for even ten minutes a day, he would quickly take the temperature of the situation. If it looked serious he would apologize, make promises, bring her flowers, take her out to dinner, and see how long that kept her happy.

After ten years, she had had it, and he didn't even suspect it. She dropped the bomb on him one Sunday afternoon in December. He had killed her emotionally, she said. She told him she would not divorce him, would not leave him, but that neither could she guarantee any emotional response to him whatsoever. He had killed every last vestige of love she ever felt for him. She was finished, defeated, deflated, and she couldn't even smile.

It was as if someone had kicked him in the stomach. When he started his promise to turn over a new leaf, she simply went upstairs to bed. He knew this was serious and that no bandage was going to make things right again. He wept, sensing, knowing finally that she was right. He begged for forgiveness from God and for a solution.

Pat was an obsessive, compulsive person, driven to succeed at whatever he set his mind to, whether it meant memorizing a verse of Scripture a day, spending an hour in the Bible each day, jogging six miles a day, building a winning basketball team, or speaking three hundred times a year. He could do anything. And now he decided to put his mind to his marriage. He was ready and willing to do whatever it took not just to salvage it, but also to make it the best it could be. He wept and wept as God brought to his mind dozens of things he should have done over the years. He was reminded of every complaint Jill had registered over the decades and he filled page after page of a yellow legal pad, determined to change his ways on every point.

God also led him to a book, *Love Life for Every Married Couple,* by Ed Wheat, and he memorized the principles that urged him to apply the BEST acronym. He was to bless, edify, share, and touch his wife constantly, not just to win her back, but also simply because it was the right thing to do. In fact, Dr. Wheat stipulated in his book that all this activity would not guarantee any response from the hurting spouse. He said, in essence, that the wounded partner may never respond after all the damage that had been done, but these principles applied anyway, and should be followed.

Pat was desperate to convince Jill that this was no typical restart. He really meant it this time. He had really heard her. He loved her with all his heart and wanted to prove it. He was so committed to his marriage that everything else in his life paled in comparison, and yet she could not bring herself to respond. She couldn't smile or even speak except in cordial, formal, functional conversation. He got no encouragement, and he said, "It was like looking into the eyes of a dead woman, a woman I had killed."

The story ends happily, of course. Eventually Pat proved himself. God forgave him and has given him the strength to maintain his commitment to this day. Jill finally forgave him and saw life and love return to her being. At the time of their marital crisis more than seven years ago they had three children. They have since had another of their own and adopted eight more!

You wouldn't think a household with a dozen children in it would be a healthy place for a troubled marriage, but it is. A miraculous transformation has taken place there, all because Pat got the message and planted hedges, albeit almost too late.

He talks to his wife a lot every day.

He spends time with her and with the children. He remembers special days.

They date frequently.

He applies a lot of nonsexual touching.

She has become the center of his life.

It hasn't been a quick fix. He knows he can never let his guard down, never slip into the old patterns. Now that he is president and general manager of a new NBA franchise and the family has moved to Orlando, Florida, the risks and temptations are greater than ever. Yet his resolve is all the stronger. Remember, these were not just leaves he turned over. They were hedges he planted deep in thick, rich soil, and they're growing strong.

IKE AND LAURIE VANDERAY

Ike is a successful independent insurance agent in the South. Laurie worked early in their marriage but became pregnant almost immediately, and they now have five children under age eleven. They were a passionate, exciting couple during their long courtship, but financial setbacks, health problems, and two miscarriages made early married life difficult.

Seven pregnancies in a dozen years have not been a problem for Laurie. She loves babies, was heartbroken over the two losses, and is even interested in maybe having one more. Both Vanderays are very active in their local church, serving in Sunday school and in the choir and on various boards and committees. Ike is also very visible in community affairs for the sake of his business.

Ike has found that Saturdays can be big in his line of work. People who can't see him during the workweek will often schedule a Saturday appointment. Laurie pleaded with him to take one day other than Sunday off, so when his business became healthy enough, he announced he was taking Mondays off.

To Laurie, this was heaven. She looked forward to their getting a baby-sitter and spending the day together, or having Ike watch the kids while she spent the day shopping and running errands. She had felt so isolated and trapped that she couldn't wait to just get away for a few hours.

There was a breakdown in communications the first time Ike took a Monday off. He agreed to watch the kids for a while, and she assumed he knew she would be gone most of the day. Many of his clients had not gotten the word of his day off, so he was trying to answer calls and do business over the phone while keeping track of the kids. The longer Laurie was gone, the angrier Ike became.

When she got home, she got an earful. Not only was she not going to have a free baby-sitter on his next day off, but he was going golfing all day. His day off, in case she didn't know it, was for his sake, not hers, and that was the way it was going to be.

"When do I get a day off?" she whined. It was a mistake to ask that just then, though it was a valid question.

"You get a day off all day every day," he said foolishly. He lived to regret that remark.

When tempers cooled, the Vanderays knew they had a problem. Ike got an answering machine that informed everyone that he was unavailable on Mondays. He pledged to baby-sit from breakfast through lunch on Mondays so Laurie could eat out with friends and get her errands and shopping done. She agreed to let him do whatever he wanted in the afternoon, and if she needed a baby-sitter so she could go with him or remain out on her own, that was OK. Monday evenings also became their date nights.

"It revolutionized our marriage," Ike says. "I feel like I'm helping her. I get time to get away and have some fun. She's happier because she gets out, sometimes for the whole day and evening. And even though we each are getting some freedom to do what we want to do, we are also seeing more of each other than ever."

Laurie says Ike seems like the same young, energetic, funny, creative guy she married. "He's less uptight, and we have fun like we used to. We talk like never before. Sometimes we go somewhere before or after dinner, but sometimes we don't. Sometimes we close the restaurant, sitting there gabbing and planning and telling each other everything all evening. We've even been known to go and park!"

OTHER HEDGES

Some couples schedule a breakfast out each week. I know a pastor and two business executives who have regular appointments with their wives booked right onto their calendars, and their secretaries know those dates are inviolable. They don't necessarily tell the caller where their boss will be, but they do know to say, "I'm sorry. That slot is filled."

To a busy man, an appointment with his wife on a regular basis is every bit as much of a hedge as mine are. Spend time talking with your wife. Find out what her deepest needs are, what she really wants and requires from you. Then plant a hedge around that, around her, around you, around your marriage. It'll be the best gardening you've ever done.